ACT Art Therapy

ACT
Art Therapy

*Creative Approaches to Acceptance
and Commitment Therapy*

Amy Backos

Jessica Kingsley Publishers
London and Philadelphia

First published in Great Britain in 2023 by Jessica Kingsley Publishers
An imprint of Hodder & Stoughton Ltd
An Hachette Company

1

A CIP catalogue record for this title is available from the
British Library and the Library of Congress

ISBN 978 1 78775 803 2
eISBN 978 1 78775 804 9

Printed and bound in the United States by Integrated Books International

Jessica Kingsley Publishers' policy is to use papers that are natural,
renewable and recyclable products and made from wood grown in
sustainable forests. The logging and manufacturing processes are expected
to conform to the environmental regulations of the country of origin.

Jessica Kingsley Publishers
Carmelite House
50 Victoria Embankment
London EC4Y 0DZ

www.jkp.com

*For my clients—I so appreciate being
in the moment with you!*

Acknowledgments

Thank you to my wonderful support team who nourish and inspire me every day:

Charlie, Oliver, and Wicket Rockwood

Ronald, Marcia, and Eric Backos

Michelle Jones, Ari Dunbar, Sarah Bowen, Sherri Hegyes, Terri Wong

The students, faculty, and alumni of the Graduate Art Therapy Psychology Department at Dominican University of California

Thank you to the people who contributed time, ideas, and stories:
Carrie McCracken, Gabriel Aleman McCracken, Darcy Crosman, Jocelyn Fitzgerald, Maria Fuster, Jordon Gonzalez, Sarah Kremer, Claudia Mezzera, Corrie Mazzeo, Kayla Ormandy, Oliver Rockwood, Gwen Sanders, Christine Shea, Juviel Vinluan, Shari Weiser, Kamaria Wells, Melanie Worstell, Erin Partridge

Contents

Introduction

I was introduced to acceptance and commitment therapy (ACT) when I was completing my internship and residency in clinical psychology at the Cleveland Veterans Administration (VA) hospital. At the time, my training was not my only challenge. Something even more significant and challenging was happening besides. Only seven months prior to entering the VA, I had become a first-time parent. I had my husband to support me, yet we faced some significant challenges in those seven months. A week after he was born, our son was admitted to the neo-natal intensive care unit for a very scary week of tests and treatments. Shortly after that, my father-in-law passed away. Then, I learned I was accepted on the national psychology internship match to a hospital over 2000 miles away from home. So, we packed our belongings and drove from San Francisco to Cleveland with our new son. As I entered my internship, I was excited, yet mostly exhausted and on edge. Being introduced to ACT was pivotal to my ability to successfully navigate the challenges I was confronting. This is because ACT principles are not only introduced to our clients for the benefit of their wellbeing, ACT therapists practice and live them as well. ACT and the much-needed focus of present moment awareness, cognitive defusion, and values arrived just in time to help me with some major transitions in my life, and enable me to hone my craft as a therapist.

So, "What brings you to ACT?" I invite you to answer the question for yourself. How did you come to ACT? What was happening in your life as you discovered the simplicity and power of ACT? How did ACT support you and your work? If reading this book is your introduction to ACT, I am excited for you and I ask you to pause and reflect on what is happening now in your life. As you continue to read, you will see and experience how the ACT concepts can support your personal and professional growth.

ACT in action

Using ACT in therapy requires the therapist's ongoing personal reflection, mindfulness, and commitment to a value-based life. Art therapists additionally commit to the value of creativity, including personal artmaking and sharing creativity for the benefit of others. Coming to ACT means agreeing to live it and continuing to grow with it as a person and as a therapist. There is nothing prescriptive about ACT or art therapy. Both involve the client *and* the therapist cultivating creativity and psychological flexibility by letting go of limited, constricted, or habitual ways of thinking and being. This leads us to think, create, respond, and behave in ways of our choosing, bringing richness and renewed meaning to our lives.

Working with students in the Art Therapy Psychology Department at Dominican University of California in Northern California has been my privilege and pleasure as we learn together about ACT art therapy. ACT concepts provide powerful tools in my work with students for reflecting on our profession and their motivation in school. Students have integrated ACT into their art therapy clinical work and qualifying exams at master's level, as well as dissertations at doctoral level. In this book, you will read about some of the ACT work being done by my colleagues and students.

We bring client-focused attitudes to the therapy office, which demand culturally humble and sensitive approaches. When I came to ACT, I was able to easily integrate the stance and theoretical approach into my prior experiences as an art therapist practicing from a feminist and antiracist perspective. I used ACT to deepen my knowledge and appreciation for my values, and I became increasingly attuned to the principles of both antiracism and feminism and how I could more fully embody them in my lived experience when providing therapy.

I believe it is critical for therapists to understand and support our clients through their social lens and avoid replicating social injustices in the shared therapeutic space. Furthermore, we are summoned in our profession as advocates for equal access to mental health across race, gender, sexual orientation, ability, age, class, religion, country of origin, and income. Our therapy approaches fail to be effective and elicit change if they are only designed for, and available to, some people, while others are alienated by the approaches or unable to access mental health services. The possibilities in therapy of healing and self-actualization are only good ideas when they are physically available and psychologically accessible to all.

At the time I began training to be an ACT therapist, I had almost a decade of experience as an art therapist using feminism, existentialism, and antiracism to guide my work. The supervisor at the VA suggested I read and completed the client workbook, *Get Out of Your Mind and Into Your Life* by Steven Hayes (Hayes & Smith, 2005). I started reading and answering the questions while riding the bus home after work, and I had the feeling I was reading a much-needed user manual for understanding my mind. As I practiced the strategies and employed the concepts, I experienced the relief of cognitive defusion. Cognitive defusion is a central component of ACT, which allows you to achieve psychological distance and perspective on your thoughts. For me, it meant that instead of being stuck in my thoughts, I was able to observe them with increased curiosity and less criticism. Instead of lingering on negative thoughts, such as my parental guilt or professional uncertainties, I learned strategies to help me quickly shift from a place where I believed my thoughts to be the truth, to simply noticing them and then deciding how I wanted to proceed in accordance with my values. Integrating feminism and antiracism into my ACT value system flowed seamlessly, and these two philosophies continue to inform my work.

Before I accessed the functional utility of mindfulness through ACT, I had cultivated a curious, observing stance in nature and through meditation and guided imagery. I experienced flow in artmaking, physical exercise, and academic work. ACT helped me build on these experiences of flow, of being immersed in the process of what I was doing, and offered me pragmatic tools to manage stress and create perspective by observing my thoughts and choosing actions that were aligned with my values. ACT strategies inform every aspect of my life and I harness these tools for daily living. I immediately set out to design art therapy projects to bring attention to each of the ACT concepts. I thought, if I can benefit so quickly with just a few ACT exercises and my sketch book, I want more! And if I could do it, so could my clients. My colleague, Corrie Mazzeo, and I set out to create an ACT art therapy group (Howie, 2017) and we facilitated many groups over the next two years with veterans from various eras and challenges, such as post-traumatic stress disorder (PTSD), substance abuse disorders, depression, and anxiety.

I continue to grow in ACT through my work in a substance abuse facility, in private practice, and as a professor. I use the skills and ACT's emphasis on values to guide my personal and professional behaviors. Using ACT and art therapy as a combined approach has been my personal and theoretical philosophy for over a decade, and I am committed to continue my growth and understanding of this unique approach.

What you can expect

The purpose of this ACT art therapy book is to provide a theoretical and practical guide for art therapists and other mental health professionals to understand key concepts in ACT art therapy and to implement art therapy interventions from an ACT approach. I am happy to share the ACT and art therapy concepts that—for me over the past several decades as an art therapist and professor—have informed my work. In this book, you will find the creativity that informs the field of art therapy, as well as the theoretical underpinnings of ACT. Historical context is offered to understand art as a tool for self-expression and the underpinnings of art therapy as a mental health profession for healing individuals, families, groups, and communities.

It is my hope that you will develop a meaningful context for understanding how ACT and art therapy align to creatively achieve psychological flexibility for you and your clients. Our efficacy as ACT therapists and art therapists depends on both our personal understanding and our practical application of these principles in our own lives. The art interventions in the book both illustrate the concepts and exist as stand-alone interventions to heighten creative potential and mindful attention to the present moment.

By the time you finish this book, I anticipate you will feel confident in thoughtfully and creatively integrating ACT and art therapy into your clinical practice. My wish for you as a therapist-reader is for you to first try out all of the ACT art therapy exercises yourself and then utilize the ones that might be helpful for your clients. ACT is an action-oriented therapy and merely reading about theory and art interventions offers insufficient cognitive understanding—you must *act* to experience the creative and transformative nature of these two approaches in your emotional and professional life. I am excited for you to experience the cognitive, emotional, and spiritual benefits of ACT and art therapy and I hope you will share with me your experience of what brought you to ACT art therapy.

CHAPTER 1

What is ACT Art Therapy?

In this chapter, ACT art therapy will be introduced as a creative therapy process to increase psychological flexibility and reduce suffering for ourselves and our clients. ACT art therapy, which combines art-based self-expression and an evidence-based modality belonging to the third wave of behaviorism, offers a potent tool to use in the therapy office. When integrated, these two modalities create a synergistic impact, which relies on action and awareness to facilitate change. Art initiates a creative therapeutic process that allows clients to dig deep into the intellectual concepts of ACT and express themselves through visual art. The combination aids clients in identifying values and transforming behavior into committed actions and a meaningful life.

The work of therapy truly springs from radical and pragmatic optimism. Why else would we be here as therapists if we thought otherwise? Psychotherapists optimistically build careers on the idea that people and society can heal and be uplifted through improved mental health. Reducing internal and external suffering for ourselves and those around us uplifts humanity, which is a worthwhile goal, both necessary and achievable.

In spite of the pain both we and our clients experience, therapists somehow have the radical notion that we can improve the lives of ourselves and others. Furthermore, we have the courage to act on the belief that one person can undeniably help ease the pain and misery of another. When we reduce our suffering and then enable our clients to reduce their suffering, we increase our individual and collective capacity for meaningful relationships and harmony in society.

Many therapists are drawn to study psychology because of the positive belief that distress can be lessened and that psychotherapy offers an effective modality for healing (Hay, 2020). This sanguine conviction serves to remind us of the importance of helping others, especially when our work is challenging or we feel unsure. Similarly, many artists study art therapy because of their lived experience of using art for self-expression and personal growth. Art therapists bring optimistic convictions about the tremendous effect of creating art in therapy to alleviate heartache and cultivate joy. These hopeful beliefs, coupled with the personal value of service, anchor and guide therapists in their work to reduce individual and collective hardship.

Art therapy offers a nonverbal means of self-expression to promote wellness and mental health, whereas ACT offers the best of the third wave of behavior therapy and is an evidence-based practice for a variety of disorders. The blending of the two approaches offers opportunities for utilizing the creative process in therapy with the support of evidence-based behavioral treatment.

Those unfamiliar with how behavior-focused modalities work sometimes tell me they are worried the treatment will be "too clinical" or leave no room for personality, creativity, and relationship building. On the contrary, I have found the third-wave behavioral approach of ACT to facilitate authentic and genuine relationships. ACT provides a necessary structure to therapy and serves as an excellent foundation for open and personable relationships with clients. Additionally, art therapy provides creative and transformative processes to support clients in expressing both wanted and unwanted thoughts, feelings, and bodily sensations. Working in conjunction, ACT and art therapy bring about psychological flexibility and creative thinking. Art therapy brings to life practical actions related to the ACT concepts of present moment awareness, action-oriented interventions, and externalization and defusion of inner experiences. The combination of ACT and art therapy offers a unique and truly impressive therapeutic approach.

Origins of the ACT paradigm

ACT was developed in 1982, and as mentioned previously, is part of the third wave of behavior therapies. For context, it may be useful to trace its development through the first two waves. The first wave includes the psychoanalytic and humanistic approaches. The second wave encompasses behaviorism and cognitive approaches. The latest wave of therapies adopted the paradigm of pragmatism or contextualism as a necessary component of understanding behavior (Follette & Callaghan, 2011). In addition to ACT, other approaches in the third wave include dialectical behavioral therapy (DBT), functional analytic psychotherapy behavioral activation, and mindfulness-based cognitive therapy (Follette & Callaghan, 2011).

ACT considers an individual with their unique historical context in order to take into account the whole person, including their thoughts, beliefs, memories, experiences, and personal and social history (Follette & Callaghan, 2011; Hayes *et al.*, 2012). This interplay of various lived experiences and situational contexts informs how we express ourselves through our behavior (Gordon & Borushok, 2017). Behavior necessarily occurs within a context, and ACT explores the wider context that makes up each of our lives.

Contextualism makes the third wave of behavior therapies unique; it stems from the assessment of both the *context* of a behavior and the *pragmatism* involved in making behavioral choices. Context includes both the inner and outer experiences and the accumulated history of each person. Radical behaviorism considered behavior to be a choice, which is selected based on accumulated history (Follette & Callaghan, 2011; Wilson *et al.*, 2011). Pragmatism essentially fashions distinctions as relevant only when they will make a meaningful difference (Follette & Callaghan, 2011). In other words, truth and meaning for each person are defined by the success of their practical application (Gordon & Borushok, 2017). In ACT, each person creates their own meaning through the therapy process and applies their individual truth in ways that work for them. Behavior, as originally conceptualized by B. F. Skinner, is evaluated by how it might make a practical difference. For example, with ACT, we ask how will any given behavior get us closer to our values?

Another way to understand pragmatism is to understand its opposite: ontology. Ontology in science assumes that truth and reality are waiting to be discovered, as though the therapist or researcher unearths behavioral truths that apply to everyone (Follette & Callaghan, 2011). In contrast, pragmatism relies on generating meaning and value based on context rather than relying on the paradigm of cause and effect in the ontological framework. You can readily imagine the impact on therapy that the shift from ontology to pragmatism had. The story, meaning, values, and behavior choices shifted away from being centered on the theory to being centered on the client. Truth and meaning emerge from the client through exploration with the therapist's support. Without the ontological framework to define individual behaviors as healthy or unhealthy, or community culture as valuable or insignificant, the client is liberated to create their own meaning, outside the gaze or judgment of the therapist, the scientific community, and society at large!

While sharing a similar influence from behavior therapy, common values, and sociological context, cognitive behavioral therapy (CBT) and ACT diverge in their approach. ACT emerges from the *behavioral* analytic tradition in behavioral therapy and enhances it by its interest in meaning and purpose (Wilson *et al.*, 2011). "ACT can be understood as a behavior analytic response to both the cognitive and existential critiques of traditional behavior therapy" (Wilson *et al.*, 2011, p.281). However, ACT differs from traditional behavioral analysis because of its pragmatic approach, which includes two key components: analysis of complex human behavior in relational frame theory and the centering of the work in domains, such as emotion, thought, meaning, purpose, and values (Wilson *et al.*, 2011).

Evidence base for ACT

ACT became my theoretical orientation because it meets both the needs of my clients and my wishes as a therapist. Gómez highlighted its utility by noting that "among all the third-generation theories... [ACT] is one of the most effective and versatile treatments" (Gómez, 2020, p.1). ACT, with its strong evidence base, has demonstrated success in both reducing symptoms and increasing psychological flex-ibility to help clients pursue a value-based life. For me as a therapist, ACT rejuvenated my commitment to therapy by helping me focus on the meaning and purpose of my work, especially during challenging situations with clients. The pragmatic utility (Messer & Gurman, 2011) of ACT quickly assists clients in making meaningful behavioral changes. The opportunity to be yourself in session by using creativity and engaging in your own values offered me greater satisfaction in my work and increased my potential for longevity.

As of 2021, ACT had had over 600 randomized controlled trials (Hayes, 2021). Three or more such studies with similar findings consti-tutes an *evidence-based* treatment (Darrell W. Krueger Library, 2021) so ACT has a preponderance of research to demonstrate its efficacy. Randomized controlled studies show that ACT has been successful in treating a variety of disorders, including depression (Ruiz *et al.*, 2020) and anxiety (Swain *et al.*, 2013). It is effective in reducing stigma (Gómez, 2020), improving psychological flexibility (Molavi *et al.*, 2020), and reducing avoidance (Thompson *et al.*, 2013), and ACT outcomes are considered equivalent to or more effective than traditional CBT (Twohig & Levin, 2017). ACT has been particularly helpful in addressing PTSD and acute traumas. As such, it is considered to be an evidence-based practice within the United States (VA) hospitals (US Department of Veterans Affairs, 2021) and its efficacy is noted around the world.

Participants who have received ACT therapy have shown exciting neurological changes. A randomized controlled neurological trial com-pared two groups of participants with clinical perfectionism ($N = 29$): those who received ACT therapy and those on a waitlist (Ong *et al.*, 2020). Clinical perfectionism includes impairment on tasks because of performance monitoring and challenges with emotional regula-tion. Participants engaged in behavioral tasks designed to elicit error detection, while researchers used near-infrared spectroscopy assess-ment to examine brain changes. Changes in the brain scans included hemodynamic response function in the dorsolateral and dorsomedial prefrontal cortex. These changes were consistent with reduced neural activity in those areas, suggesting that the group who received ACT showed greater efficiency in their cognitive processing.

In addition to the neurological evidence, several meta-analyses have demonstrated the efficacy of ACT in supporting a practical sense of wellbeing in clients. By reviewing a meta-analysis of multiple studies for outcomes in psychological treatment, we can understand the impact of ACT in different settings with various populations. A meta-analysis of 11 randomized controlled ACT trials critically evaluated studies on ACT's impact on wellbeing ($N = 1108$): ACT improved the transdiagnostic (i.e., symptom reduction across various diagnoses) outcome of subjective wellbeing in both clinical and nonclinical populations (Stenhoff et al., 2020). Wellbeing relates to affective and cognitive evaluation of one's life, including mood, satisfaction, and relationships, which are significant areas of our daily lives. The studies included five different measures of subjective wellbeing and participants with a variety of mental health diagnoses, as well as nonclinical populations. Post-treatment scores of wellbeing across the different measures were significantly higher in 10 of the 11 studies for the participants receiving ACT when compared to control groups. Most of the studies showed moderate effect sizes, showing the capacity of ACT interventions to enhance a person's sense of wellbeing in both clinical and nonclinical populations.

Another meta-analysis included 100 controlled effect sizes from 133 studies and 12,477 participants (Gloster et al., 2020). Researchers found ACT to be efficacious for treating anxiety, depression, substance abuse, and pain, as well as in transdiagnostic groups in every study. Furthermore, they found ACT to be superior to waitlist controls, placebo, and treatment as usual for each of these targeted symptoms. The only exception to the predominant findings of ACT's efficacy was when compared to CBT. However, ACT was found to be significantly more effective in 10 of the 12 of the comparison groups. These high levels of success in treatment demonstrate the efficacy of the approach and provide credibility to our work as ACT therapists. After all, we need to know if our work is efficacious in reducing mental health symptoms and whether our approach actually helps people feel better.

ACT bespeaks wide applicability and yields positive impacts across race, ethnicity, and gender (Hayes, n.d.). Researchers exploring ACT research in countries around the world for over a decade found the

ACT approach to be exceedingly impactful and successful (Bahattab & AlHadi, 2021; Cook & Hayes, 2010; Lundgren *et al.*, 2006; Woidneck *et al.*, 2012). Challenging the overuse of research samples of convenience (i.e. college students), ACT researchers are interested in understanding how the strategies apply to various populations in a variety of settings. The Association for Contextual Behavioral Science recently called for more ACT research that incorporates both pragmatism and prosocial impact, meaning research addressing real-world problems to increase social wellbeing (Hayes *et al.*, 2021).

Internalized racial oppression has been demonstrated to have deep impacts on mental health, and ACT research confronts this contextual problem. ACT techniques were found to lessen internalized self-stigma and ultimately mitigate mental health symptoms of distress in a group of Black women (Hudson Banks *et al.*, 2021). Researchers specifically noted reductions in shame, internalized racial oppression, and psychological distress. ACT combined with psychoeducation on the psychology of race has been able to demonstrate notable improvement in reducing prejudices and increasing positive behavioral intentions in young adults, with benefits superior to psychoeducation alone (Lillis & Hayes, 2007).

Evidence base for art therapy

Art therapists understand the power of art to unearth unconscious material, process upsetting and traumatic experiences, develop an authentic relationship with oneself and others, and self-actualize. Art therapy is efficacious in meeting treatment goals and is well tolerated as a treatment modality by clients. Art therapy can be tailored to work with each individual's needs and goals, in the context of an array of interventions.

There are several lines of research to suggest how art therapy can be best utilized. Randomized controlled studies have demonstrated that art therapy enhances care for clients engaged in other therapeutic approaches (Maujean *et al.*, 2014). Both qualitative and quantitative studies have found art therapy efficacious as stand-alone treatment or a single-use intervention to reduce negative mood states (Slayton *et al.*, 2010). Finally, art therapy as an adjunctive therapy enhances treatment and reduces attrition (Campbell *et al.*, 2016; Decker *et al.*, 2018). This section reports only a small portion of the peer-reviewed evidence for the use of art therapy.

Art therapy outcomes

A meta-analysis of 35 art therapy studies showed art therapy to be effective as a stand-alone treatment for a variety of age groups, symptoms, and disorders (Slayton *et al.*, 2010). The authors reviewed both qualitative and quantitative studies with various populations, including adults with learning disabilities, mothers, sexually abused girls and women, incarcerated men, people with medical conditions, people grieving, children with attachment disorders, and many others. Their findings highlighted the meaningful impact of art therapy for many populations and called for more replication studies.

A smaller meta-analysis reported positive results in seven of eight scientifically rigorous and randomized controlled art therapy studies (Maujean *et al.*, 2014). Art therapy was found to benefit a range of individuals, with notable success with people who have cancer, war veterans, and people in prison. The authors concluded that art therapy appears to be most effective when applied to specific qualities and emotional states rather than used to change a global sense of quality of life. In other words, greater success was found in changing emotions, such as reducing depression, fears, and anxiety.

Another randomized study explored anxiety levels in participants who either made art or viewed art (Bell & Robbins, 2007). Their findings demonstrated statistically significant reductions in anxiety for the people making art compared to the people viewing art. These findings are consistent with other research demonstrating that artmaking produces dramatic reductions in negative mood states. Whereas viewing art certainly has a profound impact on us, this study highlighted the benefits of making art over merely viewing art.

Adjunctive art therapy

Art therapy combined with trauma protocols provides qualitatively improved experiences for the clients, a reduction in attrition, and increased feelings of mastery over fears. The International Society for Traumatic Stress Studies describes art therapy as a useful ancillary treatment for clients in psychotherapy for traumatic stress (Foa *et al.*, 2000). When added to treatment protocols, art therapy offers unique ways to help clients process their experiences while engaged in evidence-based, trauma-focused protocols. Randomized controlled art therapy studies using art therapy as an adjunct therapy with veterans have demonstrated that clients are better able to tolerate trauma-focused therapies, and art therapy is associated with lower attrition in treatments that usually have high dropout rates (Campbell *et al.*, 2016; Decker *et al.*, 2018).

A randomized controlled study in Sweden used art therapy adjunctively with pregnant women in counseling to reduce tokophobia (fears about childbirth). While the study lacked statistical significance when comparing the treatment and control groups, in three-month follow-up qualitative assessments, women who received art therapy reported feeling calmer and stronger. The women reported that art therapy allowed them to express their birth fear in a new way and to further open up to the midwife, bringing about increased trust. Some women reported that art therapy increased their self-confidence and self-reliance during birth.

While there are many studies touting clinical success when using art therapy, making art in nonclinical settings offers simple ways for people to lower fears and anxieties when facing stress. A randomized control study of university students found that the act of coloring could reduce anxiety, increase mindfulness, and improve scores on selective attention and original ideation (Holt *et al.*, 2019). Other research supports the act of coloring, and in particular coloring mandalas, as a way to reduce negative mood states (Babouchkina & Robbins, 2015).

Why theory in context matters

Using theory to guide our work is critical for effective work as therapists. Theory is the rudder on our boats, the lighthouse in our harbor, and the map on a long journey. A unifying theory with a consistent approach by the therapist helps clients to internalize and integrate change. With therapeutic consistency, clients learn to identify and change their self-talk and behavioral strategies. When therapists utilize multiple theories or they use a combination of theories that may be fundamentally at odds with each other, I have the impression they may have lost sight of how to guide clients; they potentially struggle when presented with a challenge in therapy. Our theory, when carefully selected, is harmonious with our beliefs about the world and how people change.

However, our clients' lives and behaviors exist within a context. Each client has a unique and valuable history, including personal, familial, cultural, and generational. Their strengths and values, as well as unwanted symptoms and behaviors, also exist within a set of circumstances and contexts. Some of the external contexts include family history and culture, community, the forces of dominant society and intersecting personal identities (e.g., race, gender, sexual orientation, ability, class). Some internal contexts include a person's inner representation of their past experiences, such as internalized beliefs from parents, others, and society, the success and failure of past behaviors, and their thoughts, feelings, and bodily sensations.

Attending to the various contexts, communities, and intersecting identities of our clients allows for a greater perspective and increased capacity in the therapeutic relationships (Backos, 2021). For example, using a feminist lens or person-centered attitudes can enhance a client's experience by bringing attention to social injustices or personal empowerment in relation to the therapist's attitudes. Furthermore, using an intersectional lens (Saad, 2020; Talwar, 2019) to truly learn about, understand, and value our client's lived experience can create a therapy space that is vastly different from the circumstances that contributed to or created the problems in the first place.

Decolonizing

ACT prioritizes psychological flexibility and value-based living over pathology and symptomology. This de-emphasis on symptoms is consistent with my values of optimism mentioned earlier, as well as my wish to bring attention to ways we can build up our clients and create a more just society by working to decolonize the field of psychology. Decolonizing therapy entails shifting our approach from addressing individual mental health problems to facilitating real social change by addressing the hostile environments that *cause* mental health problems (Backos, 2021; Talwar, 2019). Providing care to reduce anxiety and depression can feel like a vicious cycle to clients, while they continue to live within the same situations that brought them to therapy in the first place. The experiences of racism, sexism, ageism, ableism, homophobia/transphobia (and many others) can lead to compromised mental health. In particular, discrimination and prejudice have traumatic effects in people experiencing ongoing oppression and microaggressions (Nadel, 2018).

Real change in the profession of therapy occurs when we first acknowledge discrimination and bias within ourselves and in the therapy space. Only having taken that step can we then empower ourselves and our clients to work towards social change and address both the symptoms and the *causes* of mental health problems. In other words, when our work offers care to the individual, as well as addressing symptoms of the much bigger social conditions that created the symptoms, we truly provide client-focused care and long-term solutions.

One example of rooting out the cause of a disorder is removing homosexuality from the *Diagnostic and Statistical Manual of Mental Disorders* (American Psychiatric Association, 2000). This came about as psychologists came to realize that homophobia is a societal problem and that a continuum naturally exists related to sexual orientation and expression. Another example of decolonization is illustrated in the steps taken by activists after the psychological term *battered women syndrome* was used to describe women who were seeking support for the distress of living in abusive relationships in the 1970s (Walker, 2009). The phrase implied helplessness and the disorder was grounded in holding women personally responsible for their inability to protect themselves or leave a relationship (Ravichandran, 2019; Walker, 2009). Grassroots activism in the following decades led to women sharing their personal experiences and working to create legislation that recognized and criminalized domestic violence and rape within a relationship. Whereas the experiences of interpersonal violence are similar across race, class, culture, the movement at that time significantly neglected and silenced the experiences of women of color, transwomen, and those of the lesbian, gay, bisexual, transgender, queer or questioning (LGBTQ+) community. The next necessary step is a decolonizing approach, which avoids the use of prescriptive interpersonal violence programs that were created using a dominant narrative and instead focuses on "an intersectional analysis since the issues facing women are constantly shifting and changing" (Ravichandran, 2019, p.147).

Intersectionality

Another example of context in therapy includes intersectionality and the inclusion of a person's full identity, such as race *and* gender *and* class *and* sexual orientation. Intersectionality offers an overarching approach to understanding and valuing clients using social and cultural perspectives in addition to the therapist's usual psychological approach (Talwar, 2019). Specifically, the approach entails understanding how marginalized identities "simultaneously intersect to create and exacerbate experiences of oppression" (Kuri, 2017, p.1). For example, a person's identity as a woman is inextricably linked to her identity as a Person of Color, while her status and the discrimination she faces are compounded by these two intersecting identities.

Fragmenting the identities of our clients by excluding a cultural and social understanding of their experiences leads to loss of understanding and perpetuates oppression and discrimination. The oppression constitutes a causal criterion or a contributing factor to many mental health disorders in the first place. Seeking understanding of others using an intersectional lens, coupled with self-reflexivity, creates an environment of respect and understanding. Part of this work includes centering the narrative of a person's life on all of the aspects *they* bring, rather than what we as therapists offer using a therapeutic lens and process within a mental health system. As Jackson *et al.* (2018) observed, "Practitioners of art therapy who regularly practice a posture of curiosity, inquisitiveness, enthusiastic exploration, and acceptance of others help to move the field forward in positive ways" (p.117). Another important component of this approach entails the self-reflective process, exploring personal, cultural, and social para-digms that influence us and our clients. In particular, *hegemony*, which is the cultural, social, economic, and ideological influence exerted by the dominant culture (*Merriam-Webster*, n.d.), must be a part of our self-reflection. The power exerted by the dominant culture affects individuals, communities, agencies, and institutions, as well as the therapeutic process.

A preponderance of art therapy literature calls for decolonizing therapeutic approaches and utilizing intersecting perspectives in our work (Ali & Lee, 2019; Crenshaw, 1989; Jackson, 2020; Kuri, 2017; Ravichandran, 2019; Talwar, 2010, 2019). It is incumbent on us to learn from art therapists with lived experience and critical analysis in the relevant areas of racism, discrimination, sexism, and homophobia. I strongly encourage you to read the work of these authors for a more detailed understanding of the need to decolonize our therapeutic approaches, using intersectionality to support our clients, and tak-ing steps to change personal practices and systems that perpetuate oppression and do damage to our clients and ourselves.

Cultural humility

Cultural humility is rooted in self-reflection and self-critique about power imbalances (Hook, 2013; Jackson, 2020; Tervalon & Murray-Garcia, 1998). Jackson describes cultural humility as "a way of developing a worldview with integrity and respect for oneself and those one works with" (p.19). Cultural humility brings "dignity to those who have felt stripped of their sense of self" and works to empower "voices [that] have been denied witnessing" (p.19). Cultural humility helps us move away from *telling* others what is wrong with them (e.g., a diagnosis and symptom reduction as the goal) to asking clients what is important to them and building on their strengths as well as their family and cultural ways of knowing. Cultural humility works in tandem with cultural awareness. "Cultural humility does not replace cultural competency and it is not an either/or situation. Both are essential to our work as therapists" (L. Jackson, personal communication, January 15, 2021).

Jackson (2020) described four core principles that guide our commitment to cultural humility: (1) making a lifelong commitment to self-reflection and critique; (2) addressing power imbalances in therapy and academic relationships; (3) developing long-term and mutually beneficial partnerships within the communities in which we work; and (4) advocating for institutional accountability. These guiding concepts apply to ACT and art therapy and help us create better therapy relationships, as well as address the causes of mental health problems.

The value of ACT art therapy integration

When I fully adopted ACT as my psychological theory and committed to being a master of the theory, my clinical work became more efficacious for clients and easier and more meaningful for me. I felt better qualified and able to help clients create a vision for their future and a way to think about and understand their past and current behaviors, and make future behavioral choices. Leaning into the theory myself and using the ACT strategies in my life proved effective, as I could consistently frame art therapy interventions with a unifying theory and clients seemed better able to integrate the work of therapy into their lives.

Furthermore, ACT art therapy positions the approach, psychological treatment, and creative process as a shared human experience. This directly deconstructs some of the power structure in the therapy office because the theory and methods of ACT are for the therapist *and* the client. Instead of a treatment or approach that is *applied to* clients and their problems, ACT art therapy offers the opportunity for two people—the therapist and the client—to engage together in the here and now as two fallible individuals. While the therapist is supporting and assisting clients with art material and psychological processes, both are seeking a way to increase their psychological flexibility, creative process, and present moment awareness to reduce suffering.

Conclusion

ACT art therapy offers a creative way to promote psychological flexibility and integrate behavioral changes to build a value-based life. The synergistic effect of using ACT and art therapy occurs because the both approaches rely on action and awareness to facilitate change. Art therapy simplifies and brings to life the intellectual concepts of ACT though client-generated metaphor. Linking the two approaches creates a powerful strategy to assist clients in making lasting behavioral changes in their lives, even in the presence of symptomology or chronic conditions. The next few chapters will elucidate the theoretical underpinnings and approaches of both ACT and art therapy, describe the integration of the two approaches, and introduce practical art therapy interventions.

Recommended resources

1. For an overview of art therapy and the many ways it can be applied: Carolan, R. & Backos, A. (eds) (2018). *Emerging Perspectives in Art Therapy: Trends, Movements and Developments*. London: Routledge.

2. A workbook that assisted me in integrating the experiential understanding of ACT with the intellectual concepts: Hayes, S.C. & Smith, S. (2005). *Get Out of Your Mind and Into Your Life: The New Acceptance and Commitment Therapy*. Oakland, CA: New Harbinger Publications.

CHAPTER 2

ACT and Psychological Flexibility

This chapter reviews the literature on the origins of ACT, its theoretical basis, and its position in the third wave of behavioral therapy. There is also an exploration of how ACT increases psychological flexibility and the strategies that can be employed to generate a value-based life. The ACT hexaflex, including the six core processes of ACT that lead to flexibility, is described, and there is also discussion of the advantages of creative thinking in ACT and how psychological flexibility can free us from negative thought patterns.

ACT is part of the vibrant third wave of behaviorism in which behavior is considered to be both outward actions, as well as inner experiences and contexts, such as thoughts, feelings, and bodily sensations. The inclusion of the inner context is the reason ACT is a part of the third wave. Gone are the ideas that a behavior is defined as an externally observable action. The modern way of conceptualizing behavior includes the consideration of inner experiences and private reactions. These internal encounters, observable only to us, constitute a dynamic and indispensable context to our lives. We are, on a continual basis, encountering these nonpublic and particular thoughts, feelings, and bodily sensations.

Using our ongoing inner reactions to past experiences creates new ways of understanding and changing behavior based on an internal stimulus. Exploring inner contexts through ACT creates opportunities in the therapy space to address the thoughts, feelings, and somatic experiences that are linked to cultural context, traumas, and past childhood experiences. ACT is especially relevant to people who experience chronic mental or physical conditions, intrusive thoughts, triggers to trauma reminders, chronic pain, or internal distress, which also create relationship challenges. ACT empowers clients by helping them place value on their inner experience and teaching them the tools to relate differently to their experiences and symptoms.

In ACT, a disliked/unwanted thought is treated as a behavior and the goal is to develop psychological flexibility in how we respond to the thought. The aim is to open up a space to respond to the thought in congruence with our personally chosen values, rather than to try to change, eliminate, or alter the thought. Psychological flexibility is supported by the six core concepts in ACT: present moment awareness, acceptance, cognitive defusion, self as context, values, and committed action. In this chapter, I will describe the underpinnings of ACT, the goal of psychological flexibility, and introduce each of the concepts from the hexaflex.

ACT basics

Humanism and person-centered approaches, which emerged in response to radical behaviorism, fell from popularity as evidence-based, manualized treatments came into vogue with large hospitals and insurance companies. Humanistic attitudes are surprisingly aligned with third-wave behavioral approaches, which fold person-centered and holistic care into evidence-based practice (McLaughlin, 2019). Because ACT is part of the contextual sciences, it considers how a behavior exists in the context of all the other experiences around it. One criticism of evidence-based practice in psychology includes the limited ways of knowing from an ontological perspective. Understanding one's self in a specific context directly challenges this limitation because it includes spirit in the therapy space, opening the process to non-Western ways of knowing, including spirituality and creativity. This integration of the humanistic and existential tradition into applied behavior analysis positions ACT as unique in the third generation of behavior therapies.

Increasing psychological flexibility is the overarching goal of ACT (Harris, 2007). Flexibility means making contact more fully with the present moment and making behavioral changes to live in alignment with one's chosen values. Making contact with the present moment constitutes having a mindful awareness of what is happening in the moment without trying to avoid, alter, or escape one's experience of thoughts, feelings, or bodily sensations. Clients may seek assistance from us because they struggle with psychological inflexibility, including behaviors, such as habitual reactions, over-reliance on a narrow range of coping strategies, and fear-based behaviors in response to a reminder of an unwanted traumatic memory. When we attempt to eschew or change our inner or outer unwanted experiences, we are avoiding the present moment and responding rigidly to what is happening internally or externally. Harris (2007) noted the importance of accepting that pain is part of living a meaningful life: "The greater your psychological flexibility, the better you can handle painful thoughts and feelings and the more effectively you can take action to make your life rich and meaningful" (p.33).

We all attempt to avoid pain and this manifests in the therapy space. Clients may wish to stop, control, or flee from unwanted emotions, the feeling of emptiness, sad memories, or unwanted sensations in response to traumatic memories. Therapists and clients both engage in a range of behaviors to avoid unwanted feelings and conversations in therapy. The telling of a traumatic memory may be avoided by the client, and the therapist may consciously or unconsciously avoid addressing a client's painful material or subtly encourage the client to avoid difficult content.

Outside therapy, we also strive to avoid discomfort. Consider the feeling of loneliness, including the discomfort that comes from our thoughts and judgments about being lonely. This is a universal human emotion; however, most of us take great pains to avoid feeling lonely. Loneliness is a feeling that often brings about sadness, loss, grief, and fear. Avoidance includes all of our efforts to change or somehow alter our present moment experience of loneliness, including the feeling in the pit in our stomach, the pain in our heart, and the unwanted thoughts such as, "Something is wrong with me," or "I am unlovable," or worse. Avoidance strategies range from ones that are mostly harmless to those that are extremely maladaptive. A more adaptive avoidance response to change our experience might be to call a friend, play with a dog, or go for a walk. While these are prosocial and constitute helpful and healing strategies, they are nevertheless steps we take to *avoid* the present feeling of loneliness we do not want to experience in the moment. Other strategies we might use to avoid, control, or escape unwanted feelings, thoughts, and sensations related to loneliness include shopping, scrolling through social media, drinking alcohol, or working many hours. There are many others you can probably think of that you as therapists or your clients may use with varying degrees of success to escape unwanted sensations. These avoidance strategies tend to be followed by unwanted consequences, such as overspending, loss of valuable time, hangovers, and missed opportunities with friends and family.

More troubling responses to avoid, control, or escape unwanted and traumatic memories include using alcohol/drugs to excess, engaging in addictions or risky behavior, such as unprotected sex, or unsafe driving. More extreme ways that people attempt to avoid, control, or escape unwanted feelings, thoughts, and sensations include engaging in verbal attacks and physically assaulting or abusing others. These compulsive behaviors reinforce mental health problems and create feelings of being a failure, even though these behaviors may be an attempt to feel better. The consequences of these avoidance behaviors essentially generate more significant problems, and clients find their lives revolving around the very thing they are trying to escape in the first place!

Engaging in more adaptive kinds of distractions and thought-stopping techniques (e.g., painting, knitting, calling a friend, walking the dog) may be suggested by traditional CBT strategies. However, although these attempts to alter our feelings may be successful in the short term, the changes remain unsustainable, because the change relies on ongoing use of avoidance strategies. Unwanted thoughts, feelings, and sensations inevitably return.

Unable to banish feelings and memories from our experience, our minds are hardwired to remember and constantly think. Having a drink, "treating" ourselves with a new purchase, or engaging in compulsive behavior might help alter an experience in the moment; however, without present moment awareness and acceptance, the upsetting feelings return and often with unwanted consequences. We are unable to fundamentally change human experiences, such as loneliness, traumatic memories, or unwelcome physical sensations, and we seem doomed to repeat this tension-reduction cycle of trying to avoid, control, or fundamentally alter our present moment experience of remembering and feeling. As previously noted, behavioral choices begin to revolve around the unwanted feelings and thoughts, making the unwanted experiences increasingly the focus of life choices.

What is the alternative? Once we are willing to step off the treadmill of striving to avoid our present moment we can exist in the now and accept what is happening. Doing so, however, constitutes a stance of *willingness* to accept our present moment experience without exerting efforts to deny or avoid our inner, private experiences. We may dislike what is happening in the now; however, accepting what is happening in the present moment is the key to resolving our deep painful issues and reducing our suffering. When we stop using avoidance and control strategies and instead fully experience our inner private sensations, we find new ways to relate to our thoughts, which can end the cycle. When we establish our own willingness to cultivate this stance of acceptance, then we can teach our clients to do the same.

Avoidance of our unwanted feelings and thoughts seems to be a universal urge, and avoidance constitutes a core symptom of PTSD. Avoidance fuels substance use disorders, self-injurious behavior, eating disorders, obsessive-compulsive behaviors, and many other problems. Not surprisingly, stopping our avoidant behaviors and accepting what is present in each moment poses significant challenges for all of us and especially for people with diagnoses and behavior strategies that rely on avoidance to manage inner conflict. This brings us back to the goal of ACT: psychological flexibility, which is the ability to be in full contact with the present moment without attempting to fundamentally alter it, coupled with the ability to adopt or persist with actions that allow us to pursue our personally chosen values.

Underlying theories supporting ACT

In Chapter 1, we discussed the essential consideration of context and the underlying paradigm of pragmatism. Pragmatism proposes that meaning and truth are created by each individual and that behavior is influenced by a wide context. The psychological theories supporting ACT include *functional contextualism* and *relational frame theory*, which provide the foundation for ACT and the rationale for therapy interventions. These theories will help you to further understand how ACT differs from other cognitive behavioral approaches.

Functional contextualism

ACT is a part of the contextual sciences, which means that the context of a given behavior is essential to predicting that behavior and ultimately to changing it. The understanding of the importance of context offers an updated and modern approach to behavioral analysis. Whereas behaviorism considers the behavior, functional contextualism considers the context of the behavior and how the behavior is *useful* in a given context. In this way, functional contextualism invites our client's context into the therapy office as a way to explore and motivate a person to try new behaviors. The context for each person has to do with their age, gender, sexual orientation, class, culture, ability, religion, country of origin, their family, their friends, society, and, importantly, their personal and cultural history, as well as many other aspects of their lives. Past and current family, work, and community environments are part of the individual's context, which helps therapists and clients understand the functional utility of any given behavior.

Functional contextualism asks the pragmatic question, "How does a behavior function in a given context?" Function relates to what *works* and the context is the certain situation in which it, a specific behavior, works (Gordon & Borushok, 2017). Consider any situation in which you are experiencing success and ask yourself, how does my behavior function in this context? Essentially, functional contextualism helps therapists to think pragmatically, to focus on what predicts and influences events through the use of empirically based rules and concepts

(Gordon & Borushok, 2017). It invites us and our clients to begin to wonder, "how does what I am thinking and doing get me closer to my values and what I want in this situation?"

ACT builds on this idea to ask, "What is the function of a thought and how does this thought and subsequent behavioral choice help get the person closer to their values?" It asks clients to determine if their current relationship to their thoughts helps them get closer to their specific goal. Thoughts and behaviors may function quite well in one context and be maladaptive in another. For example, hypervigilance, and the thoughts that inspire hypervigilance, serves an adaptive function for a soldier in the context of a war zone. Being on high alert and extremely vigilant allows a soldier to achieve the very primary goal of survival. However, these thoughts and behaviors can become quite maladaptive in a context of safety, such as after a war has ended and the soldier returns home. Thoughts and behaviors that served to keep a person alive in combat yield unnecessary outcomes, including time spent in a heightened state of anxiety and having disagreements with family members who are unable to understand behaviors such as someone insisting on sitting with their back against the wall at restaurants, reckless driving, and frequent checking for safety. While the contextual function of the behavior in combat was adaptive and kept the person alive, the strategies are no longer useful at home and in a time of peace.

For functional contextualists, the truth of a particular thought or idea rests on its utility in a person's life (Follette & Callaghan, 2011). Does the thought or behavior serve a useful purpose in this context? For the client with PTSD, the answer would be two-fold: hypervigilance served a very useful purpose while at war, whereas it serves an unhelpful purpose at home. In fact, it is so unhelpful that it leads to behavior that goes fundamentally against a veteran's goals of having a peaceful family, enjoying one's neighborhood, and feeling a sense of community. The pragmatic approach to observing the symptoms of PTSD is not to dismiss the experience of these symptoms, but rather to experience them in a way that serves to increase psychological flexibility in response to the inner stimulus that brings about the symptoms.

Relational frame theory

Relational frame theory provides the philosophical underpinnings of ACT, explaining the function of *language* in the human experience. Language in this context includes the thoughts, feelings, and private experiences a person has before selecting a behavior. The behavior of Pavlov's drooling dogs was understood as a function of hearing a bell ringing—the bell served as an indicator that food was on its way and so the dogs began to salivate. However, humans are assumed to be more complex than dogs. Our behavior is influenced by a whole host of stimuli that are not easily perceived or apparent to an outside observer (Gordon & Borushok, 2017). Essentially, we are influenced by our thoughts and the way we talk to ourselves.

Relational frame theory considers more than what is observable by two or more people, which is the traditional definition of behavior. Behavior includes thoughts, feelings, language, and other private experiences (Hayes *et al.*, 2001). These internal private experiences help to shed light on the personal and socially constructed aspects of our behavior that people bring to each situation—the inner context that influences how each person "sees" a situation based on their internal stimuli and interior language. These inner experiences include the unique learned/conditioned behavior from childhood, as well as one's wider cultural understanding and historical learning based on race, culture, ethnicity, religion, sexual orientation, and ability, among other influences. When all of these intersecting identities and inner experiences of a person are considered as relevant to the work of therapy, not only can we more fully grasp the function of each behavior in context, but we are also able to honor the dignity and humanity of each person in our office. Relational frame theory attends to the function of language and how it influences our thoughts and ultimately our behavior.

Relational frame theory considers how inner language influences behavior, and you can explore how it works right now. You are likely already aware of your self-talk and how it influences you. Now is a great time to begin or continue a mindful practice of noticing any outdated, negative, and automatic thoughts about yourself. Each time you tell yourself something unkind, just notice that language and explore how these thoughts influence your behavioral choices in the moment. See if you can develop a practice of making any subsequent behavior choices in line with your values instead of in reaction to negative self-talk. If you are having a judgment about trying this exercise, you can use that thought about the futility of change as your example and engage in value-based behaviors in line with personal growth, in spite of that negative thought.

Why psychological flexibility matters

Psychological flexibility happens when we consistently engage in the present moment and then choose behaviors that are aligned with our values (Kashdan & Rottenberg, 2010). Being flexible helps us evolve and adapt to our constantly changing environments (Kashdan & Rottenberg, 2010) and helps us to avoid engaging in limiting or rigid ways of thinking or acting. Flexibility involves using our behavior to reflect what we most desire in any given situation. It requires awareness and conscious attention to our values and then aligning our behaviors and thoughts to be in harmony with them (Backos, 2021).

"In ACT, whether a thought is true is not that important" (Harris, 2007, p.46). Instead of considering the truth of a thought, consider how helpful it is and whether it is a thought to which we want to give attention. After this consideration, we can make the best behavioral choice for ourselves and others we care about, with guidance from our personally selected values. Rather than remaining inwardly focused on our thoughts, we attend to our values and the external behavior that will bring us closer to them. In other words, psychological flexibility entails first considering our choices and values and then responding behaviorally to situations with thoughtful intention. In summary, psychological flexibility involves mindfulness and curiosity and allows us to consider each situation, how helpful our thoughts might be in any given moment, and proceed with or shift our behavior so that it is in line with our values.

Want a happy life with satisfying relationships? ACT research demonstrates that psychological flexibility can help you be happier (Moradi & Dehghani, 2018), gain more satisfaction in your home or family life (Hayes, 2016), experience a reduction in mental health problems (Hayes, 2016), and improve your relationships (Peterson *et al.*, 2009). In ACT, psychological flexibility is the all-inclusive goal and all of the strategies in ACT work in concert to support this singular experience: to empower you to freely choose behaviors consistent with your values to create a life worth living and full of meaning.

Knowing the goal of ACT is psychological flexibility helps us to integrate each of the six core processes in ACT: acceptance, mindfulness, defusion, self as context, values, and committed action. Each of these components that support psychological flexibility will be detailed fully later in this chapter.

Over a thousand studies in the ACT literature demonstrate the connection between psychological flexibility and mental health and how inflexibility predicts how severe and chronic the problems become (Hayes, 2016). Psychological flexibility is relevant whenever we use our minds, including our self-talk and our parenting, as well as when we are in communication with loved ones, classmates, and co-workers. Psychological flexibility informs how you show up as a worker, student, lover, parent, and citizen. It influences our personal sense of wellbeing, as well as how we respond to social injustices and how we manage to survive in a pandemic.

Flexibility and plasticity play a crucial role in how we respond and how we act within our closest relationships. This is why psychological flexibility is linked to greater overall satisfaction and happiness in relationships. In a meta-analysis of 174 studies with 43,952 participants, researchers concluded that mindful flexibility was linked to rewarding and satisfying relationships and strong family connections (Daks & Rogge, 2020). Specifically, parents with *higher* levels of psychological flexibility utilized adaptive parenting strategies and demonstrated less negative, harsh, or lax parenting strategies. Conversely, *lower* levels of psychological flexibility were linked to negative family dynamics and conflict, as well as parenting stress and poor child functioning. In romantic relationships, people with *lower* levels of psychological flexibility demonstrated dissatisfaction with themselves, their partners, and their sex lives. Those with lower levels of flexibility also experienced more conflict, physical aggression, and attachment-related anxiety.

Psychological inflexibility

In contrast, psychological inflexibility includes reacting to inner experiences and external situations as they arise instead of with purpose and values in mind. Psychological inflexibility occurs when we engage in avoidance behaviors to control or escape our present moment experience. It includes believing our thoughts as if they were a true depiction of reality (Harris, 2007). Rigidly applying rules that we may not even be aware of, or at least have not examined, to manage our responses to thoughts, feelings, sensations, and experiences limits our behavioral options; we essentially paint ourselves into a corner with limited behavioral choices. Suddenly, we are unable to be authentic and in the moment and instead keep performing behaviors that are unworkable and cause more problems than they solve (e.g., drinking, shopping, binging on television, social media, and/or food). If our response works, we may use it again and again, even if it is only a short-term solution and creates more problems. When we keep performing the same behaviors in response to unwanted feelings, even when we lack success or our behavior causes more problems, we are engaged in psychological inflexibility. By foreclosing on the ability to freely choose our behavioral options in any given moment, our behavior becomes rigid, inauthentic, forced, and compulsive.

Psychological inflexibility also ensues when someone uses an equivalent reaction each time they are faced with any unwanted internal stimulus. Examples of psychological inflexibility can be seen in people who have a diagnosis of PTSD when they strive to avoid the reminders, memories, and unwanted feelings that characterize the intrusive symptom of PTSD and they engage in behaviors to control or avoid their present moment experiences. As a consequence, some people may end up spending significant amounts of time avoiding their painful feelings and memories, and thus lose interest in and the ability to engage in their life in a meaningful way. Managing and controlling the unwanted feeling becomes the focus of behavioral choices instead of engaging in values to help them be the person they want to be.

CLIENT EXAMPLE

Let's explore psychological inflexibility using a client example to appreciate how responding to trauma reminders and intrusive thoughts can be conceptualized and treated using ACT and a reduction of avoidance strategies. Zee, an African American woman in her 40s, was diagnosed with PTSD after she was sexually assaulted by a stranger. She endured significant personal challenges when dealing with the symptom of avoidance. She avoided unwanted feelings, thoughts, and memories associated with the trauma, as well as people and situations that reminded her of the trauma. She began to avoid the exact location where she was assaulted and her avoidance expanded. At first, she found herself avoiding the restaurant where she was assaulted, and she quit her job there. Zee then began avoiding the street and later the whole neighborhood, as well as people similar to the man who assaulted her. She began to feel unsafe in any restaurant and started to decline invitations for lunch or dinner with friends and family.

Each time Zee was out of the house, she experienced unwanted feelings and reminders of the assault, so she would return home as quickly as possible. Her strategies of avoidance initially worked to reduce her anxiety and stop the intrusive memories. Because leaving a situation was a reliable way to feel better, she continued to employ this strategy, expanding her use of avoidance. Declining social invitations eventually led to challenges in going anywhere: the grocery store, work, and therapy. She began to stay home more often and started having a glass of wine or THC gummy candies earlier in the day to avoid the unwanted thoughts, feelings, and reminders of her trauma. The repetitive use of this avoidance strategy limited her ability to leave her house or travel in her community, and it compromised her joy in seeing friends and loved ones.

Avoidance exponentially increased her problems in the category of psychological inflexibility. The symptom of avoidance, which initially helped Zee feel better and reduce her anxiety in the moment, led to significant consequences, including loneliness, isolation, increased anxiety and anxious behaviors when she was out of her house, and feelings of being unable to manage her feelings. Fearing far more than being assaulted again, she reported feeling unsafe everywhere she went. In this example, her psychological flexibility decreased to the point where she had only one strategy to manage her distress—leave and go home or avoid leaving the house in the first place. The symptom of avoidance created a whole new set of problems because Zee was unable to engage in activities she valued and see people she loved. What began as a problem of thoughts and feelings and memories was now a problem that affected all aspects of her life: her behavior, her work, her relationships. Her dominant feelings were fear, anger, and suspicion. Her entire life came to revolve around behaviors she used to avoid her present moment feelings.

This is when her family intervened, encouraging her to talk to her pastor. They hoped she would "get over it." They prayed for her, visited her at home more often, and eventually helped her find a therapist. When faced with discomfort from an inner experience (memories and bodily sensations) or from an external reminder (seeing someone who reminded her of the perpetrator), Zee had two options. The first option was to respond inflexibly with repetitive behaviors to avoid, control, or escape the discomfort, such as leaving the situation, freezing, drinking, engaging in compulsive behavior, or getting angry. The second option would be for Zee to consider all her behavioral options, using tools to ground herself in the present moment, such as deep breathing and bringing her awareness to the current moment to understand that the abuse she experienced was in the past instead of the now. This might look like pausing, breathing, reflecting, and choosing to act in the here and now based on her values. By recognizing her intrusive thoughts as solely revolving around an event in her past (instead of perceiving the experience as happening in the present), she could situate her trauma as part of her history.

In Zee's experience, dropping her avoidance strategies facilitated the process of resolving her dissociation by recognizing that her thoughts were about the past rather than the present. She began to employ her values to motivate her to return to a life she loved and one in which she felt more safe and comfortable. While still facing her trauma memories and reminders, she found increased psychological flexibility to engage with her family and friends. Highlighting her value of family, joy of seeing her sister, niece, and parents, as well as being part of her community, motivated her to engage with her relationships.

Environmental supports for and barriers to psychological flexibility

Environmental conditions in our lives create support or present obstacles to our health and wellbeing. Barriers create significant challenges for clients by effectively hampering their efforts to increase their psychological flexibility. Examining the layers of influence over individuals and families allows for greater understanding of our clients and the barriers that may affect their movement in therapy. Ecological systems theory is informed by a convergence of biological, psychological, and social science literature. Developed by Urie Bronfenbrenner in the 1980s, ecological systems theory is still widely used, especially in social work, to consider the environmental influences on development and the lived experiences of each individual (Crawford, 2020). Environmental influences include individuals in one's immediate sphere and broader spheres, including culture, society, economy, and politics (Soyer, 2019). Developing an awareness of these factors and the proximal systems in which they interact increases our skill as therapists. Bringing our attention to the bigger picture of development and influence on each person promotes our understanding and empathy, and, most importantly, helps us avoid pathologizing clients based on behaviors that are adaptive and are enacted in response to the environment.

Microsystems, such as an individual's immediate environment and personal interactions, may include family, home, and social environments, as well as personal temperament (Crawford, 2020). Many people face significant challenges in environments in which their family lacks resources and in which mental health issues and substances are present. Larger spheres of influence, such as *exosystems*, that may limit psychological flexibility include the negative influences of parents, media, and culture on beliefs about therapy and value of the individual based on race, sex, culture, language, country of origin, ability, and religion (Crawford, 2020). Lack of financial resources may limit a person's ability to access care, and working multiple jobs can create time constraints and deplete the energy one might need to devote to psychotherapy. Finally, *chronosystems* include environmental events occurring over a lifetime, such as war or terror, economic and safety conditions in a region/country, migration, racism, sexism, and homophobia/transphobia, as well as standards of beauty and perceived societal values (Crawford, 2020). These conditions existing over time leave lasting impacts and traumas, including historical and general traumas, on individuals (Backos, 2021; Nadel, 2018).

These conditions may lead to adaptations that create psychological inflexibility, which may manifest in behaviors in and out of therapy, such as rigidly following rules, wishing to be right or correct, a low ability to tolerate emotions in self and others, engaging in logical thinking to the exclusion of emotional awareness, lack of contact with the present moment, overconcern with the opinions of others, lack of self-awareness, excessive emphasis on safety, and overattachment to one's self/ego. Without knowledge and awareness of ecological systems theory, therapists may erroneously utilize an overly individualistic model to understand clients, which could result in ascribing pathology to what are actually adaptive behaviors or traumatic reactions to environmental pressures.

Conversely, the environment may offer support and encouragement for a client to increase their psychological flexibility. The microsystem may expand to include family and friends who encourage growth and change for clients. As therapists, we can encourage healthy and supportive friendships and support clients in creating an extended support system, which includes those in our client's community who uplift them and provide support. Additional factors supporting psychological flexibility include creative thinking through artmaking and encouraging creative thought processes to generate multiple ways of approaching a situation. Art therapy facilitates creative thinking and fosters an environment in which psychological flexibility can increase through clients taking risks and trying new materials and ways of knowing through art.

Finally, advocacy by clients and therapists can positively affect the client's microsystems and exosystems. Therapists affect many systemic barriers by advocating for increased access to care through arguing for a responsible caseload, voting, writing, talking with friends and family, legislation efforts, financial donations, or volunteering. In clinical practice, we can provide care for historically underserved populations, provide pro-bono services, and supervise others who provide care for historically underserved populations. Most importantly, we must adopt an open, curious stance of cultural humility so that our work with individuals, couples, families, groups, and communities reflects truly compassionate and informed care.

Willingness

"Willingness," writes Harris (2007), "is the only way to effectively deal with life's obstacles" (p.213). Willingness is a crucial component to helping ourselves and our clients achieve greater levels of psychological flexibility. In this work, it is of the utmost importance that a person is willing to feel and experience whatever is happening in the present moment regardless of whatever is happening in that moment (Harris, 2007). Powered by choice, willingness is the inclination to accept without reluctance or be "favorably disposed" towards doing so (*Merriam-Webster*, n.d., para. 1). It is quite different from merely tolerating unwanted feelings, thoughts, and bodily sensations until they go away. One may dislike or even hate what is happening yet remain willing to fully feel the present moment and ultimately proceed in a desired, value-based direction. You regularly demonstrate willingness to give your money to the grocer in exchange for food and to your therapist in exchange for support. You are currently demonstrating, by reading this book, your willingness to keep learning about psychology and art therapy in service of your values.

We can be willing in spite of discomfort and thoughts that might suggest we give up. The term *impostor syndrome* (Chandra *et al.*, 2019; Feenstra *et al.*, 2020) is sometimes used casually to describe a feeling of personal doubt, but it is a construct that can undermine a person's sense of self-worth, as it leaves us thinking we arrived in our positions through luck or mistake. It manifests in worries of being discovered as a fake or impostor in our work, our relationships, and in love. It might manifest in doubt about our efficacy and/or knowledge in any area of our life. Impostor syndrome is not a syndrome or a diagnosis but a common experience many of us can relate to when comparing ourselves to others. When we use ACT to unpack this set of uncomfortable thoughts and feelings, we are demonstrating willingness to have the experience of impostor syndrome and proceed anyway. We dislike the experience and yet still go to school and work.

Some recent studies about impostor syndrome shed light on new ways of relating to these thoughts and feelings and address social conditions and injustices (Feenstra *et al.*, 2020). Ascribing these thoughts of doubt to an internal cause fuses us to the thought of being an impostor. However, we can relate differently to these thoughts by considering the wider context. While impostor syndrome is often linked to historically marginalized groups in the literature, carefully considering both the internal and external context that supports this feeling allows us to avoid pathologizing our clients. In ACT terms, we must consider the wider context to include how this experience of impostor is created, reinforced, and magnified by social barriers and injustices (Feenstra *et al.*, 2020). In other words, the context includes the person's experiences in their family as well as in society and the overt and subtle means by which any person of minority status is told they are less than or not good enough. Seeing how our social environment may have had an impact on our development of impostor syndrome liberates us from the internal pain of believing what it tells us and essentially defuses us from the impostor thoughts. This disentanglement from our thoughts promotes a willingness to persist, even in the presence of unwanted feelings. From this example, I hope you see how willingness plays a key role in promoting psychological flexibility.

Hexaflex

The ACT hexaflex consists of the six (hex) core concepts that lead to psychological flexibility (flex); thus, the name hexaflex (Figure 3.1).

On the six points of the hexaflex are each of the six fundamental areas that, when integrated, lead to greater psychological flexibility: present moment awareness, acceptance, defusion, self as context, values, and committed action (Hayes, 2017). It is the integration of these concepts that creates the magic ingredient that makes ACT so effective. Lines in the diagram connect each component to all of the others. Integrating each of the concepts in clinical practice comes with understanding and practice, yet we must learn each concept singularly and then build on integrating them into a whole component. As you read through each area of the hexaflex, try to think of how it may connect with each of the others.

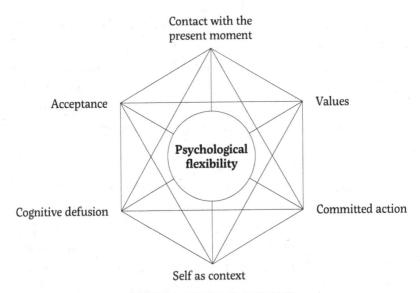

FIGURE 3.1: THE ACT HEXAFLEX

Note: The hexaflex shows the six core processes in ACT: acceptance, contact with the present moment, cognitive defusion, self as context, values, and committed action. Copyright 2017 by Steven C. Hayes, used by permission.

Contact with the present moment

Contact with the present moment refers to being consciously aware of all that is happening in the present moment, with specific intention and kindness, and without judgment (Kabat-Zinn, 1990). In ACT, contact with the present moment includes making open, accepting contact with the moment and all of the private experiences contained within each present moment (Harris, 2007). The *content* of what is happening in the present moment is different from the *awareness* of the moment. In other words, there are two things that happen in any given moment: (1) your present moment awareness (contact with or awareness of the moment), which is distinct from (2) the content you are aware of (e.g., reading this book, specific thoughts you may have, feelings, and bodily sensations). One way to anchor yourself in the present moment is to remind yourself of these two distinct phenomena and ask yourself what is happening in each area. You are observing the moment *and* observing what is happening in the moment. Kabat-Zinn (1990) tells us that we can approach each moment with kindness towards ourselves and our private inner experiences, even if the content of our inner experience is unwanted or disliked.

Acceptance

This core tenet of ACT means being *willing* to accept what is happening in the present moment without attempting to alter or change what is happening (Harris, 2007). Far from gritting one's teeth and bearing the pain of unwanted thoughts and feelings, acceptance involves letting go of the struggle with our inner experiences and embracing what exists internally. It means learning to acknowledge the presence of the unwanted parts of ourselves, including our insecurities, our cruel self-talk, and our painful memories and feelings. Acceptance also involves eventually learning to appreciate and even to love these parts of ourselves. It may sound challenging to accept and even love the parts of ourselves (e.g., experiences, behaviors, thoughts, and feelings) that we may feel ashamed or embarrassed about; however, ACT offers acceptance as a way to gently hold our sense of self and our experiences in a loving and peaceful way.

Cognitive fusion/defusion

The process of cognitive fusion occurs when a person links a thought they are having with the idea that it represents the *truth*. The process of thought itself becomes attached to the content of the thought, when in fact, they are quite distinct (Harris, 2007). In other words, when we are fused to a thought, we confuse having a thought with reality. When these things are fused, we believe thoughts are the literal truth, and the more we think a thought, the greater our belief in the reality of that thought. Fusion involves giving ultimate power to the verbal processes in the mind (i.e., thoughts). The mind dominates all other available information, such as context, behavioral regulation, and pursuit of goals and values (Pinto-Gouveia *et al.*, 2020).

Conversely, cognitive defusion occurs when we are able to notice thoughts for what they are—merely the synaptic firing in our brains, which are accurately perceived as merely thoughts. It involves recognizing that thoughts are distinct from, and often quite unrelated to, reality. A client may believe she is unlovable and that thought shapes her behaviors towards herself and others. Through the process of defusion, she recognizes that the thought, "I am unlovable" constitutes only a thought created in her mind, rather than reality or truth. When we separate ourselves from believing such thoughts are true, we are offered a reprieve from self-judgment and self-hatred, and it is why the process of defusion often comes with significant relief. It opens up new pathways to engage with ourselves and others in a value-based way.

Fusion with thoughts overshadows every other piece of information available, including objective reality. Thus, you can see why defusion is critical to psychological flexibility. When we are defused from our thoughts, we can look more objectively at *all* the information present. Using thoughts as information and merely part of our current context liberates us from the burden of a painful internal experience. It should be noted that defusion is distinct from the thought-stopping techniques of CBT. Changing our *relationship* to our thoughts, rather than attempting to change the thought itself, is the hallmark of defusion.

Self as context

Self as context is conceptualized as an extension of the principles of mindfulness, enabling "individuals to focus on a stable, grounded, and enduring sense of self that is able to have a flexible perspective" (Godbee & Kangas, 2020, p.917). Considering the self as the context for what has happened in your life creates space for objective observations of what is happening in the now. Consider for a moment that you have seen all of your experiences in life, you have witnessed and survived all of your best and worst days, and you have seen both your exemplary and shameful behaviors. Tapping into yourself as context means engaging with that part of you currently existing that has existed your entire life.

While there is limited evidence that tapping into ourselves as context is effective as a stand-alone way of managing emotional wellbeing, it works beautifully *in conjunction* with the rest of the ACT concepts to create psychological flexibility (Godbee & Kangas, 2020). Remember that an evidence-based practice includes *all* of the concepts in the approach; choosing just a few of the concepts to use in therapy is a deviation from what clients and therapists have identified as effective.

Values

Values are your unique, personally chosen principles that guide your choices and behaviors. They constitute your heart's desires for what you want to do with your life (Harris, 2009). You may be currently acting on unarticulated values, such as caring for your child or exercising. You care for your child because you value bringing up the next generation in your family in a loving way. You probably exercise because you value your health, are a therapist because you value service, and are kind to your partner because you value a loving relationship. The behaviors you do (e.g., teaching your child to tie his shoes, exercising your body, and being kind to your partner) are distinct from your values (being a loving parent, appreciating your body and health, or loving and respecting your partner in romantic relationships). Values are distinct from goals: They are the guiding principles that help you set and achieve your goals (Backos, 2021).

Committed action

Committed action is created by engaging in behaviors that are in line with one's values (Backos, 2021; Hayes, 2016). Action inspired by values makes for a meaningful and satisfying life (Harris, 2009). The action part of committed action is the behavioral component of ACT. Action could be spending time with a loved one because you value time with your family. Another example might be engaging in professional development to make your work life consistent with your values of service or professionalism.

The committed part of committed action is so significant it made it into the name of the therapy—acceptance and *commitment* therapy. Commitment comes from a personal dedication to engage with your values, regardless of how you feel on any given day. Committed action inspires therapists and clients to believe we can consistently take steps towards what we value, regardless of the presence of mental health symptoms or unwanted thoughts and feelings.

In summary, the goal of psychological flexibility is achieved through the six core processes of ACT working in combination. We can employ psychoeducation to teach each of the ideas to our clients, and our art interventions and verbal metaphors are applied to support the goal of psychological flexibility. Integrating the aspects of the hexaflex into our work requires both knowledge of all the areas and of how to identify the concept that will be most impactful for a client in any given moment. We must also have a clear sense of how the concepts integrate. For example, making contact with the present moment links to acceptance and defusion. They must exist together. It is impossible to be in full contact with the present moment if one believes that the content of our thoughts is real. In addition, defusion assists in the process of noticing the self as context and making contact with the present moment. Values exist to serve and guide committed action, which can only exist with present moment awareness and an attitude of acceptance, and so on.

How ACT differs from CBT

ACT is quite unlike other behavioral and cognitive theories for several reasons. ACT is considered a part of the third wave of behaviorism and places emphasis on mindfulness and acceptance to generate second-order behavioral changes rather than attempting to alter thought content (Follette & Callaghan, 2011; Ruiz, 2012). In other words, the focus is on living a value-based life and increasing psychological flexibility rather than attempting to reduce mental health symptomatology. With ACT, symptom reduction is *a result* of psychological flexibility and value-based committed action. ACT, unlike other approaches, works indirectly on symptoms. The expression of symptoms is mediated and reduced by psychological flexibility and value-based committed actions.

Furthermore, as part of the behaviorism tradition, ACT's modern approach to treatment includes an expanded definition of behavior. CBT typically considers behavior to be something that can be observed by two people, such as a smile, tears, or a fear response. Unlike this older definition of behavior, ACT considers private, inner experiences to be behaviors. These inner behaviors are only observed by one person—the person who is experiencing them. Broadening the definition of behavior offers a means of addressing and changing our relationship to unwanted solitary experiences, such as thoughts, feelings, memories, and bodily sensations. Expanding what we view as behavior is critical to decolonizing psychology. Using ACT to help clients define their own values amplifies the expertise of the client.

CBT teaches strategies to stop or alter thoughts about a traumatic experience, whereas ACT teaches new ways of *relating* to the memories of the trauma, which includes acceptance and defusion. In ACT, beliefs and thoughts are not correct or incorrect, rather they can be described in terms of their *workability*. We can ask, are the thoughts, beliefs, and behaviors *useful* to obtain progress towards a value-based life? Whereas mindfulness teaches us that we are unable to control the content of thoughts, we are able to control how we respond to the content of the thoughts.

ACT clients who previously received CBT therapy are typically asked to forget strategies such as thought-stopping and distraction as techniques to overcome intrusive thoughts. Instead, they are encouraged to acknowledge and accept the presence of memories as part of their important past experiences. ACT invites clients to drop their struggle with their thoughts and beliefs and to be present with themselves and what is happening in each moment. Instead of attempting to stop the memories or alter their present moment experience through maladaptive and ineffective avoidance strategies, clients are invited to be curious about what is happening in their mind each time they face unwanted memories or beliefs. Clients can then decide how to respond to thoughts that get in the way of their ability to act in accordance with their personally determined values.

A tool often used in CBT for altering present moment experience, increasing positive mood, and drawing attention to new thoughts is guided imagery. The goal of guided imagery is similar to that of traditional CBT: to alter one's thoughts and feelings. Conversely, ACT uses mindfulness meditation in which clients observe their thoughts with no attempt to alter them. The goal of mindfulness meditation is similar to that of ACT: to observe one's thoughts and create a new relationship to the thoughts.

Different from CBT, ACT is a contextual theory, meaning the work centers around the client as context. ACT focuses on how internal and external behaviors can be useful in a particular context, or maladaptive in another. Remember, the goal in ACT is for clients to increase their psychological flexibility by developing a wide range of behavioral responses from which to choose in any given situation, and to select behaviors that are consistent with their values. This is accomplished through new ways of relating to experiences without using avoidance to change, alter, or escape them. The context of a behavioral response might be a survival strategy which is adaptive in a crisis: freezing, fighting or fleeing. In the context of an abusive childhood, any of those crisis reactions may occur. Following a trauma, numbing or avoiding feelings may be an adaptive means of survival. For a child in an abusive home, this strategy allows them to survive when they are unable to leave or get help. Continuing to use these survival strategies from childhood in adult relationships reflects psychological inflexibility in a new context.

To determine the difference between ACT and traditional CBT in terms of efficacy, many studies have compared the two approaches (Collard, 2019; Niles *et al.*, 2017; Ruiz, 2012). Over time, studies have found ACT to be of equal benefit and later to be superior to CBT approaches. For example, a meta-analysis comparing ACT to traditional CBT reviewed 16 empirical studies, focusing on their effectiveness with respect to anxiety, depression, addiction, cancer, and chronic pain, with 954 participants (Ruiz, 2012). ACT was favored over CBT as demonstrated by the *mean effect* sizes (how important or large the differences are), as well as the *primary outcomes* (the most important change sought in a research study). Specifically, the author found that ACT outperformed the CBT interventions in reducing anxiety and depression and improving quality of life. In other words, this review found important differences between the ACT and CBT studies that showed ACT as being better able to help people increase their sense of wellbeing. Other studies have found that ACT and CBT yield similar outcomes. One large randomized trial (N = 208) found equivalent one-year success rates between ACT and CBT for group therapy aimed at smoking cessation (Niles *et al.*, 2017). Researchers found that ACT is equivalent to or better for incarcerated women (N = 50) with addictions and co-occurring mental health disorders (Lanza *et al.*, 2014).

Because ACT stems from behaviorism, CBT and ACT may, in practice, coexist in a treatment plan. Criticism of ACT research stems from its overlapping concepts and uncertainty about the differences between the two approaches in practice, or who might benefit from one approach over the other. In particular, commonalities between the two are related to the "implicit versus explicit attentional foci of the different models" (Collard, 2019, p.1), as well as the idiosyncratic use of language between the two approaches. In other words, some concepts may be similar in practice, even though philosophical approaches and theoretical underpinnings are quite distinct. The ACT foundations of relational frame theory and functional contextualism drive the unique research and therapy practices of ACT. Contextualism is of critical importance in ACT in that it brings into focus the many overlapping identities and situations that each client brings to therapy.

In summary, ACT focuses on changing one's relationships to thoughts, feelings, and bodily sensations without attempting to alter these experiences, by helping clients accept distress as part of life while behaving in ways that are consistent with their values. Context, internal behavioral responses, and values provide a unique ACT perspective. Unlike CBT, the goal of ACT is not to change what is happening internally but rather to respond differently and focus on value-based decisions.

Integrating personal philosophy and professional practice

When integrated with art therapy, ACT brings pragmatism to therapy for both the therapist and the client and this next quote points to the power of weaving personal beliefs into therapeutic philosophy. With over a decade of experience as an expressive art facilitator for individuals with acquired brain injuries, Shari Weiser shares why she selected ACT as her theoretical orientation. Weiser completed her master's in art therapy and marriage and family therapy at Dominican University. During the pandemic, Shari's work focused on individuals with acquired brain injuries whose psychosocial issues were complicated and exacerbated by the conditions created by the Covid-19 pandemic. Her recent research, Zoom Art Program with Adults Living with Acquired Brain Injury: The Effect of Using Videoconferencing to Deliver ACT Art Therapy Intervention (Weiser, 2021), investigated the effectiveness of group ACT art therapy sessions delivered through video conferencing during Covid-19. Weiser uses ACT to support her belief that problem-solving skills can be enhanced by exploring potentiality and actuality, building stronger communication skills, and by developing connections with others.

> I gravitated to the concepts of ACT before I knew that ACT existed. Being a person born with a noticeable difference, I will always be a person experiencing dwarfism. I realized that if I spent all my time worrying about how life would be if I were taller, I would have gotten nothing done. I had to understand who I am and develop a sense

of peace around being different from other people to be happy and thriving in the world. I had to see what I wanted to do and spend my time doing that, knowing that it would be a waste of time to dream of playing NBA basketball. It has only been recently, while in a master's program studying to become an art therapist, that I became more aware of my way of working that out; it is also the place where I came into contact with the concepts of ACT. It turns out that my internal reality is living the truth of ACT—practicing mindfulness skills, developing self-acceptance, and strengthening psychological flexibility.

For individuals experiencing chronic conditions or unresolvable personal traumas, such as the people I work with who have had brain injuries, "stuff" will come up. When it does, it can suck, and parts of it might not be resolvable. Some kinds of help are useful in that situation, while other types are not beneficial. For instance, I am a big fan of positive thinking, but it isn't always useful, especially when there is no way to eliminate the problem. ACT acknowledges what has happened. This approach offers a helpful problem-solving tool, enabling a person who has an unchangeable condition to imagine a life beyond those real or perceived confines. Having gone through my life in my skin, my embracing of self-acceptance and flexibility has helped me thrive, and ACT provides the structure to bring this philosophy to my clients.

Conclusion

The goal of ACT is to increase psychological flexibility to enable one to live a value-based life. This goal is accomplished by first making contact with, and then sustaining, mindful awareness of what is happening in the moment without trying to avoid, alter, or escape one's experience, thoughts, feelings, or bodily sensations. The six factors in the ACT hexaflex (present moment awareness, acceptance, cognitive defusion, self as context, values, and committed action) comprise the variables that must be implemented in treatment for the evidence-based practice to be effective. Values provide a road map for direction and purpose in life, as well as a tool for determining the workability of any given behavior by determining if any given behavior will move us closer or further away from our values. ACT and CBT maintain similarities. However, ACT is part of the third wave of behaviorism and offers a unique approach to changing one's relationships with thoughts, beliefs, feelings, memories, and bodily sensations, as well as providing direction for behavioral choices. ACT invites context into the therapy space, which inspires the inclusion of cultural humility as a vital necessity in knowing ourselves and others.

Recommended resources

1. Association for Contextual Behavioral Science: a worldwide online learning and research community for ACT, relational frame theory, and contextual behavioral science: https://contextualscience.org.

2. This TED-X talk by ACT co-founder Steven Hayes details how increasing psychological flexibility improves mental health: www.youtube.com/watch?v=o79_gmO5ppg.

CHAPTER 3

A Brief Introduction to Art Therapy

Building on artistic traditions found throughout all cultures, art therapy offers a unique therapeutic approach to assist clients in creativity and authentic self-expression. This chapter considers the historical context of art as a tool for self-expression and the under-pinnings of art therapy as a mental health profession. Also included are some hypothesized mechanisms of change in art therapy and how psychology and neuropsychology influence art theory and practice. Developments over the past decade in art therapy will be reviewed, including its evidence base, and a culturally humble and strength-based approach to art therapy.

Humankind and civilizations utilize art to document our existence, express beauty, communicate our thoughts and feelings, define and share spiritual our beliefs, tell a story, make a point, sell products, and protest. Furthermore, art holds an evolutionary purpose and plays a significant role in creating, defining, and advancing civilizations (Dissanayake, 1992). Establishing norms, expressing beliefs, and relating to other people or a higher power are made possible through aesthetics (Dissanayake, 1992).

While it is not possible to demark the exact time when art emerged as a tool for self-expression, the earliest documented abstract art was created using an ochre crayon on rock approximately 73,000 years ago in South Africa (Henshilwood *et al.*, 2018). The abstract and figurative art found in Europe, Asia, and Africa about 40,000 years ago represents what is considered to be the prime visual indication of cognition and behavior. The cross-hatched marks found in South Africa were present long before these figures and inspire curiosity about how people began making lines and art.

The urge to express oneself is biological and universal. Like those who created marks on the rocks 73,000 years ago, young children engage in the thrill of scribbling their crayon across paper. The act of making marks on paper is of primary importance, whereas what the marks represent (e.g., an animal, a person) is secondary or irrelevant. Adolescents and young-adult graffiti artists express that powerful urge to "make their mark" and see their name, symbol, or picture tagged on a wall.

Throughout time, art that captures the spirit of a shared human emotive state transcends the zeitgeist to emerge as a classic expression in various cultures. Ancient Greek artists defined their relationships with the gods in a way that we can still appreciate today. In modern times, newspapers share political comics, while protest and memorial murals continually emerge around the world. Businesses use symbols in art to easily convey complex information to promote sales. The sleek design of a sports logo or a social media site conveys a multitude of ideas with just one line or simple shape. There is no doubt that art, inspired by life around us, informs every aspect of our culture and daily experience.

In this chapter, I will provide a brief introduction to art therapy and how it utilizes the urge towards self-expression and transforms it into a therapeutic modality. I will include a brief overview of art therapy, the development of art therapy theory, the roles of art therapists, the mechanisms of change in art therapy, as well as neurological evidence supporting the use of art in therapy. I will weave the values of social justice throughout this chapter.

Art and psychology

Art and science came together in the early 1900s, providing an opening for creativity and psychology to merge. In the salons of Vienna, artists gathered with researchers and doctors from the Vienna School of Medicine for intellectual stimulation and inspiration. New ideas emerged about how we perceive the world and how we feel in response to what happens around us. Artists and intellecuals, such as Sigmund Freud, Arthur Schnitzler, Egon Schiele, Gustav Klimt, and Oskar Kokoschka, frequented these salons, sharing ideas and inspiration (Kandel, 2012). The connections between artists and doctors led to significant breakthroughs in art and psychology (2012). Insights generated here laid the groundwork for brain science to usher in new ways of linking art and science (King *et al.*, 2019), with both disciplines pursuing the expression of inner truths.

In the past century, the psychoanalytic tradition inspired many early art therapists, including Margaret Naumburg (1987), who is regarded as the founder of art therapy in the United States. She emphasized the use of art to encourage free association and uncover unconscious material in her patients and referred to her work as dynamically oriented art therapy (Naumburg, 1987). Many have contributed to the development and evolution of the profession of art therapy, including art therapists of color: Cliff Joseph (2006), Charlotte Boston (2005), Chantel Lumpkin (2006), Cheryl Doby-Copeland (2006b), Phoebe Farris (2006), and Sangeeta Levy (2006). Others, including Susan Langer, Edith Kramer, Doris Arrington, Judy Rubin, Harriet Wadeson, are often cited (Carolan & Stafford, 2018). Art therapy was nascent during a time when psychoanalysis dominated the field of psychology, and it has since evolved to include multi-faceted psychological approaches (Carolan & Stafford, 2018), global projects (Etherington-Reader, 2018), social justice (Harrison, 2018; Jackson *et al.*, 2018; Jackson 2020; Talwar, 2019), and a significant evidence base (Chapman, 2014; King *et al.*, 2019).

Referring to art therapists, Carolan and Stafford (2018) noted, "We have been seduced by the tremendous influence of the scientific process as a way of knowing" (p.19). Amazing new insights and developments in psychology, neuropsychology, genetics, and medicine help us understand the brain and its functions (King, 2016). This knowledge, coupled with documentation regarding the effectiveness of treatments, offers us profound knowledge and often efficacious treatments. However, art therapists have continued their pursuit of knowing using creative methods (Allen, 1995; Carolan & Stafford, 2018; Langer, 1942). Traditional materials have been supplemented with digital art and video (Andrus, 2019). Art therapists still seek to increase our awareness of culturally humble ways of knowing (Backos, 2021; Jackson, 2020), as well as exploring traditional and new uses of materials.

Art and human rights

The universal urge to express ourselves creatively not only survives but is enshrined as a human right. Around the time that art therapy emerged, the freedom and right to express ourselves artistically and creatively was captured by the United Nations Declaration of Human Rights (1948), which stated, "Everyone has the right to freedom of opinion and expression; this right includes freedom to hold opinions without interference and to seek, receive and impart information and ideas through any media and regardless of frontiers" (p.5).

Connected to the fundamental aspect of cultural rights, the human right to creativity encompasses the freedom to "seek, receive and impart information and ideas of all kinds 'in the form of art'" as well as the "right to enjoy the arts and the creativity of others" (United Nations, 2021, para. 1). Furthermore, the United Nations (2021) asserts that states are obligated to respect the freedoms necessary for creative activity and action.

The United Nations (2021) highlights the human freedom involved in art including "the right of all persons to freely experience and contribute to artistic expressions and creations, through individual or joint practice, to have access to and enjoy the arts, and to disseminate their expressions and creations" (United Nations, 2021, para. 3). The fundamental right to creative expression remains and informs the work of art therapists today. The value placed on the arts at this time by the United Nations, as well as the appreciation of the interconnection between art and science, created an open environment in which art therapy could emerge and thrive.

What is the profession of art therapy?

Art therapy emerged as a profession long after art had been used in the assessment and care of psychiatric patients. Also used as a tool in hospitals as a form of distraction, vocational activity, and therapy, creative arts traditionally offered psychiatric and medical patients the opportunity to engage in a prosocial and productive activity. Creative expression offered patients the chance to learn a new skill, soothe their mind, and engage in a mindful, insightful, fun, or distracting activity to deepen their connection to themselves and to stabilize, heal, and thrive.

Art therapy is a mental health profession that "enriches the lives of individuals, families, and communities through active art-making, creative process, applied psychological theory, and human experience within a psychotherapeutic relationship" (American Art Therapy Association (AATA), 2017, para. 1). As King *et al.* (2019) wrote, "Art therapy is a profession, not an intervention" (p.149). In other words, art therapy is a stand-alone profession whose practitioners are trained in both art therapy and psychology. Instead of using art as merely a diagnostic tool, art therapy provides a means to explore emotions and support people of all ages in addressing a wide range of challenges, disorders, and disabilities, as well as in spiritual and personal growth (AATA, 2017; British Association of Art Therapists [BAAT], 2014).

Using art materials and creative expression as the primary means of communication and personal expression, the practice of art therapy is distinct from recreational therapy or art classes (BAAT, n.d.). While often enjoyable, art therapy offers engagement in a nonverbal means of treatment to reduce psychological symptoms and promote mental health. Above and beyond what is available through verbal expression, the process engages the whole person: mind, body, and spirit (BAAT, n.d.). Specifically, art therapy empowers individuals, couples, families, groups, and communities to voice their experiences and make positive internal and external transformations.

Moving past the original influence of psychoanalysis, the field of art therapy has expanded significantly in the past 50+ years to embrace a variety of theories, including person-centered, feminist, intersectional, cultural humility, family systems, existential, cognitive, and other theories and philosophies. Art therapists work with people of all ages and all types of ability, diagnosis, or challenge. Neuropsychological research has been embraced by art therapy as a means to demonstrate or document the benefits of the creative process. Furthermore, art therapy has evolved to reflect the culture and values of the people engaged in it, notably in its advocacy of social justice and for access to mental health (BAAT, n.d.). This "cultural turn" in art therapy is vital to understanding our clients and delivering services that are culturally sensitive and that build on community and individual strengths (Talwar, 2019, p.xii).

The profession of art therapy is unlike any other. Far more nuanced than art classes, art therapy provides clients with innovative ways to unearth and explore their memories, thoughts, feelings, and unwanted inner experiences. Whereas vocational therapists at hospitals and other facilities offer important classes, including art classes, art therapists provide psychological treatment using art as the primary modality.

While the goals of art therapy are similar to those of expressive therapy, the distinction between these two modalities is worth noting. The two may look similar in terms of vehicles for expression. Art therapy includes classic and modern visual and tactile arts, such as painting, sculpture, collage, drawing, printmaking, photography, graffiti, cartoon, zine, textile, printmaking, mosaic, papermaking, eco art, digital art, as well as other culturally relevant art traditions, such as origami, altermaking, costume, and community art projects. Expressive arts use a variety of creative processes, including music, poetry, creative writing, visual art, theater, as well as dance and other movement. However, whereas art therapy emphasizes visual, tactile, and linguistic art modalities for the purposes of healing, expressive therapists engage clients in expressive arts with the aim of enhancing personal growth as well as community development (International Expressive Arts Therapies Association, n.d.). In art therapy, artmaking for personal expression and insight embodies the primary means of facilitating healing from mental health disorders, as well as personal, couple, family, group, and community healing. Art therapists sometimes utilize other creative domains to support clients and understand their unique visual art process. For example, reflection on the art process in art therapy may include creative writing, journaling, or attention to movement in artmaking to help clients fully express the emotions and thoughts that emerge in the visual artmaking experience.

Art therapists possess a master's or doctoral degree in art therapy and have significant training and supervision in clinical practice both before and after graduating. Thus, it is readily understandable why merely taking classes or workshops is insufficient training for clinicians who want to market themselves an art therapist. Many therapists use art and play in their therapy sessions. However, the practice of art therapy and the title of art therapist is reserved for professionals who follow a distinct set of ethical guidelines and principles and are specially trained in the use of media and metaphor (BAAT, n.d.).

How art therapy elicits change

The assumptions underlying the mechanisms of change in art therapy relate to the integrative neurological experiences of visual input, and kinesthetic behavioral response, as well as use of both emotions and thoughts in the creative experience. First, the cognitive, emotional, and behavioral practices that take place in art therapy can both induce and support change (King et al., 2019). Ask artists about their process and they will describe making art as absorbing, engaging, vital, and therapeutic. Offer children art materials and they often become engrossed in their creative expression. One important mechanism of change in art therapy is its unique capacity to access previously unavailable inner and outer experiences and to externalize them via art and language. In other words, accessing and expressing our inner world, which is created from our histories and our reactions, is inherently helpful for "feeling better" or reducing unwanted psychological symptoms. An abundance of literature exists about the self-reported positive benefits from engaging in art therapy (Alexander, 2020; Backos, 2021, Chapman, 2014; King at al., 2019).

A second mechanism of change emerges in the success of the visual mode of expression when language is unavailable. In particular, preverbal experiences can be expressed by children and adults using the visual modalities in art therapy (Backos, 2021; Chapman, 2014; King, 2016). A preverbal experience may occur before language develops, especially relevant in therapy in instances of neglect or physical/sexual abuse of very young children or adults abused as children. Traumatic experience also has a nonverbal component. The nonverbal nature of traumatic experience is of critical importance in working with teens and adults who have experienced interpersonal and community traumas, as well as natural or human-made disasters. Nonverbal experiences are the result of the brain's incapacity to access verbal circuitry, such as that which occurs during a traumatic experience when the limbic system, which supports emotion and memory, overrides other brain functions to use flight/fight/freeze for survival (Backos, 2021; Chapman, 2014; Hass-Cohen & Carr, 2008; Spring, 2004).

When individuals experience significant fear and trauma, the limbic system takes over and the verbal regions of the brain are inhibited (King *et al.*, 2019). Thus, verbal description and a coherent narrative of a trauma must be created, since the experience is primarily encoded in sensate feelings and visuals, rather than in a verbal narrative (Backos, 2021; Backos & Mazzeo, 2017; Chapman, 2014; Hass-Cohen & Carr, 2008; King *et al.*, 2019). In other words, the physical sensations, as well as certain sounds and visuals of a trauma, are clearly recalled and even re-experienced. Conversely, the logical sequence of memories remains fragmented and fuzzy. Lack of access to language is illustrated in trauma survivors who report a loss of words to describe what happened to them (Backos, 2021; Chapman, 2014).

Through their clinical work, art therapists are familiar with the ways in which language is often inhibited in individuals. Art therapy offers efficient access to the visual and kinesthetic aspects of memory. As Howie (2017) noted, "The hand remembers what the mind has forgotten" (p.3). Through the kinesthetic process of art therapy, clients are supported in exploring their own mind and their forgotten feelings, thoughts, and memories (Howie, 2017). Memories, especially traumatic ones, can be sensate, verbal, and visual. This access to a person's inner experiences, including thoughts, feelings, physical sensations, and bodily memories, is precisely what makes art therapy so effective in helping individuals to overcome traumatic distress (Backos, 2021).

A third mechanism of change relates to the concept of flow and how the mind engages in focused attention on a task when that task is engaging and sufficiently challenging (Csíkszentmihályi, 2008; Kapitan 2013). Artmaking offers a task that engages the emotions and cognitions, as well as the body, and these tasks can be incredibly absorbing. Art interventions in therapy provide a specific focus to help the client attend to their unique needs, strengths, and areas of potential growth. Engaging in activities that create a sense of flow provides psychological and emotional benefits as well as enjoyment. Artmaking offers practical skills that clients can utilize in between sessions and throughout their life. Without the need to recall skills or cognitive tools learned in therapy, and without the need to schedule and pay for therapy, art therapy remains relevant across the lifespan (Partridge, 2019).

The skill of artmaking in between sessions or after therapy has allowed clients to support themselves and take ownership of their feeling states and behavioral choices. Learning to explore one's inner feelings through the art is particularly effective for clients with relational traumas who may become distrustful of others when distressed. Personal artmaking helps support a client's relationship with themselves, especially in times when wariness of others might limit their perceived options for seeking support. Of course, many other forms of coping can be assigned to clients, such as taking a walk or engaging in other enjoyable, value-based activities that offer solitary ways of self-soothing. However, artmaking offers a focus and attention to one's experience that is captured in mindfulness activities with the added benefits of kinesthetic engagement, aesthetic experience, and creativity, as well as externalization of the inner experiences and insight.

The role of art therapists

Previously, I have written about the philosophical foundations of art therapy, which include the roles of healer, artist, and psychotherapist (Backos, 2018). These three intersecting identities merge into the role that modern art therapists play in their work, not only in their office and their classroom, but also in the community. As healers, art therapists create atmospheres and opportunities for individuals, families, and communities to recover, change, grow, and thrive. The inclusion of collective healing to address social injustices, such as ensuring that all people have access to mental health and creative therapies, broadens our identity as healer.

Van Lith (2020) noted that as art therapists we "can be change agents who socially and politically traverse barriers to establish new frontiers in human rights endeavors" (p.167). This is a necessary expansion of the work of therapists—one that has often been neglected by professional organizations, agencies, and individual therapists. The emphasis on Western individualism in the creation of psychological theories and in the training of therapists disregards community strengths to support and heal individuals, and, furthermore, ignores opportunities for collective healing. Talwar (2019) and others have called for "decolonizing art therapy in order to connect cultural competence to social justice frameworks and open paths for envisioning new paradigms of care that are rooted in ethical decision making" (p.11). This more collectivist approach in art therapy challenges neoliberalist approaches (Gipson, 2017) and encourages new ways of working, including radical care for our clients and communities, a care that centers social justice as a vital part of the work (Ravichandran, 2019).

Furthermore, to be a healer requires exploring our own unattended or ignored past traumas as well as examining our beliefs and assumptions about others. Our own psychotherapy, art process, and supportive environments are vital to resolving a therapist's personal and relational concerns. A healthy healer brings greater capacity to the healing art of therapy. Engaging in the lifelong process of practicing cultural humility and questioning standards of practice offers healers the opportunity to reflect on their own learning, biases, and assumptions (Gipson, 2017; Jackson, 2020; Talwar, 2019). This, in turn, helps create a more inviting, shared space in the therapy office for all clients.

As artists, art therapists engage in formal training or apprenticeship to build and master their craft and then apply these skills to the practice of therapy (Backos, 2018). In other words, art therapists are artists who utilize creative thinking and art practice as a way of working with clients, as well as to understand our own countertransference and direct our practice. Mary Huntoon, an art therapist in the United States in the 1930s through to the 1950s, focused on fostering a creative and intuitive process with her clients, whom she called students (Wix, 2000). According to Wix (2000), Huntoon espoused the notion that "all artists are practicing self-therapy. They have always been aware of the self-therapeutic power of their trade" (p.174). Art therapists engaging in the practice of self-therapy through the creative process is precisely what makes art therapy a different kind of practice from what is performed by talk therapists who use art in the therapy office. Art is the primary language in the work of art therapists. Instead of being a means to an end, art in therapy is treasured as a language, a mode of expression, and a way of knowing.

As psychotherapists, the profession of art therapy was influenced by traditional facets of psychotherapy (Backos, 2018). Using the tools of psychotherapy, art therapists utilize psychological theories and apply the most relevant and appropriate interventions in therapy. Art therapy is applied through a theoretical lens to guide the therapy process and help people heal and facilitate change. The art therapist serves as "an ally who provides opportunities for clients that encourage ownership, autonomy and integrity for clients in all areas of art therapy practice" (Van Lith, 2020, p.167). Although art therapists practice in offices, they broaden the scope of traditional frames of psychotherapeutic modalities to include spaces as diverse as museums, gardens, nature, city sidewalks, community centers, and neighborhoods.

Art therapy and psychological theory

Art therapy is an integrative practice in which the creative process is merged with psychological theory to guide the work in therapy. Art therapy relies on theories of psychological development and their mechanisms of change to direct the approach and art interventions. Each art therapist must identify the psychological theory best suited to their understanding of how a person, family, group, or community grows and changes.

While the hypothesized mechanism of change occurs through the visual art process, the understanding of how to approach the intervention depends on the psychological theory being applied. In other words, an art therapist may use psychoanalytic art therapy, ACT art therapy, CBT art therapy, existential art therapy, Adlerian art therapy, or other therapeutic approaches with art therapy. Each theoretical orientation used by an art therapist will yield different goals and treatment plans, as well as different art and verbal interventions. A treatment plan created by an ACT therapist will look different from that created by an Adlerian art therapist because the fundamental understanding of the ways people change is quite discrete. That is to say, whereas two art therapists may employ a similar art intervention with their client, the understanding, interpretation, and discussion will be underscored by their fundamentally different foundational beliefs.

Neuropsychological evidence of artmaking

Carolan and Hill (2018) wrote that art therapy "should have a basis anchored in neuroscience, and there should be a collaborative function between the two fields where each enhances the understanding of the other" (p.43). Much of our modern understanding of why art therapy helps people change arises from neuropsychological research and how the brain encodes and processes stimuli from the environment. Older ideas have included explanations of "right and left" hemispheres of the brain, with creativity stemming from the right side of the brain and logic from the left. These earlier explanations for understanding how parts of the brain become activated in creative thought or why some people are more drawn to symbols and descriptions and others prefer words and logic offered an overly simplistic view of the brain. More recent evidence points to integrative brain functioning, in which both systems and hemispheres and the plasticity of the brain is used to compensate for deficiencies of damage (Carolan & Hill, 2018; Lusebrink & Hinz, 2016).

Such evidence demonstrates that our brains do indeed possess two distinct neural systems that can be divided into emotional responses and objective evaluations (Carolan & Hill, 2018; Lusebrink & Hinz, 2016). While distinct, these two brain systems are related and integrated and, for simplicity, researchers refer to them as left and right hemispheres. Specifically, one aspect of the brain (left hemisphere) activates to help us create a sense of self, attach to others, and engage with abstract concepts. The other area (right hemisphere) helps integrate logical concepts through language and objective observations (Chapman, 2014; Gantt & Tripp, 2016). Research shows that art activates the brain in a variety of nonlocalized regions (Belkofer & Nolan, 2016; King et al., 2019). In other words, both hemispheres work together or in tandem during the creative process to create an integrated expression, conceptualization, and experience when making and viewing art.

Neurological research informs and directs the application of art therapy. One explanation for how creativity enhances our lives and promotes recovery in therapy includes its bilateral and multifunctional processes (King, 2016). Furthermore, the methodology and art materials used in an art therapy session can assist in self-regulation through the expression of emotional material in a controlled way (Chapman, 2014; Hinz, 2020). Finally, the creative process and the art product offer verbal and nonverbal communication as a part of psychological interventions. In other words, art therapy includes creating through kinesthetic movement and viewing the art object through the use of visual and perceptual systems in the brain (King et al., 2019).

Practical application of neuroscientific research in art therapy includes explaining and normalizing our emotional responses, as well as recognizing feelings that may be outside our direct awareness. Accepting that we all have parts of ourselves that are unknown to us, we can use art as a way to unearth our hidden feelings and become more authentic, emotionally healthy, and ultimately thrive. We are able to tap into these unknown emotional states partly because inner emotional experiences typically accompany changes in behaviors, such as heart rate, breathing, and other bodily sensations. These emotional and bodily variations then directly or indirectly link to formal elements of art, including color, metaphor, and symbol (Hinz, 2020; King *et al.*, 2019).

The expressive therapies continuum (Hinz, 2020) offers a unifying, neurologically informed theory to understand the phases of creative expression. Since its inception in the 1970s, the expressive therapies continuum has been widely used, and progress in neuroscience and brain development offers significant support for this model (Hinz, 2020). The expressive therapies continuum offers an important theoretical model both in describing and assessing a client's creative functioning and in assisting therapists in selecting art media and interventions appropriate to the client's creative functioning (Kagin & Lusbrink, 1978). This transtheoretical model provides pragmatic utility for therapists understanding their clients' levels of expression. The levels in the expressive therapies continuum describe three distinct stages of expression and a fourth stage that incorporates the previous three levels. These include: kinesthetic/sensory, perceptual affective, cognitive/symbolic, and the integrative stage of creative (Carolan & Hill, 2018). The expressive therapies continuum offers a schematic framework of the neurological mechanisms associated with various media (Hinz, 2020; Kagin & Lusbrink, 1978) and is appropriate for a variety of theoretical approaches (Carolan & Hill, 2018). Using the expressive therapies continuum to guide and direct our interventions allows art therapists to offer art materials appropriate to the stages of the therapy process, as well as ones that are developmentally attuned to the person making the art.

The power of projections in art

Viewing art inherently evokes emotional responses, self-reflection, and connection to others through a shared experience with the artist and others. This connection to ourselves and others, established through the viewing of art, offers the first glimpse into how art creates meaning for individuals and society. Viewing and making art generates the private events that ACT refers to as a behavior perceived by one person: thoughts, feelings, memories, and bodily sensations. The artist offers their response to something internal or external, and the viewer of the art is invited into the experience. These private events generated by viewing art may include relief, respite, beauty, truth, love, fear, disgust, and much more. Identifying our reactions to art highlights our shared humanity, ultimately connecting us to at least one other person—the artist. We can feel reassured that there is at least one other person who feels something like what we feel. The private behavioral events generated when looking at art can reduce isolation and help us identify new ways to share ourselves with others.

Our projections are powerful psychic material that sheds light on our inner experiences and beliefs. Projection is a process by which our beliefs, thoughts, judgments, and feelings are projected as an image on a screen, onto something or someone else, thus revealing our personal psychology. We can project love and happiness, or mistrust and judgment onto another person we have never even met, often with disastrous results. We can fear another person simply based on our collective and personal judgments of their skin color, religion, or country of origin. The manifestation of these prejudices are the result of stereotypes and lead to actions that discriminate, harass, dehumanize, and oppress marginalized people. As a nation, we can project our worst and unwanted parts of ourselves onto another country, making it easier to objectify and hate them, create laws against them, and wage war on them. As you can see, projections are powerful feelings and people and nations make significant and sometimes disastrous decisions based on them.

Understanding our projections in art offers positive opportunities to explore our self in therapy using projection as a tool for therapeutic growth. Exploring and harnessing our projections can serve us by reducing our biased behaviors and providing us with personal insight. Psychologists have used projection as a means of understanding the personality of their clients by presenting them with ambiguous images and asking what their client might imagine or see in the images (Eyal & Lindgren, 1977; Filho, 2020; Klumpp et al., 2020). Projections help us to understand our art and gather personal insight, and this component of art therapy links to several ACT concepts, including mindfulness and defusion. Looking at art and creating art offer clients the opportunity to explore their inner behavior by externalizing their private events (thoughts, feelings, memories, and bodily sensations).

Through the process of art, they can come to greater acceptance of their self and their inner experience.

A note of caution for therapists

While many therapists use art in the therapy process, art therapists are uniquely trained in studio experiences and media, as well as the therapeutic process. The rapid emergence of inner experiences in the creative process demonstrates an important reason why art therapy should be conducted by people specifically trained as art therapists. Observing and facilitating the art process and exploring the art product can provide important clues about what a patient might be experiencing. Art therapists are trained to notice subtle shifts in the use of materials that can suggest opportunities in therapy for growth or the need for increased support. Howie (2017) provided a variety of examples of subtle or overt shifts in patient artwork that could alert art therapists to a client's suicidal intentions. In the cases Howie noted, these intentions were overlooked/unseen by medical providers. Howie was able to identify subtle shifts in the art when compared to previous art that preceded suicidal attempts. Areas worth noting include changes in energy level, colors from changing from bright to dark (or vice versa), and the inclusion of suicidal imagery. Themes and affect include anger, hopelessness, isolation, and self-hatred (Howie, 2017). Howie highlighted important distinctions in clients expressing themselves using art as an emotional catharsis and client art displaying the hopelessness and despondency that would suggest suicidal ideation.

Many psychologists use art in therapy as part of a battery of psychological assessment, such as using the Rorschach Ink Blot test (Filho, 2020), the House-Tree-Person drawing series (Eyal & Lindgren, 1977), or the Kinetic Family Drawing (Klumpp et al., 2020) and other similar assessment tools. However, psychotherapists may also use art as a tool to facilitate change or insight when the therapist feels stuck or unclear about how to help a client. This approach, without a therapeutic aim or intent and without training to understand the art or discussion process, is akin to casting a very wide net with the intent to catch at least something. While you might stumble on new client material with this approach, it can potentially be harmful. Rapidly exposing clients to their inner feelings without the necessary observations or processing that an art therapist can provide may lead to unregulated feelings of isolation, distress, frustration, or ennui. Clients may feel they have shared something very personal and if you have ignored, misunderstood, or projected your own imagination onto their art, they can feel rejected or dejected.

It is my hope that clinicians who are interested in using art interventions with clients proceed with preparation, personal use of art, caution, and clear treatment plans. This book outlines how you can use art yourself and with clients. It is incumbent on us to make art ourselves and try out each intervention with the planned art materials before ever using them with clients. Always practice art interventions in several ways before introducing them to clients and consider the intervention from their perspective instead of from your reactions and experience. Students occasionally want to alter an assessment drawing series because they have decided some aspect of the drawings would be too challenging for their clients. On further reflection, they eventually realize that a drawing that appears especially challenging (or particularly enjoyable) for them personally reveals *their* psychology rather than that of their clients. Our reactions to an art intervention provide only some of the information we need to determine what to use with clients. After completing the art interventions yourself, make personal observations by explaining your art to someone else and/ or writing about your art and your insights. Your experience will be different from your clients, yet this step is vital to successfully using art in session.

If you are a clinician adding art to your work with clients, I highly recommend consulting an art therapist in treatment planning when considering bringing art into therapy. Consulting before you include art in your sessions allows you to address your treatment plan and goals through the art. Asking an art therapist to "interpret" drawings for you after you already have the drawings in hand will likely frustrate the art therapist and provide little insight for you. An art therapist can assist you in creating interventions that are likely to elicit the content and progress you and your clients are seeking. I have often consulted with clinicians and art therapists to assist in planning interventions and case conceptualizations, and the shared process has been fruitful for clients.

Naturally, I encourage you to work with an art therapist yourself to unearth your own creative process and unknown parts of the self! You can find a list of registered art therapists through the large professional art therapy associations around the world, as well as local art therapy associations. Make sure you find an art therapist who possesses recognized art therapy training and credentials, which you can verify through the professional organizations or the regional credentialing bodies. A list of professional organizations is included in the resources section of this chapter. Finally, if you are already a licensed clinician who wishes to become registered as an art therapist, many schools offer post-master's training to prepare you.

Conclusion

Art therapy offers a unique therapeutic approach to assist clients in authentic self-expression and builds on a tradition found throughout all cultures in creating, defining, and advancing civilizations (Dissanayake, 1992). The creative process in art therapy supports and heals individuals, families, groups, and communities. Using art to tap into thoughts, feelings, memories, and bodily sensations allows clients access to implicit underpinnings of their experiences, heightening their understanding of themselves.

Connecting art therapy to ACT allows for nonverbal externalization of thoughts and feelings. Art supports defusion by helping individuals express previously unvoiced stories and reactions. Far more than simply part of a battery of psychological tests, art expression in therapy offers an opportunity to balance oneself, learn coping skills, increase psychological flexibility, and connect with one's values in a meaningful way.

Building on art therapy and ACT concepts from previous chapters, we will further explore these concepts and identify art therapy interventions that support psychological flexibility. In the next chapter,

I will focus on integrating ACT concepts and art therapy to help you enhance your own practice with creativity to promote psychological flexibility in both you and your clients.

Recommended resources

1. Art Therapy Alliance: Documents art therapy associations around the world: www.arttherapyalliance.org/GlobalArtTherapyResources.html.

2. Art Therapists of Color: While much is written by and about White art therapists, we must ensure we learn about and give credit to art therapists of color who have advanced the profession. This link provides open access articles of the viewpoints of six art therapists of color: Cliff Joseph (2006), Charlotte Boston (2005), Chantel Lumpkin (2006), Cheryl Doby-Copeland (2006a), Phoebe Farris (2006), and Sangeeta Levy (2006): https://multibriefs.com/briefs/aata/open020118.pdf.

3. British Association of Art Therapy: This membership organization promotes art therapy and provides professional support to its members. The BAAT publishes a peer reviewed journal, *The International Journal of Art Therapy: Inscape*: www.baat.org.

4. American Art Therapy Association: Founded in 1969, this not-for-profit education and professional membership organization is dedicated to the development of the profession of art therapy. The AATA publishes a peer reviewed journal, *Art Therapy: Journal of the American Art Therapy Association*: https://arttherapy.org.

5. International Expressive Arts Therapies Association: This membership organization, founded in 1994, was created to encourage the creative spirit and support arts therapists, artists, educators, and consultants who are using multimodal arts processes for community and individual growth: www.ieata.org.

CHAPTER 4

Integration of ACT and Art Therapy

Art therapy and ACT work synergistically to create a powerful thera-
peutic approach, which relies on creativity, behavioral change, and
multiple ways for the client to better know themselves and change.
This chapter explores the goals of integrative ACT and art therapy
in working with individuals, groups, families, and communities.
What can be accomplished with these two combined approaches
is significant for clients in increasing psychological flexibility and
creativity.

Recall from earlier chapters that ACT, as part of the third wave of
behaviorism, offers the goal of increasing psychological flexibility,
including acknowledging, accepting, and accommodating the presence
of pain in our lives. ACT is unique in the field of cognitive therapies
in its goal of inspiring clients to engage in a worthwhile and meaningful life, even while living with the suffering that accompanies our
existence. Far more than merely an existential philosophical approach
acknowledging life's heartaches, ACT provides practical behavioral
interventions to increase our ability to approach life with behavioral and attitudinal options, empowering us to stop compounding
our pain with overthinking and mental suffering. The six areas of
the ACT hexaflex (i.e., acceptance, cognitive defusion, contact with
the present moment, self as context, values, and committed action)
support psychological flexibility by helping clients (and therapists)
in several ways. First, ACT helps us become willing to accept what is

happening in each moment and stay focused on the here and now. Next, it offers ways that we can accept all parts of the self—both the wanted and unwanted external events—and our inner, private experiences. Finally, ACT teaches strategies to make a commitment to our values and make behavioral choices in line with our values to create a life focused on meaning, rather than on suffering and avoidance.

ACT can then be effectively combined with art therapy, which has the goal of using creative expression to understand self, others, and our communities, increase positive emotions and behaviors, reduce mental health symptoms, and create and support lifelong positive skills and personal expression. Furthermore, creative expression leads towards self-actualization. Art creations can be used to support change in ourselves and others, including informing others about issues related to social justice. To substantiate the usefulness of ACT and art therapy, Rosal (2018) has noted that a preponderance of evidence exists to support cognitive approaches in art therapy, as well as the combined use of CBT and art therapy. This is important, because cognitive therapies rely on scrupulous research to create, test, and refine the protocols. Evidence-based treatments, such as ACT, have come to stand out in the field of psychology as both time efficient and efficacious for a variety of disorders (Rosal, 2018), and so integrating ACT with art therapy offers intriguing possibilities.

Linking ACT and art therapy offers clients the opportunity to engage in meaning-making through personal articulation of one's whole self via the creative process. The powerful evidence base of ACT combined with the universal, cross-cultural, and evolutionary supported practice of making art, fashions a holistic treatment approach with distinct processes and outcomes. Synergistically, ACT and art therapy utilize personal expression, psychological flexibility, and meaning-making to create a value-based personal expression of one's life. The blending of the two approaches offers client-centered and creative therapy with behavioral strategies aimed to create a value-based life.

Jocelyn Fitzgerald, a registered and board-certified art therapist, author, and certified practitioner of eye movement desensitisation reprocessing (EMDR), works with clients in Vancouver, Canada, Washington, US, and in Shire, Ethiopia. She trains teachers and community leaders to use creative practices for the purposes of self-soothing and stress reduction in children. Fitzgerald created the beautiful watercolor hexaflex in Figure 4.1. I invite you to return to this picture as you learn more about each ACT concept throughout the book. Remember, each aspect of the hexaflex interconnects with all the others. As you learn and understand each new concept, you will assimilate your comprehension of how psychological flexibility depends on holism and integration of all six areas.

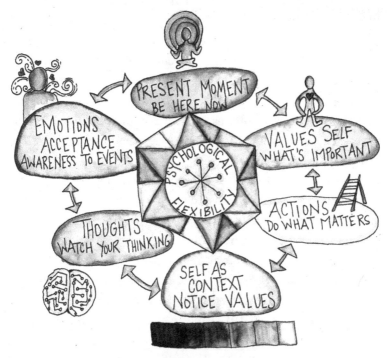

FIGURE 4.1: HEXAFLEX IN ART
Note: By Jocelyn Fitzgerald, watercolor.

In the remaining sections, this chapter introduces the ways that we can build connections between ACT and art therapy, while a fuller integrative rendering of how to combine the two is presented in Chapter 11. This chapter moves away from viewing each of the concepts in the hexaflex as distinct and begins to explore how each of the areas of the hexaflex intersects with the others.

Research

While ACT is considered an evidence-based practice for a variety of disorders due to the significant amount of research conducted on it (Gómez, 2020; Hayes 2021; Stenhoff *et al.*, 2020; Twohig & Levin, 2017), art therapy has a wealth of research supporting its ability to reduce symptoms in individuals with a variety of disorders (Gantt & Tripp, 2016; Hinz, 2020; King *et al.*, 2019). Combining art with other approaches has been shown to be effective in helping people remain in therapy longer and deepen their understanding of themselves. However, sparse research exists on combining the two approaches. At the time of this writing, there were zero articles on art therapy and ACT in the following journals: *Journal of Creativity in Mental Health*, *Arts in Health: An International Journal for Research, Policy and Practice*, and *Art Therapy: Journal of the American Art Therapy Association*. Expanding the search to research databases, and consulting with the librarian at my university revealed two journal articles found on the Academic Search Complete (EBSCO) database.

In the UK, a case study using ACT and art therapy demonstrated improvements on measures of wellbeing and psychological flexibility, as well as an increase in value-based behaviors during an eight-week intervention for an adolescent with an autism spectrum condition (Chapman & Evans, 2020). In another study, researchers combined ACT with art therapy using a transactional model of acceptance with 42 adolescent girls in India to reduce their psychological distress after the death of a parent (Davis & Tungol, 2019). Using an exploratory-sequential mixed method design, the researchers developed their method and assessed its efficacy. They found a statistically significant reduction in depression, anxiety, and grief in the experimental group who received eight weeks of ACT art therapy when compared to a waitlist control group.

Writing about PTSD in Paula Howie's (2017) book, *Art Therapy with Military Populations*, Corrie Mazzeo and I described our work facilitating ACT art therapy groups with men and women veterans with chronic PTSD at the Cleveland Veterans Affairs Hospital. We compared PTSD and depression scores before and after the therapy. The statistically significant findings in our assessment of the eight-week groups during a two-year period revealed a reduction in depression symptoms, and were reported in Maria Rosal's (2018) book, *Cognitive Behavioral Art Therapy: From Behaviorism to the Third Wave*. While changes in PTSD symptoms were insignificant, qualitative feedback revealed that art therapy was well tolerated and some veterans continued in the art therapy process after the group to support their recovery. Certainly, more research is required to better understand the synergistic impact of ACT and art therapy.

Mindfulness and art

Harnessing our mind to engage in the present moment involves the application of ancient wisdom in modern practice though the use of ACT and art therapy. Engaging in practices to bring ourselves into the current moment reduces anxieties about the future and sadness about the past. It brings truth to our experience, reminding us that the present moment is all that really exists. Our mind can trick us into time travel—we can reminisce or regret the past, as well as anticipate the future with excitement or fear (Hanh, 2010). However, none of those things is happening in the moment.

Have you had the experience of being in a perfectly good mood, only to drop into despair or anger when thoughts emerged about the past? Nothing changed in your circumstances except your thoughts, mood, and reaction. The *present* moment was spent thinking, feeling, and acting on an event from the *past*—thus we traveled in time in our mind. When we are unable to stay in the present moment, we are being the opposite of mindful and can be left with a lack of meaning, intention, clarity, or motivation.

To bring about present moment awareness, ACT encourages activities that call awareness into the body, such as breathing, movement, and actions with intention towards what is most valued in any given moment, such as being loving, kind, and supportive. Artmaking offers mindfulness in physical movement and visual stimulation, as well as personal expression. Creating lines, shapes, and colors offers a point of focus for the present moment. Next are some sample exercises that will involve just one line and engage your present moment awareness and your imagination. Art skills are unnecessary for these two exercises and they capitalize on the primitive urges for artmaking. The primary objective in these drawings is personal expression and physical movement. Form, content, and art skill are rendered irrelevant.

Art reflecting the breath

The primary, sensate expression of art is captured in this technique, which follows the breath. Melanie Worstell, ATR, received her MA in art therapy with a specialization in counseling from Seton Hill University in Greensburg, Pennsylvania. She works as an art therapist on a behavioral health unit at a large hospital in the state of Nebraska, where she leads daily ACT-based art therapy groups on the psychiatric inpatient ward. Worstall's willingness and curiosity led her to develop ACT art interventions to support her clients.

Focusing on mindfulness in her therapy groups, Worstell created this intervention titled The Breath. This simply requires a square piece of paper and black ink or sharpie pen. Each up stroke represents an *in-breath* and each down stroke represents an *out-breath*. This image captures and tracks the metaphorical form the breath takes as it changes over a brief time span (Figure 4.1).

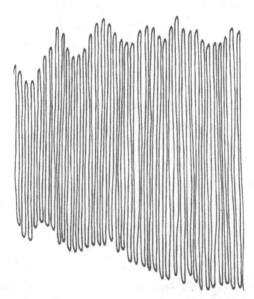

FIGURE 4.1: THE BREATH BY MELANIE WORSTELL
Note: Rendition of the exercise, ink on paper.

First, take notice of your breath for a moment and the flow of air into your lungs and diaphragm. Then begin creating a line that reflects the movement of your chest and diaphragm or that depicts how you imagine the flow of breath itself. Try this exercise a few times before you introduce it to clients. Following your breath and documenting it on paper makes a fantastic doodle that you and your clients can employ anytime, including in class, meetings, or anywhere you have a pen and paper. You can introduce other media, including tempera paint on large paper, water on a Buddha board, or digital tools using an art program on a tablet.

Just One Line

This next single line drawing is an excellent check-in with clients, and I have been using it with clients and students. I developed the idea when working with a client whose depression manifested in avolition. Creating art in session seemed like an insurmountable task for her, and I needed to create an intervention requiring little energy and movement. Relying on the primitive movement and expression and ignoring form and complexity, Just One Line provides accessibility, especially when clients have limited mobility, are concerned about their art skills, or as in the case example that follows, their depressed mood makes participation difficult.

> LL is a 50-year-old, White therapist living in California. She reported loving her profession prior to the Covid-19 pandemic. After six months of social distancing, she found herself increasingly fatigued living alone and conducting teletherapy from home. She became despondent and began to dread seeing her clients, who often shared similar fears to hers about health and safety in the pandemic. While still able to express her values in providing support to others, she reported feeling a sense of hopelessness about having any impact on her clients. She maintained some social relationships over the phone and computer, but she reported feeling isolated from friends and family as well. Pleasure in hiking and biking dwindled, and she was experiencing physical pain and exhaustion. She would get

easily frustrated with clients and family. She appeared uncertain as to where to begin talking, and apathetic when I bought up the idea of making art, so I suggested we start with just one line, which she could do on the shared Zoom screen. She agreed, and when she finished, I asked her to give it a title and describe the line (Figure 4.2). Once she drew the line, our conversation flowed and she revealed more of her thoughts. She was able to identify her values (nature and supporting her clients); however, she reported feeling overwhelmed when she spoke about acting on her values.

FIGURE 4.2: THE UPS AND DOWNS OF BURNOUT

Why does even drawing a line seem difficult? I guess I would call it the Ups and Downs of Burnout. It looks like a timeline of ups and downs of life on the left, and then after the pandemic the lines get sharp and jagged. To describe it, I guess I would say it moves up and down like life, with a few pits that seem to circle below the midpoint. If this were a message to me, I would say I am quite stressed about what is happening in my life and the pandemic, and I need time to repair myself and recuperate from a half a year of intense stress and fear. It looks frantic here on the right. I guess I am surprised to see my current stress level projected onto a line I drew on a piece of paper! It makes me think that my stress is always right there, at the surface. If that's what I see in a single line, it must be there. I think it bubbles up in other places as well—at home and at work, with friends and even being alone. It just feels so difficult to even take care of myself or want to make a healthy meal.

It's hard to even imagine what I could do right now to make things better. I have lost interest in doing fun stuff like being out in nature. Going out feels like such a chore right now. Honestly, I am trying to just survive and do my job. Thriving seems like a luxury right now. I could definitely rest my brain so that I am better able to listen to my clients. I value my work and my relationships with clients. Sometimes it helps to remind myself of that, and other times it feels scary to have people depend on me when I feel so depressed and hopeless.

LL was able to identify a few behaviors consistent with her values and we reflected on these. I provided encouragement for what she was doing well: she kept her appointments with clients and felt that her work was still important. We explored her fusion with negative thoughts, such as the futility of her work, and her fears about health during a pandemic. We also discussed her perseverance over the ups and downs she experienced prior to the pandemic, which were represented on the left side of the paper. This conversation reminded her of her strengths and how she was able to overcome her past challenges. I also attempted to normalize the anxiety of the pandemic and how therapists, first responders, and essential workers were facing significant pressures with such uncertainty over when or how things might improve. This last point sparked enthusiasm for her, as she was able to identify ways in which she was part of a community of people attempting to help others during the pandemic.

It may seem surprising to read how much LL shared after making a simple line drawing. This idea of making Just One Line was appropriate at a time in which she demonstrated difficulty talking and expressed ambivalence about making a whole piece of art. She revealed thoughts to which she was fused (difficulty imagining what she could do right now to make things better), her behaviors (staying in instead of being in nature, not eating enough, or eating unhealthy food), as well as some important values she held about her profession (value of supporting her clients). This exercise reminded me how powerfully creative our minds are when we are present and given the opportunity to use our hands for expression.

Just One Line instructions and variations

Try this exercise for yourself to experience mindfulness and projection. All you need is a pen or pencil and a piece of paper or a computer tablet.

First, take three deep breaths and bring your attention to what you are doing. Notice how your body feels, the sounds around you, and the thoughts in your head—there's no need to attempt to ignore your body, silence your environment, or stop your thoughts. Just notice whatever is going on inside and outside.

Draw one single line on some scrap paper, office paper, a note card, or on a tablet. It can be any kind of line you want and there is an abundance of possibilities; so however you do, it will be great. You can express whatever comes naturally to you. Avoid thinking too long about the directions and avoid trying to make the line artistic looking or into some kind of picture. Next, answer the questions below and write them down next to your line or on the back of the paper. Avoid the temptation of reading the questions and just thinking about the answers. The act of writing is really important in this exercise. Sharing your answers out loud with another person works just as well if they are in a position to really listen and be curious. Examples are given from LL's answers as a reminder for what you might write for each question.

1. *Title your line or give the line a name.* (For example: The Ups and Downs of Burnout.)

2. *Describe your line* in a few words or sentences. (For example: It has ups that are short and a lot of downward moving lines and a few pits that seem to circle below the midpoint.)

3. *What does that line tell you? What message can you get from it?* (For example: I am quite stressed about what is happening and I need time to repair myself and recuperate from all this intense stress.)

4. *Identify what themes, issues, or values arose in what you felt or wrote about in your line drawing.* (For example: I see my current stress level in a line I drew on a piece of paper! If that's what I see in a single line, it must really be there. I think it bubbles up in other places as well—at home and at work, with friends and even being alone.)

What was that exercise like for you? Like LL, you might be surprised to find how revealing a single line can be. I suggest you try the exercise a few more times on different days before you introduce it to clients. It is always best to first *ask* clients if they would be *willing* to try an exercise that you think would help them. You might say something like this: "Would you be willing to draw one line with me? There is a curious exercise that I found helpful for me to identify what is on my mind and how I am feeling. You may find it simplistic; however, I have used it multiple times myself and each time it revealed new things to myself about my thoughts, behaviors, and feelings."

Better out than in!

Our thoughts and feelings are best dealt with when they are outside us instead of locked away or bubbling below the surface. When I was beginning my career as an art therapist, I noticed that so many teenagers at the Cleveland Rape Crisis Center felt their experiences, thoughts, memories, and feelings were unique. Many felt misunderstood and decided that their feelings were best kept from their parents, kept to themselves, or avoided completely. What seemed massive and insurmountable inside their heads became a little smaller and more manageable once it was put into art expression and words.

Artmaking offers the opportunity to externalize inner content that previously lacked language. It allows our clients to create a coherent, linear story of their experiences, memories, thoughts, and feelings. In the exercise above where you drew a line and answered questions, I asked you to write down your answers or describe them to another person. Thinking about our inner experiences is what we already do and to fully externalize them we must create art and talk or write about them. Creating a coherent trauma narrative is vital to healing and that means we tell the story in art and words (Chapman, 2014; Gantt & Tinnin, 2009; Gantt & Tripp 2016).

Conclusion

ACT and art therapy synergistically offer a therapeutic approach based on self-expression, with an aim towards increasing psychological flexibility and meaning-making, and developing a value-based life. The creative and behavioral expressions of values that manifest in ACT art therapy will be unique to each person. Combining the approaches facilitates creative authenticity and a lively engagement in therapy.

Using just one line, you can experience how art enhances the mindful attention—to breath in Melanie Worstall's The Breath art intervention and to the present moment in my Just One Line intervention. These powerful interventions enhance and lengthen attention to present moment awareness and can bring about flow states. Simply explaining mindfulness concepts and the power of now to clients may be met with reluctance. However, using these art interventions with clients to enhance mindfulness creatively manifests the experience in the therapy space.

Recommended resources

1. Steven Hayes, co-founder of ACT, shares the importance of psychological flexibility in a TEDx talk at the University of Nevada. *Psychological flexibility: How love turns pain into purpose*: www. youtube.com/watch?v=o79_gmO5ppg.

CHAPTER 5

Be Here Now: Present Moment Awareness

In this chapter, the present moment experience will be explored, including ancient origins and modern incarnations of mindfulness practice. Present moment awareness is used in various religions, spiritual approaches, and psychological theories. This chapter describes practical strategies from ACT and art therapy, including specific examples and techniques to help clients experience the present moment and reduce anxieties and worries. Topics include: attitudes towards mindfulness: nonjudging, nonstriving acceptance, letting go, beginner mind, patience, and trust.

Are you in the present moment right now? How do you know if you are? *Being* in the present moment is experienced differently from being aware of the actual content to which you are attending (Harris, 2007). Right in this exact moment, you find yourself reading the words on this page. The words, ideas, and your interpretation are the *content* on which you are focused. Now you have an *awareness* that you are reading the words, absorbing ideas, and making synaptic connections to integrate the information into your existing knowledge base. Since the current content is about awareness, you may find yourself presently noticing that you are sitting in a comfortable position, breathing in a relaxed manner, and enjoying the learning process with curiosity. You may find that your mind is intentionally wandering to ways you can use this information in your life or with clients who you are aware could benefit from this information. When you become aware of your body, your emotions, and new thoughts, those qualities become the current content as you continually shift your attention to the ever-present, constantly evolving *now* (Tolle, 2004). Our minds and awareness shift rapidly.

Since you are reading this right now, I assume your client is elsewhere. That means your awareness is of yourself and having thoughts about your client. What you are *doing* (i.e., reading and thinking about a client) is fundamentally different from your *awareness* of what you are doing and how you are doing it.

These two distinct processes—the content about which you are aware and your awareness of the present moment—are happening simultaneously. In other words, you can be aware of both what you are doing and that you are doing it. Another way to differentiate between experiencing the content of your thoughts and awareness in the moment is to think about how therapists discuss group content versus group process (Yalom, 1995). Group *content* is what the group is discussing, such as substance abuse recovery, disordered eating, or a story from last week. This contrasts with the group *process*, which refers to how the members interact with one another, such as listening intently, leaning in, offering support, responding with empathy, and the roles the group members may play in the group. Process exists because there is content and arises as a result of the content (Puskar *et al.*, 2012).

The following cognitive defusion exercises provide training to disengage from the content of the thoughts and see thoughts for what they are—merely thoughts. While they may be merely thoughts, we often find ourselves wrapped in the content of the current moment. Our mind urges us to attend to thoughts and feelings. However, keep in mind that "you are not your mind" (Tolle, 2004, p.11). With practice, we can train ourselves to concentrate on the process of being a human in the present moment. Thoughts and feelings are only part of the now. The more we are able to defuse from our thoughts, the more we can be present in the now, utilize psychological flexibility, and move towards our values.

Present moment exercise

Still unsure about whether you are in the present moment? Try this exercise by answering these questions out loud. As you answer the questions, go slow and really savor the sensory input. This is a powerful exercise to ground you in the present moment, so take your time. What are you seeing? What are you tasting? What are you smelling? What are you hearing? What physical sensations and touch are you experiencing? You may have used this exercise with clients when you notice dissociation or dysregulation in their emotions. However, this exercise can be utilized often, as it brings the ease of present moment awareness, appreciation, and gratitude.

Before you read any further, gather a pen and paper. Draw or scribble your current awareness of the *now*. It necessarily changes and evolves even as you are creating it. What emerged for you in the now while you were drawing? Did you try to draw the previous moment or were you able to stay in the present moment? You can experiment with present moment doodles and scribbles throughout the day as a way to get connected to the now. To enhance your experience and awareness of your senses, try answering the five questions above without words—just bring your attention to each of your senses without falling into the habit of using language. Then use your pen and paper to reflect your increased consciousness.

Defining present moment awareness

Now that you have a sense of *being* in the present moment, you probably noticed how quickly your mind can become distracted and shift you out of the present moment and back into the content of a thought or a feeling. Let's explore the definition of present moment awareness and how it fits into ACT and art therapy.

Present moment awareness emerges by specifically attending to your conscious awareness of the present moment, with kindness towards yourself (Kabat-Zinn, 1990). Present moment awareness happens when we purposefully pay attention and keep our focus on what is occurring in the present, observing without judging (Backos, 2021). If we are engaged in judgmental thoughts about ourselves, we have lost the kindness aspect. For example, if we are criticizing ourselves for losing track of the present moment, we are even further away from the moment than if we just noticed we had slipped out of the moment and returned to the now. In fact, our minds normally become distracted by our thoughts as we move in and out of present moment recognition. Noticing when we have drifted away from the moment means we have once again moved into the now—the act of noticing our mind wandering *is* the moment of mindfulness. We often catch our mind wandering when we follow this moment, and we often do so with judgment. Instead, celebrate that you have come back to the moment!

Awareness in the moment will eventually include being present with both thoughts and the moment without judgment. Steven Hayes (2011), co-founder of ACT, describes being present as "being able to direct attention flexibly and voluntarily to present external and internal events" (para. 10). According to Ekhart Tolle (2004), a contemporary proponent of present moment awareness, the present moment is "a timeless state of intense conscious presence" (p.8). Tolle describes the aspect of the self that is aware of thought content as the *thinker,* while the part of the self that is conscious and attending to the process is the *knower*. The thinker remains actively engaged in thoughts, and simultaneously the knower defuses from thoughts and remains in the moment, noticing the now as well as observing the thoughts.

Thich Nhat Hanh, an exiled Buddhist monk dedicated to teaching mindfulness, describes presence as freedom and the single moment as the place in which we can truly be alive (Hanh, 2010). Hanh illuminates the workings of the mind, noting that we are often lost in our thoughts and plans, attending to regrets from the past, plans for the future, and our anger and anxiety. Like Tolle, he references the Buddha in his teachings of present moment awareness, which becomes a practice rather than a skill that is completely mastered. Essential for ACT practitioners (therapists and clients alike), commitment to the practice of mindfulness and movement towards values creates psychological flexibility and reduces suffering.

Tolle (2004), Hanh (2010), and Hayes (2011), as well as many others, refer to the activities of the mind as constantly vacillating between past and future. Hayes further described present moment awareness as being present to "external and internal events rather than automatically focusing on the past or future" (para. 10). The goal is to stay grounded in the present moment to reduce suffering and to be truly alive. ACT utilizes these ideas that emerge from Buddhism and other philosophies as a way to help us disengage from the chatter of our mind and to truly engage in the present moment. ACT overlaps with some of the spiritual and wisdom traditions that teach practical techniques to control our busy, thinking minds. We can use the mindfulness concepts in ACT to support the spiritual aspects of our clients; however, without any particular religious focus, the concepts of ACT are attractive to clients who follow a particular religion as well as to atheists.

Happiness and the present moment

Happiness requires present moment awareness. A wandering mind contributes to unhappiness and our minds wander a whopping 47 percent of the time (Killingsworth & Gilbert, 2010). This means we are engaged in our lives about half of the time and we spend the remaining time disengaged from the present moment and thinking outside the now. Research shows that allowing our minds to wander makes us very unhappy (Killingsworth & Gilbert, 2010). Killingsworth studied happiness and found that we feel happier when engaged in the present instead of allowing our minds to wander. Engaging with the present moment makes space for happiness, even when we are occupied with what we perceive to be "boring" or uninteresting activities, such as sitting in traffic or doing chores. We are simply more satisfied when in alliance with the now (Backos, 2021; Coget, 2021; Killingsworth & Gilbert, 2010; Tolle, 2004).

Joy springs from enjoying the moment. While perhaps easier to tap into present moment awareness and happiness when doing something engaging or fun, we are capable of joy in the moment any time we choose to be there (Pratt, 2016). You can likely recall exciting events where you were engaged in the present moment, such as a graduation, marriage, or reuniting with friends after an absence. When was the last time you found yourself in the present washing dishes, vacuuming, or waiting at a red light? Being in the moment requires practice, and lots of it. The foundational pillar of ACT includes engaging in the now and this particular strategy offers an important tool in building a positive mood as sustaining ongoing happiness. Are you currently in the present moment?

The present moment in ACT

ACT offers a precise definition of present moment awareness that can inform our therapy practice. It is the accepting, open contact with the present moment, defused from thought, in combination with the private inner experiences happening in that moment (Harris, 2007). Specifically, the awareness is experientially distinct from what is being noticed in the moment (Harris, 2007). As mentioned previously, the content of what is being noticed is different from the process of noticing.

In ACT, present moment awareness refers to the ongoing contact with the present moment that is accepting rather than judging. Furthermore, it includes contact with your own psychology, as well as the environment. Finally, one's attention can be voluntarily allocated in a fluid and flexible way of one's own choosing (Harris, 2007). In other words, being in touch with the present moment has the pragmatic advantage of allowing us to direct our attention. We can choose to focus on whatever inner and outer aspects of the present moment are most important to us in that specific context. This ability to choose control over our attention brings us closer to the ACT goal of psychological flexibility.

With flexible attention, which is the ability to attend to what is most important in a context, we can begin to use language and thinking in a more cognitively defused way. Mindful awareness gives us the opportunity to freely move our attention around while staying focused on accepting what is inside and outside us in the moment. We can then reflect on our self-talk and language with others in a way that is focused on the process (having a thought) rather than the content (the subject matter of the thought). This shifts our attention to what is happening with an attitude of curiosity rather than using language to judge and predict what will happen next.

The goal in working with clients is to help them make ongoing and flexible contact with the present moment (the external environment and the internal psychological experience) in a way that is nonjudgmental. For example, a client shared his experience of anxiety and immediately began sharing his self-talk: "I should not have this anxiety" and, "I need to be more efficient to stop all this procrastination." I asked, "Would you be willing to explore your anxiety together with curiosity so we can understand it together?" When he agreed, I asked him to focus on the feeling of anxiety and withhold judgment about the anxiety and what it meant to him while he explained his experience. I asked him to quickly scribble the feeling as he was experiencing it at that moment. He proceeded to describe and make more drawings of what anxiety felt like to him. The freedom to be in the moment without judgment allowed him to open up and genuinely share his experiences in the moment, instead of reporting his past anxiety or judgments.

Cultivating a mindful stance

There are seven attitudes that comprise a stance of mindfulness: nonjudging, nonstriving, acceptance, letting go, beginner mind, patience, and trust (Kabat-Zinn, 1990). Here we will explore each of these concepts and how they might be applied in therapy to increase clients' psychological flexibility and ability to stay in the moment to choose actions that get them closer to their chosen values.

Nonjudging

This attitude creates a space that allows and welcomes all inner private experiences, as well as external situations. Nonjudging is accomplished by reserving judgment and criticism of self or others to fully embrace whatever exists.

Nonstriving

To strive towards feeling better or avoiding the present moment is the opposite of mindfulness. Nonstriving means dropping attempts to avoid, change or stop one's experience in the moment. This is fundamentally different from CBT, which helps clients alter and challenge thoughts.

Acceptance

This involves actively attending to and embracing private events without attempting to alter them. Acceptance of the present moment provides an alternative to the struggle of trying to avoid the present moment. Acceptance of the unwanted thoughts, feelings, or bodily sensations creates an opportunity to look for the potential gift in the moment. Researchers describe post-traumatic growth as developing a life far richer after trauma than could have been experienced without the distress and the traumatic experience (Kabat-Zin, 1990). For example, a person who is able to advocate for women could perhaps be such a strong advocate because she experienced discrimination or harassment. That is what I mean by looking for the possible gifts of the unwanted experiences. In ACT, acceptance is a means to an end. Remember the goal of ACT is to engage in value-based living and being accepting of the present moment allows for space to explore values and make a decision in the moment that will get us closer towards what we value.

Letting go

Releasing attention and attachment to our emotional or physical pain begets relief. For example, a man experiencing chronic pain can accept the presence of ongoing pain and let go of the *struggle* with his pain in order to live a full life with his family. This involves recognizing and accepting the pain without adding his judgment and additional suffering to it. The pain remains; however, the struggle dissipates, leaving space for value-based behavioral choices.

Beginner mind

The attitude of a beginner's mind brings a fresh perspective to each moment, without carrying the baggage of past experiences into the present moment. Shunryu Suzuki, a Japanese monk and meditation teacher, helped popularize Zen Buddhism in the West. He founded the first Zen Buddhist monastery outside Asia in central California, as well as the San Francisco Zen Center. In his 1970 book, *Zen Mind, Beginner Mind*, Suzuki described how to cultivate a fresh perspective in each moment: developing a beginner's mind. In a beginner's mind, many possibilities exist for approaching the moment, a task, or a relationship, whereas the mind of the expert sees fewer possibilities and is often full of judgments and preconceived ideas (Suzuki, 2020).

Patience

Committing to a lifelong practice of mindfulness requires a great deal of patience. The ongoing work of mindfulness requires practice, persistence, and evolution.

Trust

When we trust ourselves and the process of being mindful, we can develop confidence that the work will be fruitful and meaningful. Letting go of fears and judgments leaves space for trust in the process of mindfulness as a way to relieve suffering.

Gratitude and generosity

The daily practice of writing down what you are grateful for fosters optimism, alertness, enthusiasm, and energy. A gratitude practice also yields fewer unwanted physical symptoms, and less stress and depression.

Present moment and flow in art therapy

Have you ever been so preoccupied in thought that you missed what you were just reading or what someone was saying? Perhaps you have had the experience of speaking to someone who seemed to miss what you were saying? A conversation that lacks present moment awareness looks like two people just waiting for the other person to stop talking so they can say something. This is an example of losing the present moment and becoming preoccupied with internal thoughts, feelings, and reactions.

Present moment awareness in artmaking may ebb and flow as we, as well as our clients, become engaged in an activity or keenly aware of some quality of the medium. Artists and clients alike may slip out of the present moment, become self-conscious, and critically judge their art skill, or become distracted by a thought or feeling and lose the focus of the present moment. Staying engaged and mindful in art is a choice. I have seen some students work as quickly as possible to finish a class art project and then pick up their phone, while others keep working and have trouble stopping at the end of the hour. The students who remain engaged certainly seem to enjoy themselves more!

Flow is a mental state involving being fully immersed, completely engaged, absorbed, with an energized focus, with full enjoyment of the process (Csíkszentmihályi, 2008). Undoubtedly, you have had an experience of flow before. Perhaps you felt it when making art, exercising, or being fully engaged in a hobby or work project. Many artists and art therapists are familiar with the concept of flow, because artmaking expands our capacity to engage in present moment awareness and flow (Backos, 2021; Rappaport, 2008, 2013). When present moment awareness is combined with an engaging process or activity, a deeper state of flow may ensue.

Mihály Csíkszentmihályi (2008), who was interested in understanding the absorption of artists in their creative process, coined the term *flow* in 1975. The concept includes an interplay of six areas, one of which includes present moment awareness. Specifically, flow happens when the following are present: focused concentration in the present moment, a loss of reflective self-consciousness, merging of one's awareness with action, a sense of loss of personal agency in the situation, an altered sense/losing track of time, and an intrinsic sense of reward.

Art clears the effluvia in my head

As discussed previously, the energy of art to increase insight and awareness manifests through engagement with the present moment. Maria Elena Fuster is a Cuban American marriage and family therapist and board-certified art therapist in private practice in Southern California. As a doctoral candidate in art therapy psychology at Dominican University of California, she blends her extensive clinical and personal experiences with her research regarding Latinx women and cultural integration. We talked about the role of present moment awareness in her clinical work and how artmaking can lead to "truth and reality." In Fuster's essay for this book, "Mindfulness in art therapy," she muses about choice and control of materials to "unlatch unconscious material" for the client.

Present moment awareness, or "mindfulness" is defined as being consciously aware of the present, in an accepting and nonjudgmental way (Kabat-Zinn, 1990). By allowing thoughts, feelings, memories, and somatic sensations to come and go without having to engage with them contributes to the creation of a sense of self that is distinct from the content of consciousness (Hayes *et al.*, 2012). Research has demonstrated that mindfulness improves a sense of wellbeing and decreases anxiety, negative affect, and depression (Brown & Ryan, 2003; Campenni & Hartman, 2020). As an art therapist and an artist, I find the practice of present moment awareness, or mindfulness, to be an integral part of creating and healing.

Artmaking facilitates relaxation that is similar to being in a meditative state (Sandmire *et al.*, 2012; van der Vennet & Serice, 2012). The creative process requires and promotes aspects of mindfulness, such as attention and focus (Edwards & Hegerty, 2018). With the guidance and "witness" of an art therapist, the client is able to engage in art in a way that encourages them to be present in the moment, with their thoughts, emotions, and bodily states. This practice of awareness, in a safe, therapeutic environment, facilitates defusion and engagement in acceptance.

As an art therapist and marriage and family therapist, I see the creative process of the client in session as an important tool in assessment, informing me of challenges the client may have with cognitive fusion and psychological flexibility. There is a sacred space within the art therapy room that allows for the client to engage in present moment awareness as their stories unfold in their search for healing. The art materials entice the client and give them the freedom to choose what they need in the moment. These material choices also inform me of how the client would like to express themselves, whether through fluid media with less control, such as watercolors, that can be more affective, or pencil and marker, for more control. The body language and the way the client sets up their art materials also informs me of the state of comfort or discomfort. As the creative process unfolds and the client begins to engage in the artmaking, the space is held for the client to become aware of thoughts, emotions, and sensations in the body. The media is manipulated and directed in ways that only the client controls or allows for no control, as they begin to unearth the images from within and reflect on what is revealed.

As the client works, I watch the client and the art meld together and flow in the experience. I check within myself and watch the process and reflect on what I know, what I intuit, and what brings about curiosity in the work and images. I also listen to what the art is telling me, through the jabs, swishes, scrapes, and stitching. The movements may tell another story, as the sensory and somatic merge together and begin weaving memory and emotions in the telling of their narratives and the meaning-making that they are sharing with me. There is something alchemical that occurs, where transformation and insight begin to formulate and become concrete. There are no words, only knowing, searching, trying to articulate that which has no words. The art becomes the invited guest in the room and the client shares the experience.

Creating art can act as a catalyst for change, as it forces the client to be present in the moment of creating, slowing them down and noticing sensory experiences as they engage in the materials. It allows the awareness of fusion, witnessing the thoughts that want to take over and learning to watch in a detached way, as the thoughts emerge and dissipate. The artmaking process can also allow for the client to have a closer connection to self and accepting self. The artmaking process encourages the development of skills of noticing and focusing, along with the use of the media, which is conducive to unlatching unconscious material and somatic sensations. The artmaking also acts as a grounding mechanism, keeping the client from dysregulating. This process can also reveal the truth and reality of any given situation that the client may have been perseverating about, allowing for psychological flexibility to occur.

Art in therapy engages a way of knowing that goes beyond the talking, where a sense of wholeness can be achieved (Langer, 1942). Susanne Langer (1942) believed that the arts are a language of emotion and that this language is used primarily to express the artist's intuitive knowledge of human feeling. It corroborates our intuition that art can tell us much—not only about what clients feel, but also about how they see life and the world—their unique flow of one feeling into another and the deep structure that underlies this flow of feeling.

"Art affords different ways of knowing in areas that include the therapist knowing the client, the client knowing oneself, and the knowing of human mind and experience" (Carolan & Stafford, 2018, p.19). It engages a range of ways of knowing through experience, felt senses, intuition emotion, and imagination. This way of knowing in the use of art can activate the mind-body and help integrate the whole person in the process of discovery (Carolan & Stafford, 2018).

In my own work as an artist (see Figure 5.1), creating art is a form of meditation, as I work intuitively, paying attention to thoughts and feelings as they ebb and flow in the moment. My process tends to start with materials that "speak" to me and compel me to create in order to gain understanding. The use of textiles, found objects, and other tactile materials elicits images to emerge and narratives to be created. The art grounds me and allows me to stay present; it slows me down, and clears the effluvia in my head. It allows me to notice the visceral feelings that have no words and digs deep until the art reveals the truth, gives me clarity. This mindfulness art practice strengthens my awareness, allows me to trust my intuitive self, and is the foundation that teaches me how to be present with my clients as I guide them on their own journey of self-awareness and self-acceptance.

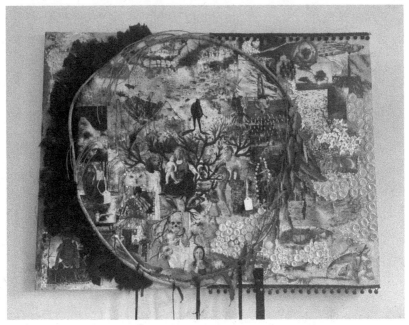

FIGURE 5.1: EL BOSQUE BY MARIA FUSTER
Note: Mixed media 36" × 48".

Questions to facilitate a curious, nonjudgmental observation of a feeling

When you notice that a client has judgments about a feeling or psychological symptom that exacerbates the experience, you can use this intervention to promote an open and accepting psychological stance. This is an opportunity to explore the unwanted feelings in the moment. This exercise help clients stay in the present by reminding them to create the art and answer the questions as they relate to the here and now.

Materials: 10–12 sheets of paper of various sizes, oil pastels/cray-pas, glue stick, scissors, stapler, tape.

Optional: cookie-cutter body shape for client to trace onto the paper, and feeling chart with a list of many feelings.

You can ask your client to make a quick response to the directives below or space them out for a week's worth of homework between sessions. Feel free to modify the directions to tailor them to your client's specific needs.

1. What emotional and physical feelings are you aware of right now? Where do you experience that feeling in your body? Describe any of the places in your body where you experience them. Do a quick drawing of a body and show the feelings in lines, shapes, and colors. Stick figures are fine, although a larger figure will allow for more expression. (*To therapist: You can provide a cookie-cutter body shape for your client to trace.*)

2. On a new sheet of paper, zoom into the lines and shapes you made in the previous body drawing and create an image or scribble to depict the internal experience of feelings in the body. Pay attention to the color, size, and texture and how these express the feelings. Point out the parts of the feelings depicted in the art that are related to judgments or pain, which comes from trying to avoid, control, or escape feelings.

3. On a new sheet of paper or on the same one, create an image using lines, shapes, and colors to show what is or could be different about the feeling when you subtract judgments and control strategies. What changes in the art when judgments are dropped? Focus specifically on acceptance and lack of judgment, which reflect your feelings, just as they are.

4. On a new sheet of paper or on the same one, create an image using lines, shapes, and colors to show what is different about the feeling when you subtract your *strategies to avoid, control, or escape* the feeling (e.g., drinking, shopping, cutting, yelling, controlling). Focus specifically on the problem, pain, or feelings as they are, without any judgments about them.

5. In words, how are you experiencing the feeling right now, in this moment? (*To therapist: You may wish to provide a list of feeling words for clients as a prompt.*) Focus specifically on the present moment. What is it like right now to share your feelings in words and art?

6. On a scale of 0–10, how intense is that feeling right now? (1 being very little and 10 being an extreme and intense feeling.)

7. Invite the self as context to observe what is happening. What does it feel like to *talk about* the feelings and *make art about* them right now? You may wish to provide a list of feeling words as a prompt. This question elicits awareness, knowing, and defused observations of feelings, rather than the content of the feelings.

8. Are there any *other feelings* that came up during this exercise? What else are you aware of right now?

9. In discussion, explore the differences between the inner unwanted experience with judgment and what the experience is without the added self-judgments. Using words, describe what you might do to *accept* the feelings next time you experience them. How might the way we think about our inner experiences make them worse when we struggle? How might a new way of relating to our feelings and thoughts be helpful?

10. Create a *new 3-D piece of art* that integrates all the artwork created in this exercise. Cut out, crumple up, fold, bend, or twist your art pieces and attach them with glue or tape to one another or onto a new piece of paper. This is designed to change your relationships to the feelings in the same way that defusing from thoughts changes our relationships with our thoughts. How might this new way of relating to your thoughts and feelings assist in accepting and being aware of the present moment?

Try this directive yourself to explore one of your own unwanted feelings before taking it to your client. You can use this directive to foster flexible attention and curiosity to create a less judgmental way of experiencing thoughts, feelings, and other private events. Add to your art or get a new piece of paper to reflect the answers to the questions above. You may discover some fantastic variations that will help you make this exercise more tailored to your clients. You might want to write a list of all the prompts to take with you into your session, and you can modify them to suit your client.

Integrating mindfulness and cultural humility

Juviel Vinluan is a master's student in art therapy psychology at Dominican University in the San Francisco Bay Area. When she was five years old she and her family immigrated to the United States from the Philippines. Her personal experiences inspired her passion to be a therapist and work with immigrants. In Vinluan's thesis research, she supported recent refugees fleeing political violence in Nicaragua using altered books and an online platform. I asked her to share what was most important to her as a researcher and art therapist. She wrote the essay below titled, "Cultural humility and mindfulness in art therapy," in which she taps into mindfulness, self as context, cultural humility, as well as her values and committed action. Her essay demonstrates how each of the areas in the hexaflex are interconnected, and you can view her self-portrait in Figure 5.2.

> Migrating to another country, I realized that connecting with other human beings was one of the primary resources for survival. Since age five, when I moved to the US, I was constantly trying to acculturate into my new environment, by changing my language or the food I would bring to lunch at school. A fond memory I had of coming from the airport was seeing the massive apartments in Los Angeles, thinking they were mansions. I was not used to being in a car on a freeway because my mother and I would either walk or ride in Jeepneys or tricycles to our destination. There was cultural shock everywhere I went. Immigration is not just a government policy; it affects generations of families and basic human rights.
>
> As an immigrant kid, I felt the pressure of the world on my

shoulders because I had no connection with who I was or where I was going. Over the years, this pressure led to my questioning in self-reflection who I wanted to be and why I was doing what I was doing. I was fused with my parents' idea of me, while staying curious of the new world I was in. This led to the confusion of who I was and what my plans were for the future.

I had the opportunity to work with Nicaraguan refugees seeking asylum in Costa Rica for my master's thesis in art therapy at Notre Dame de Namur University/Dominican University of California. Through the nongovernmental organization, Viva Nicaragua Abroad, I met with the refugees online for several months, reflecting on three primary questions: "Who are you? How has your journey been so far? What are you looking forward to in the future?" Using a cultural humility framework for the art therapy process created an open space for the participants to collaborate freely in art and in discussion. Cultural humility helps bring awareness to the importance of understanding one's culture without misinterpreting it or changing it. It helped plant a seed in their lives to reflect, accept, and understand what was currently going on in their lives.

As a researcher, I practiced a cultural humility framework through engaging in open-minded discussions about race, identity, and human rights. It helped me reflect on triggers of biases and assumptions. Creating art with the participants unraveled many emotions that I had to reflect on through a parallel process. The altered books that we all individually created as a group opened up questions of my intentions as an advocate for social justice and as a human being. I realized that my identity is constantly changing every day through the conversations we have with one another, the beliefs that we hold, and the environment we are privileged to stay in. Over the years, I have acculturated as an American, but that does not change my cultural values of the Philippines. Immigration creates this label and this bondage over basic human rights that should just be given to us by default.

FIGURE 5.2: SELF-PORTRAIT BY JUVIEL VINLUAN
Note: Charcoal on paper.

Mindfulness when viewing art

Viewing art can be a tool for self-soothing, personal growth, and a means to find balance in life (de Botton & Armstrong 2013). Even those who feel they lack artistic inclination can have a good, long look at a piece of art to promote creative thinking. De Botton and Armstrong (2013) asserted that viewing art can provide powerful solutions to what ails us. Rather than using museum standards to define what works are relevant from an intellectual and historical context, they suggested we reframe how we use art. A pragmatic approach encourages us to view art to soothe our emotions, help us reflect, and reach resolution from challenging emotional issues in our life.

De Botton and Armstrong's (2013) words resonate with me and I spend a moment each day letting my mind wander into the picture that hangs above my desk. It is a watercolor city scape, which used to hang in my parents' home. When I was a child, the picture inspired my imagination and I wondered where I might venture in that urban environment and what people might be doing in the high-rise apartments depicted in the background. On reflection, the urban landscape I viewed as a child on the wall provided the perfect balance to the pastoral landscape I saw when I looked out of the window at woods and our garden. You likely have a similar experience of being moved and balanced by a piece of art. De Botton and Armstrong recommended purposely using art to establish balance in our lives by pausing and reflecting on what we see.

However, visiting museums and viewing classic art is only one way to benefit from viewing art. In fact, seeking out unknown artists offers tremendous benefits for us emotionally (Bennington *et al.*, 2016). Many groups of people lack opportunities to have their art seen and become widely revered in art history books or museums because they are marginalized due to racism and classism, among other forms of societal oppression. Fortunately, we all now have the chance to seek out opportunities online to view past and contemporary art from disenfranchised groups to help us understand the breadth of the human condition and see our feelings reflected in the art. Consider what art you have in your home and therapy space. How does it offer balance to you and your clients?

Gazing at art offers opportunities for balance and emotional reflection, yet how much more significant is it to observe our own art as a means of discovering ourselves and how to heal? Exploring the relevance, hidden meanings, and projections of our own art elicits empowerment. Making art with an art therapist provides the opportunities mentioned earlier for self-reflection and unearthing emotions and solutions to problems. Additionally, clients in therapy can utilize their own artmaking to communicate with themselves, generate their own solutions, and take ownership over their own healing. In other words, the art empowers clients to create a positive relationship with themselves and take ownership over their healing and growth. Viewing art promotes defusion from thoughts and offers perspective. The next exercise picks up on the idea of viewing art as a tool for insight and involves mindfully creating digital photographs.

Digital art therapy and mindfulness

Sarah Kremer believes passionately in the power of art and intentional relationships for healing and growth at any age. Kremer received her bachelor's degree in visual art, her master's in art therapy from the School of the Art Institute of Chicago, and her doctorate in art therapy psychology from Notre Dame de Namur University. She serves as art therapy faculty member at Dominican University of California and coordinates their continuing education program. Kremer is a trained SoulCollage® facilitator and serves on the Advisory Board for First Exposures, a nonprofit photography-based youth mentoring program in San Francisco. She provides direct services, supervision, support, teaching, and training based on building resilience in young people and the adults around them. Through youth development, photography, and therapeutic healing approaches, she addresses trauma, mental health issues, and family conflicts, and builds resilience. She fosters creative growth with adolescents in psychiatric care, community mental health centers, substance abuse day treatment programs, alternative school settings, dance camps, juvenile probation, and mentoring agencies. Her essay and mindful photography exercise below uses digital art as a means of fostering present moment awareness, defusion from thoughts, and psychological flexibility.

Mindful photography

Being mindful and creating photographs are naturally aligned; both provide the opportunity to be in the present moment and selectively focus your attention. This photography-based mindfulness activity was inspired by an art therapy colleague, Chris Chiochios, and adapted from the "Relax, Allow, Observe" meditation by Alexis Santos (n.d.) from the Ten Percent Happier app.

This photography intervention, originally created for art therapists, has been adapted for use with graduate and doctoral students, other clinicians, and photography mentors. The goal is to strengthen the ability to be in the present moment through acknowledging thoughts, engaging the senses, and creating photographs. Reflecting on the experience afterwards increases awareness of the thinking and sensory experiences.

Some people who have experiences of trauma may feel discomfort or a retraumatization when asked to bring their attention to their inner selves. For clinicians, it is critical to know how to best support our clients through a modified meditation process as needed. You can modify by asking clients to keep their eyes open, and adding in grounding interventions, such as bringing their attention to objects in the room, sounds they hear, and so on. Be sure to practice this meditation yourself a few times before introducing it to clients.

Meditation

Make a voice recording of yourself reading this meditation, pausing for a few breaths between each paragraph. Find a comfortable place and then play it back for yourself, allowing yourself to fully experience the meditation.

Begin by settling into a comfortable position: sitting up or lying down. Draw your attention to your breath, noticing the air coming in through your nose or mouth, and the air going out of your nose or mouth. After a few rounds of breath, let go of breathing with attention and let your breath return to your natural rhythm.

Relaxing means settling back, knowing that it's okay to be exactly as you are, even if you're not getting everything right. Can you relax into your body in this moment, feeling okay with being exactly as you are?

Allowing experiences, in mindfulness, means that you allow the moment to be exactly as it is without trying to change it or wish it could be different. This allowing is noticing that whatever is happening is already happening and this applies to your breath, mind, body, and emotions. Can you allow and recognize whatever is happening to happen without resistance?

Observing what is happening by simply being aware is the last step of this meditation. Mindfulness is being aware of and noticing the present moment, in each moment. When we hear sounds, we are hearing sounds; whatever we see, we are simply seeing. Mindfulness helps to strengthen this quality, bringing more awareness to our everyday moments. Can you relax into pure observing in the present moment without brining any judgment to your experience?

Bring your attention back to the breath, noticing the quality of your breath on the inhale and exhale. After a few rounds of breathing, bring your awareness back to being in your body and in your physical space.

After the meditation, take a ten-minute walk in any direction without your camera but with the intention of being open to images that are presented to you, that draw your eyes and your focus. During this walk, stay present with this process, noticing any avoidance of escaping to the past or the future. Avoid self-judgment of your process or experience. After ten minutes, return to your seat for a brief breath-focused moment, taking five to ten full inhales and exhales, focusing on your breath.

Next, go on a second walk with your phone camera, taking ten images that came to your attention during your first walk. With digital devices, it can be tempting to create more. However, the limit supports mindfulness about the quality of what you are seeing, allowing, and observing.

After creating ten photo images on your phone, spend time responding to the following reflection prompts, either writing your responses or sharing them with another person:

- How does it feel when you look at the images?

- What do they say about who you are?

- How do they express your state of health (physical, emotional, mental, and spiritual)?

- How close or far removed are they from how you present yourself to the rest of the world?

Depending on the structure of the group, participants may share their experiences and photographs with others in pairs or small groups and then with the larger group. This activity can be done with individuals or groups and can be a repeated activity to reinforce bringing mindfulness to every moment and to reflect on another way of being mindful. Common responses from previous participants include feeling a shift in intention and drive to "be creative" or make photographs in their usual style and instead feeling relaxed and free to notice more.

The actual photographs may be the same as what was noticed on the first walk or they may be completely different from those initial mindful moments of observation. One participant, an art therapy student, reflected on how the images they made were different from what they initially observed, but that the photographs more truly reflected their emotional state of wanting to take a breath and a break after noticing their level of exhaustion on the first walk.

People who have more experience in creating photographs may become aware that they are seeing anew, making images that are nothing like their usual work. A professional photographer who focuses on "street photography" and urban scenes in their work found that their style was completely different in this exercise. The photographer completed this exercise as part of their volunteer work as a photo mentor for youth. They were surprised to discover they noticed and photographed nothing street-based in this exercise. The experience opened their mind to another way of seeing, which they associated with a new way of seeing their youth mentee and their relationship.

Mindful photography example

Oliver Rockwood is a 13-year-old, Caucasian, public middle-school student in in San Francisco. He has been practicing mindfulness for several years with an emphasis on gratitude and present moment awareness. He participated in the mindful photography exercise a week before he returned to school after 18 months of virtual learning due to the pandemic. His hobbies include video games, reading, making art, and playing with his dog. Below, Oliver describes his photos and answers the questions from the mindfulness meditation after walking around an academic center.

This was fun! Some of the pictures I took are funny, some happy, and some sad. I took a picture of a map of the campus. I suppose it is to tell you where to go. Maybe you can think of it as a map of YOU. There is the athletic field and tennis court—that could be your athletic self. There is some parking— to make room for what you are learning and to bring stuff in. There is a high school, elementary, and early learning center—this is about how you learn. There is housing—that could be where you store your good memories you don't want to forget. Here is where we are—it is "where we are."

With the pictures of the fire extinguishers, I suppose there is a story going on (Figure 5.3). Maybe there was a fire or something and they used up all their fire extinguishers and had to get more in case there was another fire. Maybe the driver of the truck in another photo I took got out of the truck to have lunch and went missing, and then a detective had to go find him. I think it is funny I took these pictures pretty far apart on opposite ends of the campus. Maybe that goes back to the map area—the extinguishers were near the houses where you keep your memories and you don't want to forget them. We have to put out the forget-ness fire!

FIGURE 5.3: FINE EXTINGUISHERS
Note: Mindful photograph by Oliver Rockwood.

This picture (Figure 5.4) says Equal Ethical Education—did students make this? Maybe I see it a lot and I guess students are asking, "Can we get equal, ethical education?" There are poles holding it up and along the fence. I think it's about how they feel.

FIGURE 5.4: EQUAL ETHICAL EDUCATION
Note: Mindful photograph by Oliver Rockwood.

I think I am open about most things. If I don't like something, I say I don't like it. If we go somewhere cool, like in my picture where I have played, I would say I would like to go back there because it was fun. I took a picture of the payphone near where I used to play because it looks cool and old (Figure 5.5). I don't even know if it works. You could still put coins in it. There is a box here—I don't know what that is for. It is just hanging there—locally, five minutes for $1, and long distance is two minutes for $1. This could mean that the closer you are to a person, the easier it is to get in touch with them.

I remember the things we did a lot of times—like going to the pool (Figure 5.6). I remember things we did just once too. There are some interesting things too! There are some sad things that happen—like I took a picture of where the pool used to be. This is the filled-in pool. I loved going to the pool and then they filled it in and no one can use it. It is just chairs and concrete. The changing rooms are still there. It is sad the pool is closed. But you can still find fun things to see and do. You can still be happy after something bad happens.

FIGURE 5.5: PAYPHONE

Note: Mindful photograph by Oliver Rockwood.

FIGURE 5.6: CLOSED POOL

Note: Mindful photograph by Oliver Rockwood.

Conclusion

Mindfulness stems from ancient wisdom as a way to achieve peace of mind, detachment from worldly concerns, and even achieve joy and enlightenment. When applied as a tool to reduce mental health symptoms within the context of a healing therapeutic relationship, the concepts of mindfulness emerge as a tool for both therapist and client. ACT emphasizes present moment awareness as an integral part of the therapy process, demanding that both therapist and client be present for the work. Artists and art therapists have long related to the concept of flow, the artmaking equivalent of present moment awareness. Using art as an object of projection brings forth awareness of the present moment and the inner state.

Recommended resources

1. *Zen Mind, Beginner Mind* offers easy to understand ideas related to the Zen concept of the beginner mind, as well as how and why to meditate: Suzuki, S. (2020). *Zen Mind, Beginner Mind: Informal Talks on Meditation and Practice*. Boulder, CO: Shambhala.

2. *You Are Here* offers simple truths about the ways we can be present with ourselves and others: Hanh, T. N. (2010). *You Are Here: Discovering the Magic of the Present Moment*. Boulder, CO: Shambhala.

CHAPTER 6

Creative Approaches for Reducing Avoidance and Increasing Acceptance

This chapter explores the concept of acceptance in ACT and its application in other approaches, such as spirituality, mindfulness, and 12-step work for people in recovery from substance abuse and other addictions. Acceptance includes (1) awareness of a problem/situation/ behavior, (2) acceptance of its presence, and (3) personal accommodations to create growth and ease in managing one's experience of the problem. Acceptance concepts apply to personal, family, group, community, and global situations, and this chapter includes practical and clinical examples. Psychological and creative art therapy approaches lay the groundwork for utilizing acceptance, and specific art therapy interventions are included. A range of examples include how to address individual problems, and ways to contextualize personal experiences to understand how we are impacted by systemic problems in education, government, and access to resources.

I don't want this! I am so sick of this! I am done with all this! We have likely all expressed something like this ourselves, and we have heard clients exclaim similar sentiments about their predicaments. It makes sense that we try to rid ourselves of what we dislike or find bothersome, and this is easy enough in many aspects of our lives. When we are bored with a TV show, we change the channel. When we are cold, we put on a sweater and many of us can turn on the heat. When we are hungry, most of us can find something to eat.

For the most part, when used in moderation, control strategies provide an acceptable way of dealing with distress (Harris, 2007). While we are often adept at making practical changes and controlling our external environment, we encounter hefty challenges and consequences when we try to control our feelings and thoughts. Lest we think only our clients try to avoid, control, or escape unwanted feelings related to their mental health, remember that we all use control strategies in an effort to manage, dodge, or alter difficult feelings.

Fun and healthy activities can become unhealthy avoidance strategies if used too much. Recall that psychological defenses are universal and provide feelings of safety and control in the moment; they are only pathological when overused or when someone relies on only one strategy to cope. For example, you might reach for cookies when you are anxious. This is okay in moderation. However, over-indulging in sugar has significant health consequences. You might exercise every day to help you feel happy and relieve stress. Again, this is really good for you unless you overdo it, resulting in injury or compulsion, or it becomes your only strategy for coping. Some people watch TV or have a drink to unwind. This might be fine in small amounts or when you have the time. However, if you are doing this because of stress before a big day, you can end up feeling worse by losing time you need to prepare or feeling foggy in the morning from the alcohol or lack of sleep.

Avoidance vs acceptance

These two divergent concepts of avoidance and acceptance offer insight into how we and our clients might change. Psychological flexibility is enhanced through making behavioral choices of acceptance and letting go of avoidance strategies. Understanding the function of avoidance and the value of acceptance promotes psychological flexibility. Each of these is discussed in the text that follows, followed by a beautiful example of using art for acceptance.

Acceptance

Acceptance means being *willing* to accept what is happening in the present moment without attempting to alter or change it (Harris, 2007). Accepting is an ongoing practice, involving letting go of denial and struggle with inner experiences. It includes acknowledging the presence of the unwanted parts of ourselves and ultimately appreciating and even loving these aspects of ourselves. Acceptance in ACT is a way to gently hold our sense of self and our experiences in a loving and peaceful way (Harris, 2006). When we willingly come into contact with private events, we are able to behave more effectively and achieve desired outcomes (Moran & Ming, 2020).

We are all exposed to private events that can be perceived as stressful. Our reactions to triggering reminders of past traumas, chronic microaggressions, and living under an existential threat of a pandemic are generally perceived as incredibly uncomfortable. The private moments can become clinically relevant when our mental health is compromised. Fortunately, acceptance is a skill that can be learned (Moran & Ming, 2020).

Acceptance is generated by encouraging openness to and acceptance of psychological events (Larmar *et al.*, 2014). By influencing people to regulate behavior successfully while in the presence of private events that we may perceive as stressful (Hayes *et al.*, 1996; Moran & Ming, 2020), acceptance uniquely contributes to the ACT goal of psychological flexibility. Unlike many Western conceptual models in psychology, which view humans as fundamentally healthy, ACT makes the assumption that for most people, psychological processes can be quite destructive (Harris, 2006; Larmar *et al.*, 2014). Furthermore, ACT assumes that pain is a necessary part of the human condition. For example, CBT focuses on changing maladaptive thoughts, whereas ACT focuses on *just noticing*, accepting, and eventually embracing private experiences. ACT's primary purpose is to "encourage individuals to respond to situations constructively, while simultaneously negotiating and accepting challenging cognitive events and corresponding feelings, rather than replacing them" (Larmar *et al.*, 2014, p.217). Noticing thoughts and feelings supports psychological flexibility, which in turn allows individuals to focus on what ACT considers to be pivotal:

engaging in behaviors to create desirable outcomes (Bach & Hayes, 2002; Harris, 2006). In other words, the primary goal is to accept all of our psychological experiences, whether unwanted or wanted, and then make constructive behavioral choices in line with personal values.

Avoidance

Avoidance is the enemy that we are all fighting against. Some veterans I worked with identified their trauma, the military, or their PTSD diagnosis as their enemy. Using ACT concepts, we reconfigured the real enemy as the strategies used to avoid the substantial pain that is present because of their traumatic experiences in the military.

As tempting as it might be to give in to the automatic impulse of avoiding pain, these attempts are ultimately futile and the consequences are significant. When faced with a crisis, the aftermaths of a traumatic experience, or stress, aversive private events will occur, including both conditioned and unconditioned fear, sadness, and worry (i.e., feelings). Additionally, adverse private verbal behavior (i.e., thoughts) develops and the thoughts and feelings reinforce each other in an unwinnable cycle (Harris, 2007; Moran & Ming, 2020). Avoidance of the negative thoughts and feelings is both individually desired and socially reinforced as an acceptable coping strategy. However, research shows that engaging in avoidance strategies to control or escape private experiences contributes to ineffective behaviors, which can potentially exacerbate clinically relevant behaviors (Moran & Ming, 2020).

Subtle avoidance in therapy may include the therapist or client shifting to another topic—away from trauma or other unpleasant material—or adopting an intellectual approach when talking about feelings. More blatant examples include a client who regularly needs to leave group for the bathroom each time they feel uncomfortable or regularly introduces the content of a new crisis at the expense of working toward their goals of psychological flexibility and value-based behaviors. I would avoid using the word *resistance* when conceptualizing our clients and how they present in therapy. Consider that avoidance strategies are not the client resisting you or the treatment. Instead, these strategies are the behaviors we aim to reduce in therapy.

Acceptance through eco-art

Carrie McCracken is a mother and social justice activist and advocate who currently resides in Costa Rica. Her degree in sociology and the cultural geography of Latin America led her to create VN! Abroad (Viva Nicaragua! Abroad), a study abroad organization that strives to promote social justice and cultural competence through needs-based community work. Originally from the San Francisco Bay Area in California, McCracken moved to Costa Rica in 1998 and then to Nicaragua in 2001, where she founded Viva Nicaragua! In 2018, she and her nine-year-old son were forced to leave Nicaragua, along with many other Nicaraguans, to escape socio-political unrest. She returned to Costa Rica and continued her work in global education and advocacy for vulnerable populations, including migrants, asylum seekers, and refugees.

McCracken collaborated with Gwen Sanders and myself to bring art therapy students to Nicaragua and Costa Rica. Through these experiences, McCracken worked with us to utilize art for community building, cultural humility, and social justice work. The pandemic forced VN! Abroad to suspend programs and find virtual spaces to connect with community. During this time, McCracken and her son embarked on a multi-week eco-art project as a means of grounding into the present moment to transform their isolation and fears into appreciation and transformation. In her essay below titled, "Grounding and finding peace through natural art," she describes her gradual incorporation of acceptance and how it changed her relationship to her thoughts and perceptions of the pandemic.

> The collective understanding of loss and pain during the first year of the pandemic gave me a feeling of support. Despite the distance and isolation, we knew that we were "all in this together." The world felt loss, isolation, fear, and uncertainty.
>
> When vaccines became available, there was hope. My friends and family in the United States had access to vaccines, whereas vaccines in Costa Rica and other countries were not available. The experience was no longer a shared experience. Others were vaccinated and spoke of the light at the end of the tunnel. Without access to vaccines, I did not see that light. The experience was no longer a shared experience.

I was happy that my family and friends and so many were now protected. Yet, I suddenly felt more isolated and alone. I surrounded myself with negativity and only focused on the problems I was facing because of the pandemic. Anxiety, depression, and negativity consumed me.

When I was approached to contribute to this book, I was taking care of a house at the beach. I was living on a tropical beach, yet I wouldn't allow myself to enjoy the place or the time with my son. I allowed the anxiety caused by the pandemic to take over all of my thoughts and emotions. I could not value the crashing of the waves, the monkeys above my home, the afternoons playing with my son at the beach, or the magnificent sunsets. I did not allow myself to enjoy the moment and the place.

I decided to use art to ground myself and focus on my surroundings and stop the negativity that was consuming me and my thoughts. My son and I created a collage to reflect on our time and how we spent our day. We didn't have my art supplies with me at the beach, so we used what was around us for simple and natural materials. Every day, we walked along the beach and forest and picked up at least three objects that grabbed our attention. We then glued the objects randomly to a cardboard background, and talked about what we liked about the object, the place we collected it, or what we were doing when we collected it. The collage connected us with the place and with the moment. Each day, I began to look at my surroundings in a new way: as pieces for my collage and as pieces of the place and beauty that surrounded me.

The collage was a process that we worked on for several weeks. As time passed, some of the leaves and flowers dried up and no longer had the meaning they had when I first collected them. We replaced what no longer functioned in the collage with new objects. With each piece I replaced, I found new beauty and created a connection with new moments. One day, a bird landed on the collage and starting collecting coconut pieces to build its nest. I did not stop this, allowing the coconut to be taken for a new purpose and replacing it with a new object and a new memory.

Every day I collected, created, and became more connected. Daily, I found beauty in the place I was and all the beauty around me. I valued the place, the nature, the process, and the time shared with my son. This process helped me to stop focusing on the pandemic, a situation I could control or change. I found joy and peace with life and with all that surrounded me (see Figure 6.1).

FIGURE 6.1: NATURE COLLAGE
Note: By Carrie McCracken and her son. On cardboard.

What are we trying to escape?

We all strive to avoid unwanted feelings and thoughts or utilize strategies to master and have control over what is uncomfortable. However, living with extensive existential concerns is a part of life. Existential fears relate to our health, the health or illness of loved ones, death, and loss. The inescapable reality of death leads to existential anxiety, and it is natural to want to employ strategies to avoid these anxieties. The fears and anxieties manifest more intensely in the context of natural or human-made disasters, climate change, poverty, lack of human rights, the Covid-19 pandemic, traumatic interpersonal events, and fears related to the damage caused by hate and oppression, which have a range of forms, such as racism, sexism, homophobia, xenophobia, and poverty. These omnipresent anxieties coupled with personal struggles, such as relational problems, mental or physical health disorders, social inequality, and trauma reactions, create a personal and community environment in need of relief and ripe for avoidance strategies.

ACT acknowledges the presence of pain in our lives and postulates that we all work hard to avoid our unwanted thoughts, feelings, and bodily sensations. We attempt to avoid feeling uncomfortable, fearful, inadequate, incompetent, ashamed, and bad. We try to control thoughts that we are not good enough, worthless, and stupid. We attempt to stop sad or terrible memories regarding what we have done or what was done to us. We create complex and elaborate behavior strategies to stop bodily sensations by limiting where we go, what we do, what we eat, and how we relate to others. We can be overwhelmed by unwanted feelings related to our physical and mental health, the concerns of our family and community, and the ongoing existential concerns, such as climate change, poverty, and racism.

It is normal to want to feel better when we are sad or unhappy. However, avoiding the underlying problem and attempting to fix only a *symptom* of the problem means the problem remains. If we have a toothache and take a painkiller, the pain will temporarily go away, yet if we want to fix the problem, we need to go to the dentist. Burying a problem under attempts to reduce symptoms only makes the problem bigger. For example, if someone is plagued with thoughts and feelings of being inadequate, then a new job, outfit, or partner only offers a short-term boost of happiness and feeling of adequacy. The problem of feeling insufficient persists and new strategies are constantly employed to keep the feeling from getting out of control.

What does avoidance look like?

Avoidance plays out in our lives and the lives of our clients in many ways—both individually and collectively. For example, many people drink alcohol or use drugs excessively to escape unwanted memories and uncomfortable feelings. Approximately 164.8 million people in the US struggle with a substance use disorder (Substance Abuse and

Mental Health Services Administration, 2019), and the consequences can range from loss of work, money, and time to loss of friendships, family members, and home. Other ways to avoid thoughts, memories, and feelings include overworking. People who work excessively neglect their physical and mental health and sacrifice their peace of mind, as well as time with family and friends. Significant unwanted feelings lead us to spend noteworthy amounts of time and money avoiding our feelings and our discomfort, often sacrificing our values and happiness in the process. We can see avoidance on a large scale from corporations and governments who ignore the need for social justice and dismiss environmental concerns.

Although personal avoidance strategies may seem less damaging or insignificant compared to those that occur on a global level, which have led to catastrophic results, individual attempts to avoid feelings can create loss, emptiness, dissatisfaction, and ongoing pursuit of new avoidance strategies. Focusing on one's health and diet, purging the house of unwanted and joyless items, or reading self-help books could be positive steps towards a simpler and happier life—or they could merely be strategies for avoidance of thoughts and feelings related to dissatisfaction with the self. We can be more or less successful in losing weight, cleaning out our closets, or changing our habits for a period of time. Yet, we will struggle to maintain change if the only purpose is to avoid unwanted thoughts and feelings and put a band aid on what is causing discomfort. Stepping off this treadmill of avoidance strategies is the first move towards accepting one's self and what exists within us or in the world.

Remember, acceptance refers to the acknowledgment of what exists. We are not required to *like* what we accept. A client of mine struggled to accept that she was being physically abused by her significant other. She initially denied the fact that she was being abused by saying it was a "one time" event. She excused his anger by pointing out how difficult her behavior might be, and she focused on the future and her belief that he would never do it again. These strategies of avoidance created barriers to making decisions that could help her. We explored avoidance in other areas of her life and discussed how acceptance has nothing to do with liking a situation and that acceptance helps us make a realistic action plan for living our values. She had an "aha" moment when she realized that avoiding her feelings by excusing his behavior was profoundly damaging her chance of making a change. Once she noticed that accepting the problem of his behavior was a way for her to see clearly what was happening, she began to shift her behaviors to make choices that were consistent with her values.

People facing anxiety tend to overly rely on control strategies to reduce it, which generally makes the anxiety and the situation worse. If you are feeling anxious at a party, you can take a few deep breaths and find someone to talk to, offer to help the hostess, drink alcohol, see if there is a dog to play with, look at your phone, hide out in the bathroom, or you can leave. Any of these might be fine and acceptable to you. These approaches might work in the moment, or you may end up feeling worse.

If someone with anxiety keeps leaving social situations to escape the discomfort of talking to strangers, that behavior becomes reinforced as a strategy that "works" to relieve distress. If leaving helps individuals feel better, they are more inclined to try that strategy again or even start skipping social events altogether. I have worked with clients who came to rely on the coping strategy of leaving to the exclusion of other approaches. It became increasingly difficult for them to leave the house to see friends and family. Eventually, leaving the house for necessary errands, such as grocery shopping or seeing the doctor, became a significant challenge.

Repeated use of control strategies leads to less psychological flexibility in choosing how to respond to what is happening internally or externally. In other words, a person can become focused and even fixated on using the strategies that serve to avoid discomfort. Ultimately, these strategies create a life that becomes all about avoiding feelings, which comes at the price of neglecting what is most meaningful and valuable. The alternative is to accept the inevitable discomforts of life and choose from a host of healthy coping strategies that move us towards our values.

The process of acceptance

When you learn how to be mindful, you learn to lessen your suffering (Hanh, 2010). The Buddhist roots of ACT highlight the undeniable pain of life and teach us to create internal peace, regardless of personal internal or external distress. While we are unable to change the pain that exists, we can learn to alter our relationship to private events. Therefore, rather than teaching ways to alter our thoughts, feelings, and bodily sensations, ACT teaches new strategies for relating to our thoughts. Because ACT assumes as a premise that we are unable to successfully utilize control strategies to fundamentally alter our inner experiences, ACT offers strategies to accept the presence of our private events and respond gracefully in ways of our choosing.

Acceptance involves an ongoing process that occurs in each moment and with each behavioral choice. Eliminating avoidance strategies and continually returning to the present leads towards acceptance. For example, for many people, there is potentially some unpleasantness involved in writing a long paper or report—it takes time, focus, research, thought, and patience. The difficulties can be expanded into suffering through procrastination and avoidance, which can occur due to failing to create sufficient time to complete the project or complaining about it. Other avoidance strategies might be good for you yet bad for getting the project done; for example, cleaning the house, exercising, or calling a friend constitute healthy behaviors when done at another time. Within the context of a looming deadline, these behaviors increase suffering and lead to the potential deleterious consequences of increased stress and running out of time to complete the report. Additional avoidance behaviors further compound suffering; for instance, drinking in the evening to relax instead of starting the project, or picking a fight with a friend to externalize the anxiety can lead to increased suffering. To paraphrase Thich Nhat Hanh, acceptance of the task at hand and mindfulness about it creates less suffering about completing the project.

Mindful action plan (MAP): Art and written intervention

Accepting unwanted feelings requires preparation and a response plan. The *mindful action plan* (MAP) offers a checklist in the form of a sentence that clients can use to help them strategize in the moment (Morgan & Ming, 2020). Morgan and Ming (2020) use the following sentence to guide clients into the present moment, accept their private events, defuse from thoughts, and move towards their values: "I am here now, accepting my feelings and noticing my thoughts while doing what I care about" (Morgan & Ming, 2020, p.1). Linking the cognitive aspect of this exercise to art therapy creates a well-rounded intervention that helps clients ground their thoughts and feelings in the present moment, through creativity and the kinesthetic experience of artmaking.

The MAP sentence can be taught, assigned as homework, and addressed regularly in therapy sessions so that clients are prepared to utilize it during moments they perceive as stressful. The MAP can be applied readily to both wanted and unwanted acute external events (e.g., a job interview, a discussion with a loved one, a disagreement) or ongoing situations (e.g., loving relationships, chronic pain, parenting, pandemic), and it works just as well with private events likely to bring up avoidance behaviors (e.g., feelings such as fear, sadness). Morgan and Ming (2020) offer a free worksheet you can share with clients to flesh out their unique plans for mindfulness. The strategy is designed to bring ourselves into context, make contact with the present moment, accept and defuse, and ultimately engage in behaviors that are in line with our values. Before you introduce this to clients, try using it yourself four to five times in situations you perceive as relaxed and ones you find stressful.

> *I am:* This is an invitation to notice the influence of any unhelpful thoughts about the self.

> *Here now:* This invites present moment awareness of what you are doing with the goal of letting go of aspects of the situation outside your control and bringing focus exclusively to components relevant to your behavior and helpful actions.

Accepting the way I feel: This invites the acceptance of any emotions that are present, without trying to alter or control them. It involves a willingness to experience any feelings you might be experiencing as you move towards value-based behaviors.

Noticing my thoughts: This asks you to notice any thoughts that arise and prepare to distance your actions from any distracting thoughts while you move forward in a meaningful way.

Doing: What you are doing/intend to be doing right now.

What I care about: These are your personal values that motivate your current behavior and your aims for value-based behavior.

Here is an example I wrote during a break from teaching a research class.

I am here now in my home in San Francisco teaching and learning about writing and art therapy. I am aware of myself as a context for this experience. I accept my feelings of worry about my students in a pandemic. I notice I am presently having thoughts about the future—about tonight, next week, and next year. What I am doing and want to do is help to actualize my students' fullest potential in writing and hone their values as art therapists. This work supports what I care deeply about: being of service to others and bringing art and creativity to therapy.

I invited art therapist and author Jocelyn Fitzgerald to complete the MAP written response and art intervention (Figure 6.2):

I am here now in my home in Vancouver, Washington, about to start my day of seeing clients. I'm excited to create art alongside my colleagues. I'm accepting the way I feel, which is excited and nervous. My book is doing well and the adrenaline is flowing. I'm noticing my thoughts of trying to focus on one thing at a time and not get ahead of myself as I want to create art that is present focused. What I'm doing is looking at my art piece and thinking about how I can add magazine clippings. What I care about is creating art and embracing my unconscious through my art. Connecting to my spirit and my soul through art and colors.

FIGURE 6.2: MINDFUL ACTION PLAN
Note: By Jocelyn Fitzgerald, watercolor and ink.

The MAP sentence can be creatively written on paper or canvas and hung in your therapy office as a reminder for clients to integrate the components of the ACT hexaflex. You can make a point of referring to it in sessions regularly and identifying each area as you are addressing it in session. For example, if a client is struggling with acceptance as reflected in expressions of self-judgment about their feelings or behavior, you might refer them to the sign and ask what they are noticing in their thoughts at that moment. The sign becomes a way for clients to integrate the concepts in the hexaflex into their daily lives and can be a daily practice for homework.

Instructions for MAP intervention

After you have taught the MAP and used it in therapy, you can ask clients if they would like to create art as a creative response or as a written sign to use as a reminder at home. Using words in an art project is often well received, especially for clients who are reluctant or intimidated by the creative process. This project is best suited for two sessions so the painting can dry before the second layer is applied. The intervention could also be assigned as homework.

Materials

Medium or thick watercolor paper (18″ × 24″ or 9″ × 12″), watercolor or watered-down acrylic paints, medium-size paint brushes, water, spray bottle with water, paper towels, natural sponges, permanent markers (Sharpies). Optional: metal straight edge, letter stickers, hole punch, yarn.

Provide smaller pieces of watercolor paper for clients to practice using watercolor techniques, and show them various approaches to the paint. Begin by wetting the paper with a spray bottle. Using lots of water on the paint brush, start by dabbing colors onto the page. Using generous amounts of water will allow the colors to bleed into one another, creating interesting colors and designs. Use the paper towels and sponge to remove excess water and these can create interesting textures as well. If the paper becomes saturated, you may want to let it dry for a few minutes before continuing. Encourage your client to fill the entire page with color—they may want to fill several pages.

Allow the paper to dry completely before introducing the permanent markers to write. Depending on how saturated the paper is with water, you may need to wait until the next session. Provide the MAP sentence for your client to copy or suggest they make up their own sentence to remind them of the steps. "I am here now, accepting my feelings and noticing my thoughts while doing what I care about."

Variations

With any extra paper a client painted, they can create bookmarks or cards using the MAP or other meaningful quotes. Tearing watercolor paper by using a straight edge adds physical movement and creates a beautiful deckled edge. You can use a hole punch and attach yarn with a slip knot for book markers or at the corner of the sign to attach yarn for hanging.

You can create the MAP sign in a variety of media using colored pencils, collage, and so on. If dexterity is a challenge, you can assist in writing or provide letter stickers and clients can stick down the letters to create the words. Ask your client to purchase a small blank journal or provide one for them. Daily homework could include the MAP written statement followed by an art response. On the left side of the page, ask clients to complete the written MAP response with as many details as possible. On the right side of the page, ask clients to complete an art response to what they wrote. This could be done in any materials, including pencil, markers, watercolor, or as a collage.

Acceptance and engagement through photography

Avoidance creates a host of additional problems for us. However, we must be realistic about the limitations of ourselves and our clients and identify ways to engage with our values even when experiencing unwanted feelings, lacking art supplies, or being physically unable to engage in what feels meaningful. Relapse prevention in therapy provides opportunities for clients to predict future challenges or triggers and identify strategies for self-care when feeling low or under duress.

Christine Shea, an art therapist and photographer, is a doctoral candidate in art therapy psychology at Dominican University in the San Francisco Bay Area. She graduated with a master's degree in marriage and family therapy and art therapy from Notre Dame de Namur University, and her recent research focuses on photography as therapy to help lower stress in women experiencing role overload. She specializes in therapy with women, adolescent girls, veterans, and historically underserved youth. She also works as an outpatient therapist running partial hospitalization groups with adults.

With a passion for social justice and therapeutic photography, Shea engages in activist art and loves and writes graphic novels and comic books. I asked her how she utilizes phototherapy and she shared the story below about indoor photography providing relief and respite. Her essay, "The power of therapeutic photography indoors: Seeing the unfamiliar in the familiar," was inspired by a quote from Ansel Adams, "You don't take a photograph, you make it" (Xplore, n.d.).

The use of photography is gaining momentum in the world of art therapy, as the camera has quickly become one of the most accessible creative tools clients have in their possession (Wheeler, 2013). Everywhere we go, we are accompanied by photography; we see it outdoors, indoors, in print, and on screens. We hold photos in our hands, carry them with us, create albums, access them on our phones, and often share them in person or on social media. Family photos, beautiful landscapes, pets, past adventures, lost friends, and sentiments of the past, all speak to the way we personally experience the world (Weiser, 1993). Even though these photos may be artifacts of the past, we respond to them in the present (Krauss, 1983).

Photography provides an opportunity for us to see the world and our surroundings from a new perspective; it allows a new way of learning about, engaging with, and perceiving our environment, our loved ones, and ourselves (Craig, 2009). The act of photographing permits us to capture what exists in the external world and provides an opportunity to reflect on it internally (Martin, 1997). Perhaps most importantly, it creates acceptance of the moment we are in, providing a personal narrative or a metaphor about who we are, how we feel, our belief systems, and what is important to us (Gibson, 2018).

When we think of photography, and in particular therapeutic photography, we often assume it will take place outside, whether exploring a landscape, attending an event, or finding subjects to focus on which we find interesting. The outdoors can provide so much in terms of mindfulness, healing, grounding, and reflection, but what if there are circumstances that don't allow us to go outdoors? By exploring how we look at and value indoor photography, we can still engage successfully in the act of "seeing through a different lens." As art therapists, we can still suggest ways for a client to identify emotions, regulate mood, and engage in mindful calming activities in much the same way as going outdoors might provide.

There are a number of reasons why we might not be willing or able to leave the space we are in. For example, we may feel too anxious or depressed to leave the house, we might not have the time to go for a walk, we might live in an unsafe neighborhood, or perhaps we don't have the physical ability to leave the house. Other reasons might be that we are in a clinical setting, such as a therapist's office, residential facility, or hospital. Or, as in the case of my former client, we are a teenage girl with a strict mom who will not allow us to leave the house after school or on weekends. As I write this, we are currently experiencing a pandemic in which we are advised to "shelter in place." Most individuals are working from home, staying inside, and are unable to feel a state of calm and relaxation outdoors. Many who work on the frontlines may have to quarantine alone.

When considering a client's indoor environment, we can start by humbly bringing focus to some of the things we might take for granted. For example, what feels like a safe place? Where are you able to relax and take a break? By photographing these spaces, we develop a consciousness and a physical presence in a space we define and give value to, and we begin to see it in a new way. When considering a different therapeutic focus, we can think deeper about our personal spaces and find a mindful and grounding practice within them. What are the textures you haven't noticed before? What is soothing to you when you are upset? What colors do you surround yourself with that make you feel good? These are all ways to develop and participate in grounding techniques that can be called on again when feeling distressed, whether by looking at the photos themselves, or being present in the space you've designated as soothing, calm, joyful, or safe. There is also the power of engaging in metaphor. How can you represent your mood through lighting and shadow? What do you see before you that might characterize your feelings? Are there items in the space that embody a meaningful moment? Make a self-portrait out of objects in the home or objects in your purse. How does the space tell the story of your experience? Exploring why a photo is meaningful, and finding an opportunity to engage with the client in understanding and accepting that significance of it, provides a powerful opportunity to reflect.

Maria began therapy with me when she was 15 years old. She had been in trouble at school, and due to that, had to seek counseling as part of her commitment to do better. Maria never had counseling before and did not want it, but she knew she was depressed, angry, and not making the best choices. After building rapport, validating her feelings, and finding out what really happened, I discovered that her actions were ultimately a way to vie for attention from her family. Mother worked more than full time and Maria was expected to care for her little brother, do the household chores, and cook after school. Maria's mother also installed cameras outside the home after Maria had got into trouble, to make sure she stayed inside the house as was now expected of her. My client's emotions about this scenario fluctuated from angry and anxious, to sad, feeling trapped, and untrusted. She would often explode with a burst of anger towards her mother.

Maria loved doing creative artwork, but she did not have access to art materials, especially at home. She loved photography, but gave up on it because she was stuck indoors. We identified her phone as a way for her to express herself and we started to use it as a way to reflect and process her feelings internally. Engaging with her familiar environment in a new way, Maria was able to ground herself and identify aspects of the home that reflected a range of her emotions as she felt them. Examples of some of her photographs (recreated for anonymity) taken in her apartment express her negative feelings, such as "Sadness" (Figure 6.3) and "Stress" (Figure 6.4); she then counterbalanced those emotions with what made her feel at "Peace" (Figure 6.5) and with what made her "Happy" (Figure 6.6). Viewing the photographs together in therapy allowed an opportunity for Maria to reflect, gain insight, accept the situation, and find refuge in her home, which had once only served to make her feel trapped and angry. She was able to better understand herself and how to cope, and in turn, was able to see her mother's point of view. Through therapy, mother and daughter were able to work together towards a more trusting and rewarding relationship with each other.

When our internal world feels overwhelmed, particularly when we are in a space that might feel small, crowded, mundane, frustrating, or too familiar, photography can provide a sense of expanse by offering an opportunity to ground, reflect, grow, be mindful, accept, and create. The use of simple prompts that integrate unique aspects of what photography can do, such as zooming in or out, playing with the power of light and shadow, and utilizing editing effects, can be a potent way to experience creative flow. Photographing abstract colors, textures, and patterns can be a commanding way to ground and be mindful of ourselves in context to our surroundings. Creating metaphor by photographing symbols, building a still life with meaningful objects, developing a narrative or story, or simply sharing photos of friends, family, memories, and inspiration, can serve as an incredibly powerful way to engage in self-reflection and help a client develop future goals (Ziller, 1990). The act of using photography in therapy has proven its efficacy, including its unique ability to provide art therapy in some of the most challenging of circumstances.

FIGURE 6.3: SADNESS
Note: Photo by Christine Shea.

FIGURE 6.4: STRESS
Note: Photo by Christine Shea.

FIGURE 6.5: PEACE
Note: Photo by Christine Shea.

FIGURE 6.6: HAPPINESS
Note: Photo by Christine Shea.

Intersections of ACT art therapy and cultural humility

Acceptance can help us become more culturally humble practitioners, scholars, researchers, and teachers. Accepting our inner experiences (e.g., thoughts, feelings, and bodily sensations) related to race, class, culture, country of origin, body size, religion, and sexual orientation creates the first step towards cultural humility. Recognizing our assumptions and beliefs about others creates the opportunity to grow in the area of our values. An honest personal inventory allows us to decide which of our beliefs we want to carry forward and which ones we need to shed to live according to our personal and professional values.

We can build on this and use acceptance to recognize our client's intersecting identities. Recall that ACT is a contextual practice and that understanding the whole experience of a person—both the private and external events—is critical to the work. The acknowledgment and appreciation of a person within all their intersecting identities occurs when the client and therapist are open and accepting (rather than denying or avoiding) of their psychological and external/circumstantial events (Larmar *et al.*, 2014).

Using a contextual model creates possibilities to see others for who they truly are without ignoring or undervaluing aspects of their experience that are important to them (e.g., race, gender, sexual orientation); we may be unable to initially see these aspects because they seem to be ill-fitting or they are outside our (the therapist's) narrative. This section reviews cultural humility and how it links to the foundations of functional contextualism in ACT.

Cultural humility

Cultural humility creates "a way of developing a worldview with integrity and respect for oneself and those one works with" (Jackson, 2020, p.19). Cultural humility is highly relevant to the tenets of ACT because it expands our contextual awareness of ourselves and our clients. The concept was coined by Tervalon and Murray Garcia (1998) to broaden the ways in which medical providers were trained and to make central the client/patient experience and expertise.

Cultural humility involves (1) committing to lifelong critical self-reflection and critique; (2) re-addressing the patient–provider power imbalance; (3) developing mutually beneficial partnerships with communities; and (4) addressing institutional accountability (Jackson, 2020). These are initial steps in getting to know ourselves and the strategies to bring our best self to our work using approaches that truly serve our clients. Cultural humility helps us shift away from strategies that rely on our acquiring knowledge and learning cultural competence skills—these strategies too often come at the expense of cultivating our cultural awareness.

The idea of cultural competence suggests that with training (i.e., academic learning), one person (the provider) might become proficient and skilled in understanding the experience and cultural nuances of another person (the patient). However, considerable limitations exist when cultural competency is the only model for learning how to care for others. Primarily, it is impossible to become "competent" in any culture because of the huge variations among people in any group. Furthermore, people experience their lives differently, and thus, culture or identity status affects people in different ways depending on a myriad of variables, such as where they grew up, their access to resources, their education, and many other intersecting identities, which include gender, age, race, class, ability, immigration status, and where they fall on the sexual continuum.

Cultural competency as a model falls short by elevating the knowledge of the practitioner over the lived experience of the client. As Rober and De Haene (2014) noted, by emphasizing the cultural distinctions between the therapist and client, as well as the knowledge the therapist may have about a specific culture, the cultural competency model "may underestimate the importance of the social dimensions of the issues involved. Furthermore, highlighting cultural differences may obscure the shared humanity present in a transcultural encounter" (p.1). Competency without humility may result in removing the expertise each person possesses over their life and place authority over what is real and true in the hands of the provider. While it is essential to strive to understand the cultural histories and traditions of our clients, the initial step to knowing others involves exploring ourselves and how our own culture influences us. The past limitations of cultural competency in art therapy education can be challenged using "personal reflection, immersive engagement with social justice practices of naming difference, asserting counter narratives, and following the leadership of people impacted by systemic violence" (Gipson, 2015, p.1).

Cultural humility offers the antidote to the antiquated indoctrination of providers as experts in the culture of clients (Gipson, 2015; Rober & De Haene, 2014). It moves away from the idea that a provider possesses knowledge and expertise about their clients, and helps providers avoid making assumptions based on limited information or appearance. However, cultural humility and cultural competency are *both* necessary for providers (Jackson, 2020). Cultural humility serves as a *complement* to the competency training and knowledge a provider needs to work with various people. These concepts fit within the ACT framework, with its underpinning of functional contextualism, which is outlined in the text that follows.

Functional contextualism and cultural humility

Cultural humility corresponds with ACT's foundation of functional contextualism. A reductionist approach that focuses exclusively on understanding dysfunctional behaviors or pathology is rejected by functional contextualism (Hayes, 2004; Larmar *et al.*, 2014). Instead, ACT explores common behavioral responses within a historical and contextual position (Hayes, 2004; Larmar *et al.*, 2014). ACT and cultural humility both focus on and value internal and external events as relevant to a person's experience and context.

Functional contextualism includes (1) a focus on the entire event as it occurs; (2) a sensitivity to how context affects the nature and function of an event; (3) a focus on pragmatic truth; and (4) an evaluation of the truth against a particular goal (Hayes, 2004). In this case, the pragmatic truth is compared to one's inner reaction and how useful the internal events are to behavioral actions. ACT utilizes these built-in contextual features to embrace the intersecting identities of our clients by valuing the whole psychological event and its context as it occurs.

Our ability to understand the wider context of a client's thoughts, feelings, and behaviors can be significantly constrained by the therapist's blind spots and biases regarding race, culture, class, ableism, heterosexism, sanism, to name a few. Like any other psychological or educational approach, ACT benefits from the application of the practitioner's cultural humility. This includes therapists using cultural humility to engage in critical self-reflection, as well as learning about the values, strengths, and limitations of their own culture and the culture of their clients.

ACT calls on practitioners and clients to address the whole context in order to help a client reflect on, understand, and accept their inner experiences and make behavioral choices in line with their values. As ACT therapists, we must utilize cultural humility to comprehend a client's intersecting identities, as well as the wider context in which a client exists. If therapists understand a client's feelings, thoughts, and behaviors exclusively as an intrapsychic phenomenon, we lose sight of the impact their family, community, and wider society. Each person develops in the context of their personal, community, and society's collection of experiences and interpretations of those events. To deny the monumental influence of society on the individual in the therapy space misses the point of cultural humility and functional contextualism. For example, to neglect the influence of society on the private events of a Person of Color would be to deny the truth of racism and limit the ways in which we can understand that client, their context, and the pragmatic truth of their life. Similarly, ignoring the impact of sexism on women misses an important context and may preclude opportunities for greater understanding and healing. Attending to how society affects our clients and ourselves brings richness and depth to understanding our context. Unfortunately, neglect of the wider impact has been a common practice in psychological theories and Western individualist ways of knowing about people.

Conclusion

Strategies to avoid, control, or escape one's feelings exist on a continuum. We all engage in strategies to change or escape our mood in mild ways by focusing on the external (e.g., a clean house, new clothes), or stopping our thoughts (e.g., watching a movie, consuming alcohol, eating sugar). The greater the discomfort, the more we attempt to avoid the thoughts and feelings. Memories of a significant loss, intrusive symptoms of PTSD, or thoughts arising from depression bring about distress and increased efforts to control. Increased efforts to avoid uncomfortable feelings reduce our psychological flexibility and lead to greater rigidity in behavioral choices.

Internally, acceptance involves receiving the present moment without trying to change, escape, or fundamentally alter the experience. Externally, acceptance involves seeing others and accepting them for who and what they are in that moment, without trying to alter their experience to fit our own narrative or undervalue what they value.

Acceptance thus requires each of us to know ourselves, our culture, and our values. Functional contextualism links with cultural humility to help the therapist and client understand the whole context. Cultural humility helps us notice, acknowledge, and make repairs when we fail to accept the truth of the context or project our own or society's insecurities onto others. When we engage in unkind, biased, or discriminatory behavior towards ourselves or others in an effort to avoid, escape, or change our own experience, cultural humility helps us to recognize and repair.

Recommended resources

1. Jackson, L. (2020). *Cultural Humility in Art Therapy: Applications for Practice, Research, Social Justice, Self-Care, and Pedagogy*. London: Jessica Kingsley Publishers.

2. Hayes, S.C. & Smith, S. (2005). *Get Out of Your Mind and Into Your Life: The New Acceptance and Commitment Therapy*. Oakland, CA: New Harbinger Publications.

CHAPTER 7

Cognitive Defusion: A New Relationship with Our Thoughts

In this chapter, the role of cognitive fusion in exacerbating problems will be explored. Further, the goal of defusion to separate our self-worth and decisions from automatic thoughts is highlighted. Concepts from behaviorism contain examples to illustrate how with ACT we can utilize novel ways of relating to thoughts. Art therapy and behavioral strategies will be introduced to help develop a functional and healthy way of relating to one's thoughts—as merely thoughts rather than the literal truth. Also introduced are psychological and creative art therapy interventions that offer inviting ways to sustain defusion and reduce fusion with thoughts.

Regardless of the subject and content of therapy, we are dealing with thoughts, and, fortunately, these can be changed (Hay, 2020). The humbling actuality, which also brings great relief, is that we are unable to create *truth* in our mind; we can only create thoughts. Because we typically think the same thoughts repeatedly for most of our lives, we start to believe them. However, seeking truth in our thoughts can lead us away from our values, causing suffering, misunderstandings, and lost opportunities. Recently I saw a bumper sticker that read, *Don't believe everything you think*, which perfectly captures the spirit of cognitive defusion.

As discussed earlier, the goal of ACT is to increase psychological flexibility—to make contact with the present moment so we can choose from a wide variety of behavioral options to advance us towards living a value-based life. In this chapter, I will focus on the role of cognitive fusion in exacerbating distress. Defusion is a functional tool to increase psychological flexibility by changing how we *relate* to thoughts. Rather than attempting to alter the content of the thought, reduce the frequency of thoughts, or change our sensitivity to the situations when the thoughts occur, the goal is to change our *relationship* with our thoughts and the undesirable functions of those thoughts (Harris, 2007).

When we experience *cognitive fusion* with our thoughts, we start to believe them as true and real, rather than as a product of our minds. We have likely experienced the same thought patterns for a long time and the more we repeat messages to ourselves, the more likely we are to ascribe truth to the content of the thought. *Cognitive defusion* involves the ability to take perspective on thoughts and become aware of the thinking process (Harris, 2007). This metacognitive experience includes seeing thoughts for what they are—just thoughts. Increasing psychological flexibility, the primary goal in ACT, directly relates to defusing from our thoughts because doing so frees us to consider a variety of possible behavioral responses in any given context and our choices are independent from our ongoing, habitual thoughts. This next section explores cognitive fusion and defusion with some practical examples to help you practice defusion, a critical aspect of the hexaflex.

Cognitive fusion

Let's start with how our minds typically work and the challenge of using our thoughts to direct our behaviors. *Cognitive fusion*, a word unique to ACT, happens when we relate to our thoughts as if they were literally true instead of merely the product of our mind (Gordon & Borushok, 2017). Cognitive fusion, moreover, is "the dominance of verbal processes over behavior regulation, in detriment of being sensitive to contextual contingencies and pursuing valued life goals" (Pinto-Gouveia *et al.*, 2020, p.1). To unpack that definition, fusion essentially relies on verbally based thoughts to inform us of practical truths, while neglecting the context. This over-reliance on our thoughts to determine truth deters us from engaging in value-based behaviors. For example, thoughts of "I can't handle this" can begin to feel like the truth and lead to behaviors that confirm the thought, such as leaving a party, drinking more than intended, dropping out of school, or ending a valuable relationship. These behaviors can be centered around or in direct response to thoughts similar to "I can't handle this." Of course, many other contextual factors impact our behaviors, such as past experiences, fears, or anticipatory anxiety. For this example, it is believing the thought to be true (being cognitively fused to the thought) that reduces psychological flexibility and limits our behavioral choices in that moment to a narrow way of dealing with the thoughts.

Fusion with our thoughts links to experiential avoidance and the two work in tandem and create worry and stress. *Experiential avoidance* involves an "unwillingness to remain in contact with distressing internal experiences along with...attempts to control or avoid distressing internal experiences" (Hayes-Skelton & Eustis, 2020, p.115). Experiential avoidance is associated with procrastination, fear of negative evaluations, worry about the meaning of one's thoughts, concern over somatic experiences, and fears about traumatic events (Hayes-Skelton & Eustis, 2020). Attempts to control our inner experience only serve to increase distress, anxiety, fear, and they limit our behavior and awareness of behavioral choices. Judgmental and negative thoughts, as well as experiences of trying and failing to suppress anxiety, reinforce experiential avoidance.

In both clinical and nonclinical populations, research has found a bidirectional association between fusion with thoughts and experiential avoidance (Cookson *et al.*, 2020). Essentially, cognitive fusion and avoidance of inner experiences lead to worry and distress (Cookson *et al.*, 2020). For those with anxiety and depression, the approach used in the *early* stages of therapy depends on the severity of the anxiety and depression (Cookson *et al.*, 2020). Clients who have clinical levels of depression and anxiety can benefit from a two-pronged approach in the early stages of treatment, addressing both cognitive fusion and experiential avoidance. However, clients with subclinical anxiety and depression benefit most from early interventions to promote cognitive defusion exclusively. Cookson *et al.* (2020) concluded that those with high levels of experiential avoidance can be helped when the clinician focuses on defusion, whereas high levels of cognitive fusion can be helped by attending to acceptance.

CASE EXAMPLE

Lou was a quiet student who rarely spoke up in her college classes. She felt anxiety each time the teacher asked a question, even when she knew the answer. She wanted to raise her hand and contribute to class discussions, but she stopped herself because of her heart racing and thoughts of "people will laugh at my answer" and "I have been humiliated enough in my life. I don't want to be humiliated in class too." She was *fused* with these thoughts, believing she would indeed be humiliated if she spoke in class. Lou knew she was missing accumulating participation points by remaining silent in class, which added to her worries. The longer she went without saying anything, the more she believed her *avoidance* strategies (silence, sitting in the back of the class, avoiding eye contact) would help her circumvent humiliation.

While she was able to avoid humiliation through experiential avoidance and remaining silent in class, her anxiety increased as she focused more and more on avoiding her own imagined humiliation. She found she was missing things the teacher or other students were saying in class. One day, she was so preoccupied with managing her anxiety, she missed the teacher giving a direction to break off into small groups for discussion. She was left sitting by herself while the rest of the class began dividing into groups. A fellow student called to her to, "Wake up, daydreamer! You're supposed to be in our group."

Because Lou was so preoccupied and *fused* with her thoughts about being humiliated, she ended up feeling humiliated precisely because of her efforts to *avoid* feeling uncomfortable. To add insult to her humiliation, she received zero participation points and felt even more disgraced when she realized she would have got an A in the class if she had earned even half of the participation points that were possible. These problems were present in many other areas of her life as well, including personal relationships and work. For Lou, this experience in the classroom created a tipping point to bring her into therapy.

Lou was both fused to her thoughts and engaged in experiential avoidance; therefore, she needed a two-pronged approach addressing defusion and acceptance. We utilized the Shoe Shoe Shoe exercise (instructions follow) to explore defusion, and used art to engage in mindfulness and acceptance. We set small goals to reduce avoidance, beginning with talking to a classmate before class and visiting the teacher during office hours.

ACT works on several areas at a time, as each area of the hexaflex is integrated. Changing one area also changes other areas. For example, the avoidance intervention to talk to someone in class provides evidence to defuse from thoughts.

Fused beliefs

Fused thoughts are both insidious and believable and require special attention to notice them. Lou, in the example above, was unaware that humiliation was the key to understanding her fused thoughts when she first came to therapy. When we can begin to see thoughts for what they truly are (just thoughts), we can then begin to relate to them as thoughts rather than as the truth. When we can do this, it is as if the veil has been pulled away to reveal the impostor—the thoughts have been masquerading as reality. It is akin to discovering that the great and powerful Oz in *The Wizard of Oz* is really just a man behind a curtain. Though our thoughts may seem as true and confident and as real as *The Wizard of Oz*, the reality is that our thoughts are just thoughts inside our heads.

It is often easier to identify cognitive fusion in others, such as a client who adopts negative self-talk about their worth as a person. Someone with constant self-devaluing thoughts tend to treat themselves as unworthy, worthless, and unlovable. They accept relationships that confirm this belief and may find themselves in relationships in which they are undervalued or unable to get their needs met. For example, many clients who were sexually or physically abused as children will often hold the thought that they are "damaged goods" or "unworthy of love," and these beliefs lead them to treat themselves as such and expect the same from others. From my perspective as the therapist, I easily recognize and believe they are worthy and deserving of love from themselves and others. Yet, their cognitive fusion leads them to believe these thoughts as *the truth*. It can be heart-breaking to hear the self-loathing thoughts of clients. As therapists, we too may be cognitively fused to negative thoughts about ourselves and to our beliefs about the world. Thus, we can also can benefit from defusion techniques.

Discovering that thoughts are just thoughts, instead of reality or literal truth, fundamentally changes the ways we experience, relate to, and respond to our thoughts. You may feel quite liberated on learning that only you are in charge of how you relate to your thoughts and what you choose to do with them. The concept is simple; however, the practice is ongoing. Like yoga, meditation, knitting, drawing, painting, pottery, parenting, or any other worthwhile pursuit, it requires a lifetime of practice.

Cognitive defusion

Cognitive defusion from thoughts means seeing thoughts for what they are—just thoughts and the firing of neurons in our brain. Being curious about thoughts instead of believing the content of the thought as *the truth* about our lives leads to psychological flexibility and the freedom to choose from any number of behavioral choices. This liberation from the tyranny of our own minds frees us to consider any number of actions that propel us towards our values and the life we wish to lead.

Defusion is the process of cognitively focusing your awareness on your private experiences (e.g., thoughts, feelings, memories, bodily sensations), your reaction to them, and the consequence of your response. Gordon and Borushok (2017) noted, "Defusing creates space to pause and notice the effectiveness of a response to a private experience rather than being reactive or automatically trying to eliminate or avoid them with poor results" (p.12). Creating distance from thoughts allows us the opportunity to consider a variety of other thoughts and reactions and then select reactions that are most in line with, and bring us closer to, our values. In behavioral terms, defusion is the "reduction of stimulus function transformation that occurs through verbal relations... Defusion aims to minimize the influence of verbal relations, such as thoughts, on behavior, when doing so leads to adaptive behavior and valued living" (Assaz *et al.*, 2018, p.405).

The goal of defusion is, in part, to help clients develop an accurate awareness of their thoughts and emotions (Larmar *et al.*, 2014); the overarching goal is to increase the psychological flexibility to make behavioral choices in line with values (Assaz *et al.*, 2018). Whereas CBT challenges thoughts and encourages clients to challenge cognitive distortions with evidence, ACT elicits none of these strategies to alter or control thoughts. Instead, clients are asked to change their relationship to their thoughts: any type of thought or feeling is allowed to simply exist alongside one's freely chosen value-based behaviors. It is unnecessary to control thoughts in order to move towards one's values. For example, a client who had chronic intrusive memories of his military trauma altered his relationship to the trauma memories by using ACT defusion techniques. Instead of struggling with the memories and altering his behavior to control the thoughts each time the memories emerged, he altered his relationship to them. He began to defuse from the thoughts and memories, seeing them for what they were—thoughts and memories. The change in relationship allowed him to focus on what he wanted to *do* based on his values (i.e., laugh with his children, care for his family, enjoy his work), instead of taking action based on what reactions to his thoughts and feelings inspired him to do (i.e., leave a situation, fight, drink alcohol).

Shoe Shoe Shoe exercise

Experiencing the concept of cognitive defusion can be accomplished in two minutes or less. The Shoe Shoe Shoe exercise was inspired by an intervention in *Get Out of Your Mind and Into Your Life* (Hayes & Smith, 2005). Helping clients experience the limitations of language in self-talk promotes defusion from those thoughts. Hayes *et al.* (2012) wrote, "Language has a very limited capacity to apprehend and decipher personal experience; however, we are taught from childhood onward that it is the grand tool for developing self-understanding" (p.246). The creative application of language can demonstrate how limiting language can be when used in self-talk.

The way it works is that you select any word and say it over and over until awareness of the word's meaning or symbol fades away and is replaced by just the sounds emanating from your mouth. It's best to start with a neutral word, such as shoe, apple, or mug and repeat it for at least a minute or until your full awareness relies only on the sound, rather than the meaning of the word or a perception of what the word means. After the neutral word, you then move on to an emotionally charged word related to unwanted private events. Set your timer for two minutes and try it now. Say the word "shoe" repeatedly until the timer rings. What did you notice about the word after repeating it for two minutes? You may have noticed that the word lost its literal meaning and the sound became the focus of your awareness. What happened is that you experienced defusion from the meaning of the word.

Next, select one word related to challenging thoughts. It can be any word that gets repeated in your mind frequently; it can be related to self-judgments or a fear-based word. Repeat that emotionally charged word until your awareness rests fully on the sound and all meaning of the word has dissipated. Set your timer for two minutes and try it now. What did you notice this time? Variations can enhance the process: try repeating the word in a funny voice or singing the word to create even greater distance from the meaning and potentially introduce some lightheartedness to the process.

The Shoe Shoe Shoe exercise is designed to create distance from unwanted thoughts by generating a new way of experiencing the thought (Hayes *et al.*, 2012). This exposure technique can be used in therapy after rapport is established and fusion and defusion have been introduced. The Shoe Shoe Shoe exercise can be helpful throughout the therapy process as awareness of new fused thoughts emerges. Remember, always try exercises yourself a few times before introducing them to clients. You can practice this exercise with friends and family, and turning it into a game with children can be fun. Always ask your clients if they are willing to engage in an exercise about defusion before you introduce it. Take care to ensure your client feels safe before addressing a painful word in this exposure exercise, so they are able to follow through and avoid stopping while still feeling the meaning. Help them follow through until the awareness is on the sound rather than the meaning.

Finally, add creative techniques to deepen your clients' experience of defusion in the session and allow them to begin to employ the technique *in vivo*, which is to have them practice it in their life outside therapy. Adding a movement or body position to express the word brings more awareness to the private experience of the word and thoughts. You can ask clients to position their body (i.e., a pose) in a way that reflects the chosen word before the Shoe Shoe Shoe defusion technique. After they have repeated the word for two minutes and you have helped them process their awareness, ask your clients to position their body in a way that reflects how they feel about the word after completing the exercise. You can invite clients to engage in a repetitive line drawing until their awareness shifts away from form to focus on color and movement. Photography can also support the defusion process, whereby the lens of the camera becomes the new way of relating to what is seen and photographed. As always, try each of these ideas a few times before you bring it to clients.

Defusion art intervention

Melanie Worstell utilizes collage material to illustrate defusion in her ACT art therapy groups. With just one picture from a magazine, she invites her clients to cut the page into ten or more pieces and then rearrange them to create a new image. In Figure 7.1, Worstell selected a full-page desert scene from a magazine, cut it into pieces, and then glued the pieces onto a blank piece of paper to create a beautiful new image. This intervention reinforces the ACT idea of changing our relationship to our thoughts, rather than trying to alter the content of our thoughts or stop them altogether. The exercise offers reinforcement for clients who are uncertain as to how they can engage with their thoughts differently or who are curious about how a change in perspective might help them. They may wonder how changing their perspective could improve a relationship or challenge their perceived stance as a victim of circumstances. You might wish to first select a picture from nature or one related to the content of the problem. Landscapes or other emotionally positive pictures would serve best for an initial collage. A second collage could utilize a more emotionally laden image from a magazine. For example, a client who is struggling with negative body image might employ a picture of a body in their second collage. Recall that collage and artmaking can submerge clients quickly into their emotions, so starting with a positive or neutral image can illustrate the idea of defusion before a more emotionally challenging image is selected. Remember to try this a few times yourself before bringing it to your clients.

FIGURE 7.1: DESERT IN MOTION
Note: Melanie Worstell's example of the defusion art intervention.

Materials needed for this collage art project include: pre-cut full-page magazine images, scissors, glue stick, blank paper, and markers. Cut full-page magazine images from the magazines and offer a variety of images from which your client can choose, including landscapes, abstract images, and appropriate content-related images. I suggest having 20–30 or more images from which a client can select, and more images are necessary for a group. Ask clients to select an image and really study it in a mindful way before cutting it into ten pieces. Give them sufficient time to create an attractive arrangement of the ten pieces. Encourage them to try different arrangements before deciding on a final image and gluing down the pieces. After they are done, ask them to look at the new image and notice what has changed. Ask them to give the piece a title and three words or phrases to describe it. Encourage them to describe their art in as much detail as possible.

Intervention to promote defusion

According to Hayes *et al.* (2012), "The fundamental challenge of being human involves learning when to follow what your mind says and when to simply be aware of your mind while attending to the here and now" (p.243). Understanding when to attend to the content of our thoughts and consider them seriously and when to disregard them requires the ability to defuse from thoughts. This strategy links with acceptance and awareness of the present moment. A variety of defusion techniques exist in the ACT literature, and one I especially appreciate requires dispassionately observing a negative thought and repeating the identified thought aloud until the "sting" of the words is habituated and the only reaction is to the sound of the words (Hayes *et al.*, 2012). These thoughts can be treated creatively and described as an external object by giving them form, color, shape, speed, or size. Other interventions include thanking one's mind for providing such interesting, albeit unhelpful, thoughts, or providing distance from thoughts as mentioned previously by adding in awareness. For example, you can teach clients to say, "Thank you, brain, for that very interesting thought. I am doing other things right now so I am unable to respond to what you are suggesting."

Another tool to create psychological distance from our thoughts involves shifting the thought away from the content of the thought and onto the process of thinking. Attending to the *process* of thinking (awareness of the thought), rather than the content (what the thought is about), offers a new way to relate to thoughts and increase psychological flexibility. Remember, fusion is "the pouring together of verbal/cognitive processes and direct experience such that the individual cannot discriminate between the two" (Hayes *et al.*, 2012, p.244). For example, once a client identifies an unwanted thought, you can teach them to shift their attention from the content of the thought to the process of thinking. I use this next strategy myself and frequently ask clients to engage in the process. All you need is a piece of paper and a pen.

Step 1. Identify a thought

Ask your client to identify a particularly troublesome unwanted thought to which they are fused. You can try this with any thought and later in therapy, you may aid clients in identifying a core fused thought by asking them to explore their beliefs underlying frequent thoughts. For example, if the client shares a thought of, "I am unable to decide what to do," you may ask what that means about them; this line of inquiry may reveal a thought about self, such as, "I am incapable of making important decisions" or "I am unable to take care of myself." Ask your client to write down their thought at the bottom of a piece of paper (see Figure 7.2).

FIGURE 7.2: THE FUSED THOUGHT

Step 2. Step away from the thought

Ask your client to take a deep breath and as they exhale to imagine themselves stepping away from the thought and observing it from a distance of three to five feet away. Instruct them to write in the middle of their paper, "I am having the thought that" and then rewrite the fused statement. For example, the sentence in the middle of the page would read: "I am having the thought that I am unable to take care of myself" (see Figure 7.3).

FIGURE 7.3: HAVING THE THOUGHT

3. Create defused thought

Finally, ask your client to take another deep breath, and as they exhale, ask them to imagine they are moving even further away from the thought and observing it from 10–20 feet away. Instruct them to write at the top of their paper, "I am aware that I am having the thought that" and then rewrite the fused thought. For example, the sentence now written at the top of the page would read: "I am aware that I am having the thought that I am unable to take care of myself" (see Figure 7.4).

Ask your clients to explore the differences between the fused statement at the bottom of the page and the same thought written in a defused matter in the top sentence. The top line still contains the original, unwanted and uncomfortable thought. A new way to relating to the thought is introduced by including the awareness of having the thought. This strategy for creating cognitive defusion can be assigned as homework to be completed once a day for a week or a month. Encourage your client to use this technique any time they notice thoughts to which they are fused. Deeper exploration could include an examination of the thoughts, feelings, and memories that have historically occurred when that thought arises. Remember to practice this exercise yourself before introducing it to your clients. I suggest you complete this exercise once a day for at least a week or longer to reap the benefits. Once you experience defusion using this technique, share it with clients.

FIGURE 7.4: AWARE THAT I AM HAVING THE THOUGHT

This same exercise can be used to explore feelings by using art instead of words. Using lines, shapes, and colors, depict a feeling at the bottom of the page and name the feeling such as "worry." In the middle of the page, create defusion by writing, "I am aware that I am experiencing feeling of worry" and use lines, shapes, and colors to depict the feeling of worry. Finally, at the top of the page, write, "I am aware that I am having the experience of feeling worry" and use lines, shapes, and colors to describe this new level of defused awareness. Again, try this yourself before bringing it to clients.

Art therapy intervention to promote cognitive defusion

Art therapy provides a unique way to explore and defuse from unwanted/unhelpful thoughts. Hayes *et al.* (2012) wrote, "Another way to defuse language is to objectify it" (p.250.) Art makes a great tool to externalize and objectify our thoughts. The use of art materials and the resultant art product provide even further psychological distance from the thoughts, and the Passengers/Monsters on the Bus intervention that follows provides a creative way to objectify thoughts. The externalization of thoughts and feelings through art, for both clients and for me, has a much greater impact than merely talking about, engaging in dialogue with, or describing features of the thought. The externalized product creates a visual separation from the thought and both the artist and therapist can look at the thought with greater curiosity and less judgment. Furthermore, discussion about the art can bring increased objectivity related to the truth and functional utility of the thought.

Passengers/Monsters on the Bus art therapy intervention

Corrie Mazzeo and I created this intervention to creatively promote defusion from thoughts for our veteran clients. Our goal was to develop an intervention that would be a fun way to observe one's nagging thoughts and beliefs that interfere with life and create movement towards value-based choices. The concept of the monsters on the bus came from an ACT metaphor called, "passengers on the bus" about dropping the struggle with negative and limiting thoughts to make value-based decisions, in spite of the thoughts (Hayes *et al.*, 2012, p.250). Rather than trying to change the unwanted thoughts and feelings, which is never the goal in ACT, the aim of this intervention is to observe the thoughts in a lighthearted and curious way. Ideally, the exercise creates opportunities to generate choices the client likes, instead of being directed by the unwanted thoughts, feelings, mental health symptoms, or bodily sensations.

The rationale of this intervention is based on the concept of defusion to increase psychological flexibility (Hayes *et al.*, 2012).

Specifically, it relies on the idea that thoughts, feelings, and symptoms will likely persist, yet we can still make movement towards the experiences and relationships we want. We do not encourage our clients to alter their internal experiences. If it were possible to change our unwanted thoughts, we and our clients would have done it by now! However, we typically find that symptoms lessen or dissipate because we assist clients in changing their *relationship* with their thoughts, rather than trying to change their thoughts. The goal of this defusion exercise is to help clients relate differently to their thoughts. The exercise can be used as many times as a client is interested and they continue to benefit from it in their need for defusion.

In treatment planning, Monsters on the Bus can be used to achieve defusion and to expand our client's attention to thinking and experiencing as an ongoing behavioral process. Because thoughts change constantly, we can highlight them as an ongoing process, instead of how we usually experience them: as a causal, ontological way of being. The purpose is to perceive thoughts for what they are (just thoughts) instead of focusing on the content of the thought. In other words, *thoughts* related to concerns of safety differ fundamentally from the actual experience of *being* in an unsafe situation.

Monsters on the Bus is ideal if, for example, a client experiences a lack of psychological flexibility and limits their behavior choices when they have fearful, trauma-related thoughts. This intervention would also be successful when a client is struggling with beliefs about independence/autonomy, or experiencing fears about judgments from others. This intervention is appropriate for children and adults and the language can be modified to fit your clients. Determine whether your client is receptive to a defusion technique through the art process by asking them. You might say something like, "It seems as though some specific thoughts are getting in the way of you moving towards your values and doing what you want to do. Would you be willing to try an art intervention to explore some of the thoughts and see how you might be able to relate to them differently so they stop interfering with what you want to do?" Once you and your client have decided that a defusion technique would be appropriate and your client is willing, you can try the intervention that follows.

Monster/Passenger on the Bus instructions

- Imagine you have a job as a bus driver and you are tasked with driving a route and picking up passengers. You have a specific route you travel to reach your goal at the bus terminal. Your bus route/map represents your values and how you want to be: a loving and patient parent, sober, caring partner, loyal friend, and so on. The passengers you pick up represent your unwanted private experiences (e.g., thoughts, feelings, bodily sensations), or an old negative story. You are still tasked with driving your route, regardless of which passengers get on the bus.

- Imagine your inner, unwanted experiences that seem to board your bus when you are working on your values. For example, you might be working on being a loving and loyal partner and old thoughts arise, such as, "I am unable to trust anyone," or, "I am going to screw this relationship up," or you experience feelings of shame, anxiety, and fear. These might cause you to engage in behavior demonstrating mistrust, such as jealous lashing out at your partner or yelling. Another possibility might be that when working on parenting values of patience and love, unwanted memories of shame from childhood may emerge, causing unexplained anger at your child. Perhaps when working on your value of health and beginning to exercise, you may say negative, unhelpful statements that push you away from exercise and towards unhealthy choices. This kind of self-talk might include, "I will never succeed at losing weight," or, "What's the point—it has never worked in the past?"

- Identify three of your unwanted feelings, stories, thoughts, or bodily sensations that are getting in the way of moving towards your values. These can be written or discussed in therapy. Select three to use in the art intervention.

- Depict each of these thoughts, feelings, or bodily sensations as passengers/monsters who are going to get on the bus while you are driving towards your values. Imagine these are unruly passengers shouting at you or whispering in your ear the unwanted thoughts and feelings. They really make driving difficult and start to tell you to turn right, when your bus route says to turn left. These are the thoughts that really get in your way. For example, a monster might encourage the driver to go to the bar when in fact the driver is planning to stay sober. You can create the monsters using almost any medium: drawing, painting, clay, digital drawing, collage, fiber, or found objects.

- After creating three passengers/monsters to depict the unwanted thoughts and feelings, it is time to do some writing and talking about the passengers/monsters and help the monsters tell their story. Here are some questions you can use to tell the story of the monster passengers, You can make up your own backstory and add more details: What is the monster's name? What does the monster say? How old is the monster? How long has the monster been with you? When does the monster show up in your life? Who are the monster's best friends? When does the monster need to calm down? What does the monster wish would happen when it shows up? What is the monster afraid of? When is the monster helpful to you?

Figure 7.5 depicts a monster from the Monster on the Bus exercise, made with watery acrylic paint blown through a straw with cray-pas and glitter to enhance the image. I created this image with my group of clients at an in-patient substance abuse facility. Making art with my clients served several purposes: an art example, using paint in unusual ways, and revealing a human component in therapy. Sharing your already-explored and resolved examples of monsters with clients goes a long way in building rapport and helping them see the universality of struggling with thoughts. If you are able to make art with clients, while staying focused on them, and avoiding getting lost in the process, it can be a helpful intervention and way to share the art process.

FIGURE 7.5: MONSTER ON THE BUS
*Note: Rendition of the Monster on the Bus by Amy
Backos, acrylic paint and cray-pas, glitter.*

Considerations when using the Monsters on the Bus intervention

Before introducing this intervention, remember to practice it yourself so you know what to expect. Consider in advance whether your client has sufficient ego strength to manage explorations of these unwanted parts of the self when exploring what gets in the way of living their values. This intervention has been incredibly well liked by clients and students; however, I worked with one young man who had experienced so much abuse and powerlessness in his childhood that his fused thoughts led him to feel certain that he was a monster instead of the bus driver. We paused to return his focus to the present moment and take a more active approach to defusing his new thoughts of being a monster before he decided to continue with the art. While it is useful to consider which clients would benefit the most from this intervention, externalizing negative thoughts into characters through the art allows many people to be playful with their negative stories. I like to include stick-on googly eyes and show examples to my clients to demonstrate how they are welcome to get silly and have fun with the art. For clients who are highly fused with their thoughts and whom you suspect may be unable to engage playfully with the art, changing the language from monsters to passengers may be helpful. I always wait for clients to demonstrate their willingness to have fun in this intervention, and I follow their lead in how serious or silly it is for them.

In ACT, we avoid asking clients to try and stop the monster from getting on the bus. Instead, we are asking them to *relate* differently to the monsters when they get on the bus, which in turn allows them to pursue their values regardless of whatever thoughts, feelings, and sensations present themselves. Consider other ways that you can creatively externalize the thoughts—maybe through play, creating characters from clay, or making puppets of the passengers. You could use this exercise with sand-tray characters as well. Remember, the goal is to be defused from the thoughts by externalizing them. This is what removes some of the sting from the thoughts and helps clients increase their psychological flexibility by changing how they relate to their thoughts.

Conclusion

Cognitive defusion techniques in a therapy session are used to change the unwanted/undesirable outcomes or *functions* of the thoughts and inner private experiences (Harris, 2007). Unlike traditional CBT where the goal is to change or reduce the frequency of the thoughts, the goal in ACT is to alter the way the person *relates* to their thoughts and thus alter the function the thoughts serve. Once the person is able to see the thoughts for what they are (just thoughts), defusion typically yields a change in attachment to the thoughts and a reduction in how much they believe the thought to be helpful in moving them towards their values. As a result, the person can weigh the behavioral utility of a thought ("Is this thought useful right now? What behavior will I select?") instead of immediately reacting to the content of a thought (e.g. "I am going to be humiliated") as if it were true. Thoughts are context dependent: while some thoughts can be helpful in a given moment or context, others are unhelpful. Defusion allows the person to become aware of the utility of the thought, as well as the context, before making a conscious behavioral choice based on that awareness.

Recommended resources

These cartoons are less than five minutes in duration and depict the ACT metaphor. You can prepare for the art intervention by watching these videos and suggesting them to your clients.

- www.youtube.com/watch?v=Z29ptSuoWRc

- www.youtube.com/watch?v=NdaCEO4WtDU

CHAPTER 8

Self as the Context
for Our Lives

This chapter defines and explores the spiritual aspects of ACT and art therapy, which tend to be overlooked in other approaches. Self as context offers therapists and clients tools to tap into their core self and these aspects of the self can be used to support and sustain personal growth and deepen creative expression. Taking perspective on ourselves increases awareness of the present moment and expands ability to maintain psychological flexibility.

Who are you in the context of the universe? How would you describe your transcendent, spiritual experience? Who are you at your core? Though these questions may arise in therapy if the therapist or client is curious and interested in the spiritual self, these issues are overlooked in most psychological theories. When I was in school, one professor noted sadly that the religion of most psychologists is psychology. Certainly, religious counseling and many alternative healing practices attend to the spiritual aspects of the self, yet in psychology, these concepts are often overlooked or under-utilized. Buddhist principles for psychological improvement are captured in mindfulness CBT and other mindful-based therapies, and some of these concepts are present in ACT as well.

ACT utilizes mindfulness approaches from Zen Buddhism and explicitly invites the spiritual self to the therapy process. In addition to bringing the cognitive, emotional, and contextual self into the therapy, ACT encourages exploration of oneself as a context for a much larger, fundamentally spiritual experience. ACT utilizes a variety of approaches to facilitate an understanding of the self in the context of the greater whole of the universe by inspiring curiosity about the transcendent aspects of the self. This exploration is strength-based and positive. Instead of only focusing on the pathology of our clients and changing behaviors, this area of the hexaflex promotes psychological flexibility by connecting with a part of the self that is universal. Furthermore, addressing self as context brings personally and culturally relevant ways of knowing to the therapy space.

Relational frame theory

Relational frame theory provides a "functional contextual theory of human language and cognition" (Hayes *et al.*, 2012, p.39) and helps us understand the ideas related to self as context. The study of language can be found in many disciplines and explores how we use the symbols of language in evolutionary beneficial ways. Relational frame theory differentiates between verbal and cognitive events and other psychological events; its definitional framework lends a perspective in which language is at the root of human achievement, as well as human suffering (Hayes *et al.*, 2012).

Relational framing is a behavior in which associations and comparisons are made in our mind, linking language, objects, behaviors, and reactions (Hayes *et al.*, 2012). The ease at which associations and comparisons are present in our minds can be problematic because we may readily respond to these ideas, or thought stimuli, as if they are a reality we must react to. Responding to them can cause grief because a thought can trigger avoidance behavior when the thought is associated with traumatic memories. Conversely, we can utilize our mind's preference for comparisons to deepen our relationship with ourselves or to a higher power or a universal source. Ideas such as "here and there" or "I and you" parlay into an exploration of the spiritual aspects of human existence by comparing the self to one's higher power. *Nondualism* is a Buddhist concept of interconnectedness among us all (Hanh, 2010), and it can apply to how we work in therapy. Our language positions the "self" in relation to "other" and for many people, that "other" already includes God or a higher power. Bringing this aspect of the divine self into the therapy office with direct application of theory and empirically validated approaches lends credibility to the idea of spiritual experience in psychology. In other words, ACT incorporates the whole self and all its parts into the practice of psychology, thus doing far more than just asking about religion as a cultural variable. ACT practitioners welcome cultural beliefs about religion and spirituality into the office and make these beliefs and practices an important part of the contextual exploration of the person in therapy.

Three ways to understand the self

Relational frame theory includes three ways of understanding the self: self as content; self as process; and self as context (ACT With Compassion., n.d.). Process relates to the experience of the self in any given moment, whereas content relates to judgments about the self.

Self as content

This refers to how we might describe ourselves and create a conceptualized self (ACT With Compassion, n.d.). "The conceptualized self is the direct byproduct of training in naming, categorization, and evaluation" (Hayes *et al.*, 2012, p.81) This is the same process we might use to describe an object. However, while descriptions of an object may be an accurate way to conceptualize an object in the world, we treat our descriptions of the self as if they were also true and unchangeable. These are thoughts about the self to which we are fused. In other words, we are highly attached to these descriptions and thoughts of the self. Examples of our content might include external descriptions and judgments that relate to appearance (e.g., tall, short, attractive, ugly). The self as content also includes internal judgments about personality, value/worth, and judgments such as kind, cruel, lovable, unlovable. When clients are fused with the content of the self, they are focused on their perceived identity or judgments about the self. You can get in touch with the idea of self as content by describing your appearance, personality, job, as well as roles you play which you perceive as important.

The dominant descriptions of the self as content are "rigid, evaluative, and evocative" (Hayes *et al.*, 2012, p.111). The conceptualized self tends to override the other aspects of the self. Examples where this can be observed is feeling the need to be right, being highly defensive of the story we tell about ourselves, or focusing attention and attachment to the origins of our suffering. According to Hayes *et al.* (2012), "ACT views this form of self-knowledge as not only highly flawed but also very much a threat to the client's life vitality" (p.111). ACT helps providers and clients to shift their awareness to other aspects of the self.

Self as process

This relates to your ongoing awareness of experience in each moment (ACT With Compassion, n.d.). The awareness of the self, in this case, refers to both the present moment experience itself and your description of your thoughts, feelings, behaviors, and bodily sensations. "Healthy living requires a continuous and flexible verbal self-knowledge of the present moment" (Hayes *et al.*, 2012, p. 223). Essentially, self as process is awareness and observation of the self without judgment. ACT encourages clients to "see what they see as they see it, without unnecessarily judging or justifying what is present" (p.223). For example, you can take a perspective of the self as an ongoing process, experiencing constantly changing thoughts, feelings, behaviors, and physical sensations.

Self as process includes using language in a defused and non-judgmental way to relate to thoughts, feelings, and any other inner experiences. This stance allows us to differentiate our inner and outer experiences and helps us make contact with the current moment (Gordon & Borushok, 2017). You can get in contact with the self as process in this moment by asking yourself, "What thoughts, feelings, and bodily sensations am I aware of right now?"

Self as context

This describes a dynamic stance of connecting to "a sense of personal wholeness, transcendence, interconnectedness, and presence" (Hayes *et al.*, 2012, p.224). This refers to *you* being the context for all the things that you have experienced. It is different from the self as process or self as content. The self as context allows a perspective of yourself from a point of view, distinct from what is happening and how it is happening (ACT With Compassion, n.d.).

Self as context includes flexibly changing perspectives or points of view depending on the situation. "Seeing from *I-here-now* is an action of perspective taking because there is no static mental position from which perspective is granted" (Hayes *et al.*, 2012, pp.223–224). Seeing the self as a context for all that is happening and has happened in that life enables emotions such as compassion and empathy to emerge. Self as context and the observing self can help clients relate to a higher power or their transcendent self.

For those who are interested in spirituality or religion, self as context offers ripe content for discussion about relationships with higher power/transcendent self as a way of fully understanding our personal context. Self as context serves as an extension of mindfulness because the idea is to invite our clients to be mindfully aware of the self as a context for all that has happened in their lives. Ideally, awareness of the self as context enables us to focus on a "stable, grounded, and enduring sense of self that is able to have a flexible perspective" (Godbee & Kangas, 2020, p.1).

Self as context in action

Kayla Ormandy, an associate marriage and family therapist and provisional art therapist in the San Francisco Bay Area, works at a pain management clinic using ACT to support her clients. I asked her to reflect on self as context and how she understands this concept and applies it in her life and work. She makes reference to self as process, content, and context in her essay called "Wise Tools."

> I've come to think about the brain and the body as intelligent, primordial, innately wise tools that feed me information about what I am experiencing. This finely tuned body helps me to feel my emotions through my stomach, my heart, my throat, and my limbs. My delicate

brain has evolved to process information at incredible speeds. These two tools help me to interact with the world and make sense of my experience, but they are not who I am.

The brain, as I see it, is just another organ. The lungs bring in oxygen, the liver filters out toxins, and the brain thinks thoughts. We just happen to be more acutely aware of our thoughts than of the contents of an inhale, so it can be easy to get enticed into believing that what we think is who we are. Instead, these thoughts are simply a presentation of information. They are information about a current experience, are informed by previous experiences, and provide an understanding from which we can react.

I still have a self that I have conceptualized. I am a certain height, have a certain hair color, grew up in specific circumstances, and have certain hobbies. Through practicing self as context, however, I have come to hold this idea of who I am more lightly. For example, I can be a person who dyes their hair, or I can be a person who tries a new hobby. This space allows me the ability to reconstruct my worldview as I learn and grow. There was a time in which I believed that I had to be smarter than everyone to be worthy of friendship. Since that time, I gained new role models and vastly different experiences that allowed me to let go of that concept. I now strive to be compassionate and humorous in my friendships, while knowing that I am inherently worthy of friendship just as I am.

When I am working with clients to help them become more aware of their thoughts, I talk about the human system like a car. I drive my car to all sorts of places. There have been days when I've spent more time in my car than with people! But I have never identified myself as my car. In this metaphor, the body is the car we drive every day of our lives. It needs food, tune-ups, and replacements. Sometimes it gets into a fender bender and never drives quite the same way again. Yet it constantly remains the sacred vehicle that animates us, allowing us to engage physically in the world in order to achieve our goals. It allows us to interact with the world and to receive information, but it is not who we are.

Similarly, I have had lots of passengers in my car over the years. Some sat in the back, some have chosen to sit in the front, and sometimes every seat was filled. My car has transported people, animals, boxes, and art supplies. There have been many instances when the passengers meowed, hissed, or gave directions. Sometimes they wanted me to change the music, to make a pit stop, or just loudly talked among themselves. But I have never identified myself as being my passengers. These passengers inside our cars are metaphors for the thoughts our brains think. Our brain gets distracted by passing cows or by the idea of stopping for a snack, or upset by pressure changes and car sickness. Our thoughts, too, vary over the course of a day. Our thoughts are information about possible ways to interpret events and what we might need to do in response to feel safe. Sometimes these thoughts dwell in the past and look in the rearview mirror, or scurry off into the future and get anxious that we aren't there yet. Thoughts are a constant flow of information from our brains.

A trick I was taught by various teachers is to look at thoughts with gentle kindness, as though a child were setting a freshly picked flower into the palm of my hand. Some phrases I use to hold my thoughts as lightly as a flower are, "Isn't that interesting that I had that thought again?" "How curious!" and, "I'm so silly." This helps to listen to thoughts with a gentle distance, at once both accepting the thought for arising, and then choosing what to do with that information. "Do I need to stop at that fast food restaurant or can I make it home for dinner?" "Are these $500 pants in my budget?" "Am I actually overweight?" "Is it more important in my relationship to be right or to be kind?"

Like most of us, I went through life believing my thoughts and identifying with my emotions. This became self-limiting when I believed thoughts like, "I don't belong," or, "I'm not good enough." (What did this keep me from doing?) That was, until I started practicing a more loving approach towards myself. One of the ultimate practices of self as context is to see oneself as whole, worthy of love and belonging, and secure from being harmed. A capital "S", Self can witness difficult beliefs without being married to them, can feel difficult emotions and not be stained, and becomes a Self that is Home. I'm still practicing this one, knowing that no one gets it perfectly.

Self as context becomes possible through mindfulness—through becoming aware of our thoughts, having self-compassion to accept our thoughts and emotions as passing information, and through persistent practice. What I have found to be most beneficial to strengthen my ability to act from a place of self as context has been the presence of patient teachers: kind individuals who consistently bring my attention back, over and over again, to the truth of who I really am. And from this space of viewing myself as context, I can lead a more empowered and fulfilling life.

The observing self

The place from which you view your private experiences of thoughts, feelings, and bodily sensations is your *observing self*. It can be called "pure awareness, because that is all it is: awareness" (Harris, 2007, p.159). Your observing self is fundamentally different from your thoughts, feelings, and bodily sensations. It is the awareness of those aspects of the self. Without your observing self, you would lack any self-awareness.

We change constantly. The sensations of thoughts and feelings ebb and flow, continually evolving. Your attention shifts from one project or experience to the next. Your body changes constantly, growing from baby, toddler, tween, teenager, young adult, adult, middle age, older adult, to elderly. Your body creates new cells and you grow new hair and nails every day. Your roles evolve as you grow, and they even change throughout your day: daughter/son, partner, parent, aunt/uncle, grandparent, student, worker. Through all of this, your viewpoint from the observing self remains the same. It is the part of you that has seen everything about your life. Your observing self has watched you survive your worst days and seen you experience your happiest moments. It is always there for you as your source of awareness.

The observing self is by definition, perfect acceptance. "It cannot be improved on in anyway; therefore it is perfect" (Harris, 2010, p.161). That part of you sees you and what is happening for what it truly is and without judgment. Thus, concepts like good or bad are nonexistent from the perspective of your observing self. Your observing self is aware with zero judgment of your thoughts, feelings, how your body feels, and what is happening. Once the mind begins to judge, it has moved away from the observing self. The observing self is unable to be improved on and is safe from harm (Harris, 2010). Safety exists here because it is only observing, without judgment or change. Even when we are unaware of the observing self, or feeling out of touch with that part of ourselves, it still exists.

What a relief to know there is a part of each of us that is perfect, all accepting, and without judgment. For clients who relate to a religion or spirituality, this aspect can be related to the soul or the universal part of the self. Using ACT, we can tap into this part of ourselves to increase psychological flexibility. Connecting with this part of the self creates relief from distress and reaction to what is happening. We can help our clients tap into this source, even when they have felt alienated from themselves or feel that this part is somehow missing. Through self as context, we can experience respite from distress.

Observing self-exercise

Staying present with the observing self requires attention and practice. Our thoughts typically crowd into our mind, fighting to be noticed and relevant. Our body sensations or plans and worries for the future compete for our attention as well. Practice noticing your mind as often as you can. Hanh (2010) offers a simple, albeit often difficult, tool to access the observing self. He teaches awareness of the self with these two sentences: "Breathing in, I know I am breathing in. Breathing out, I know I am breathing out" (Hanh, 2010, p.1).

Try the exercise below yourself three to five times a day for a week and then you can introduce it to your clients.

Close your eyes and breathe at your normal rate. It is unnecessary to alter or change the pace of your breathing. As you are breathing in, say out loud, *Breathing in, I know I am breathing in.* As you breathe out, say out loud, *Breathing out, I know I am breathing out.* On the next breath, repeat the sentences in a whisper. After that, say the sentences silently in your mind while your attention is focused exclusively on your breath.

Thoughts and other awareness will inevitably wander into your mind. When that happens, you can say, *Breathing in, I am aware of the thoughts* or *Breathing out, I am aware of how my body feels*. It may seem to you that your observing self leaves when your attention is drawn to some thought or feeling. However, you may trust that your observing self is omnipresent, perfect in its acceptance, nonjudgment, and awareness. Simply return to your breath. Breathe in, saying, *Breathing in, I know I am breathing in.* As you breathe out, say, *Breathing out, I know I am breathing out.*

You can create your own mindfulness awareness meditation by making a recording on your phone of the two sentences and play it several times a day to get more familiar with your observing self. You can also record yourself reading the two paragraphs above at a slow pace and listen to it in the morning and before bed. Other variations include designing an artistic sign which reads: *Breathing in, I know I am breathing in. Breathing out, I know I am breathing out.* You can give credit for the saying on your sign to Thich Nhat Hanh. You could hang the sign in your office and invite your clients to create their own sign to hang in their home.

Wait! What am I?

The creative metaphors art therapists can draw on to help clients come into contact with their observing self to begin to adopt a stance of viewing the self as a context are unlimited. Here is an artistic metaphor you can use to get in touch with the self as context. Before you read on, pull up a picture on your phone of a painting you enjoy viewing. For example, you might like to look at a painting by Frida Kahlo or Jean-Michel Basquiat, artists whose work I find beautiful and meaningful.

Ask yourself, if I were this painting, what part would I be? Might it be the figure in a Basquiat painting? The most colorful section? The most textured? Possibly you relate to the paint itself? Might you most relate to one of the animals in a Kahlo painting? Perhaps you identify with the person in a self-portrait?

What if, for the purpose of this exercise, you could identify as the canvas. The gesso, paint, thickener, dust, and whatever else you add to the canvas represent your experiences, situations, roles, and beliefs. The media on the canvas are fundamentally different from the canvas—the canvas is the base, and the layers made by the gesso and paint represent parts of the painting. Each medium or layer adds to the whole, yet the canvas is fundamentally still intact, supporting the layers of paint. Imagine you are the canvas that supports the painting. Your *self as context* is the canvas itself. Each of us is distinct and unique from our past, the roles we play, the jobs we have, and our beliefs about ourselves and others. You, and your context, are the canvas, while the paint and anything else on the canvas are your experiences, roles, and beliefs.

Perhaps you might prefer to identify as the creator of the painting, and you would still be right. The painting can be housed in a museum or in your home and that might be your community. If you believe in a higher power, you might see your higher power as the craftsperson who built the stretcher on which the canvas rests, or the building itself where the painting hangs might be your higher power. In whatever way you decide to relate to the painting—as the canvas or as the artist—you would be correct. The point is to dis-identify with the gesso, paint, thickener, and so on, on the canvas and to identify with the context on which the paint relies—as the canvas, stretcher, or artist. What other metaphors can you think of to represent yourself as the context of your life?

Why metaphors?

Metaphors in therapy offer a way for clients to understand abstract or difficult concepts (Blenkiron, 2005). Furthermore, using stories and metaphors in therapy allows the client to draw their own conclusions, which brings more of their thinking process to the therapy room (Monestes & Villatte, n.d). When concepts are integrated in the therapy office, material and insights are better retained. Metaphors in ACT are considered an important tool because they facilitate coherence of the concepts and content (Monestes & Villatte, n.d). For example, you will likely have an easier time recalling concepts related to self as context since you completed the exercise looking at a piece of art and imaging yourself as all the paint and the canvas. You might forget that it is called self as context, yet I suspect you will be able to recall this metaphor when you desire distance from the content of your life to focus on your transcendent self.

Metaphors are such a central part of ACT in practice precisely because they can illustrate many of the obtuse concepts in therapy and help clients with psychological flexibility (Stoddard & Afari, 2014). While occasionally used in CBT therapy, metaphors provide an important tool for ACT therapists to help clients challenge their rule-bound behaviors and hyper-focused attention to their symptoms. For example, I have had clients who defined themselves by the content of being broken, sick, unwell. They over-identified with having a disorder such as PTSD, depression, chronic pain, or anxiety, to the exclusion of other aspects of their life, including their work and their relationships with partners, children, and friends. Metaphors bringing awareness to self as context were incredibly useful for the clients. Contextualizing their medical or psychiatric disorder as only a *part* of who they were created new space for choice, enjoyment, pleasure, pride, and increased capacity for relationships.

I worked with one veteran who kept wearing his full uniform each day, long after he was discharged from his service. People all around him reacted to his uniform and people assumed he was "on duty" instead of a veteran shopping for groceries or coming to the hospital for an appointment. We worked together to explore his conceptualized self and move towards his self as context. He came to realize that his over-identification with who he *was* in the military (conceptualized self) overshadowed his self-concept. He had, until our work together, only been able to see himself in that light. The more we worked with self as context, the more flexible he became in this area until one day he arrived in session wearing a new, casual outfit. We discussed how this dramatic shift in his clothing signaled a willingness to engage in the here and now and to let go of his past conceptualized self. Other providers in the hospital noticed and he found that people began to relate to him differently, opening up opportunities for him to relate differently to himself and others.

Metaphor in art therapy practice

Gwen Sanders received the American Art Therapy Association Distinguished Clinician Award in 2019 and the student nominated George M. Keller Award for teaching excellence in 2016. She is the Clinical Practicum Director at Dominican University of California and has been teaching in the Graduate Art Therapy Psychology Department for over 20 years. She is an Honorary Life Member and Past President of the Northern California Art Therapy Association. Sanders has extensive work in trauma, including working abroad as a military family life consultant for the US Army in Europe in Germany and Italy, and in Nicaragua and Costa Rica, working with multigenerational survivors of war trauma. She serves as a consultant to various agencies, presents nationally on her clinical practice, research, and international travel, and recently authored a chapter entitled "Emerging paradigms in art therapy: The use of art therapy" in *Emerging Perspectives in Art Therapy* (Carolan & Backos, 2018).

Sanders and I discussed the use of metaphor, such as how an artist might illustrate an abstract concept or a therapy client might understand a new idea. Each summer she teaches a class called Metaphors of Psychopathology in Children and so I asked her to share her ideas about how her private practice clients used metaphor to illustrate emotions, thoughts, change, desired change, and new direction in therapy during the Covid-19 pandemic. Her essay that follows, "Belonging as a metaphor of place, the silence of siloed existence," illustrates how memories and feelings can be sorted into art and stories.

> Art therapists intuitively utilize metaphors and symbols that align with verbal narratives to capture the essence of visual constructs, connecting our client's inner world to the universal language of emotions. My clinical work with adults during the Covid-19 pandemic has deepened our connection through the use of their words as art to communicate adeptly through a virtual screen. Metaphors of living are rife today with emotional imagery concerning love, action, inaction, worry, loss, depression, and anxiety related to being siloed by the pandemic. These feelings overshadow, like a fog, the darkness, solitude, suffocation, and emptiness encumbered by the silence. The lack

of connection to others in the community does not create a sense of belonging. Sensory deprivation from the void of regular physical contact with others beyond one's family does not meet the needs of togetherness. The flat screen is the connection.

These metaphors of suffering have crystallized during the global pandemic to inhabit a historical isolation, amounting to the siloed self in existential angst. The solitary self often uses the words, "I, me, myself" as a mark of insignificance, an inability to touch others or to reach out, thus this egocentrism exudes a self-wrought deprivation that comes from feeling left out, overcome, overshadowed. Instead of the usual mirroring from society, which often depicts images of the self as loved, creative, connected, the reflection has been lost. Thus, self-defeat of negative metaphors may flourish. A siloed existence is compromised with self-deprecating stories such as, "I don't know how, nor want, to reach out," "I don't feel loved," "No one cares what happens to me," "I should disappear; no one will notice," "I am undesirable," and on and on. To belong is a human condition, of having a "place at the table," which encompasses the yearning for love and having a voice that is honored. This limited existence is metaphorically mirrored in the Black Lives Matter movement to shine the light on White supremacy, which has silenced many People of Color within the global community.

This is the work—art, voices, eyes, words, and symbols hold the stories of one's lived experience, encouraging action and change. The movement of therapy helps to gain traction towards transformation, the slow re-creation of the stories of our life appears to be a piece of our lifelong narrative; it is profound and has indelibly marked us all—differently.

Our work as art therapists is to open up dialogues and doors that hold hope, to encourage the language of opportunity and belonging, to help our clients find their voices. Taking action encourages movement and engagement, requiring energy and focused intent. Art and words help us to evolve from isolation and despair to honor resilience as an adaptive means to accommodate to the world as lifelong learners. Altering our stories creates new stories we name as our own.

"I can't imagine being anything if I am unable to be that!"

Conducting an art therapy workshop for the Northern California Art Therapy Association in 2019, I taught ACT art therapy concepts and the most energy and excitement in the room was generated when we all worked on letting go of our attachment to our perceived identities of ourselves as content. This exercise was designed to produce psychological flexibility by creating distance between the actual self and our thoughts and beliefs about ourselves (Backos, 2021).

We start with the personal, *I am*—making three statements about our identity, ranging from temporary states like "I am sitting" to more permanent/ongoing roles, such as "I am a parent." Then we rank the statements by degree to attachment to our conceptualized self.

Here are examples of my three statements that start with "I am" and the order increases in attachment to my identity. Let's break down each of these statements and you can see how attached I am to each of these "truisms" as part of my identity. The first one feels like a low-level attachment to my identity. I feel more attached to the next statement and the last "I am" statement that feels challenging to distance myself from.

I am sitting outside.

I am a psychologist and art therapist.

I am a mother.

Low-level identity: "I am sitting outside." It was easy to acknowledge that my identity is different from my physical position of sitting outside. I will eventually stand up and go inside and that piece of my current identity will change. I will still be me when I move inside.

Moderate-level identity: "I am a psychologist and art therapist." This feels more integral to my identity and my perceived purpose of sharing art therapy with others to help improve the world. I see myself as someone who is devoted to service and this feels central to my conceptualized self and the content of my identity. I like this part of my identity and I spend many of my days in this role. However, one day I will retire and I will still be me. So, while this feels incredibly integral to how I spend my time, I will still exist after this role has run its course.

High-level identity: "I am a mom." This statement describes a role I have and this one is very important to me and my family. I am committed to parenting the best I can, I think about it a lot, and I live with my child. However, I have other roles that may take priority over this role at any given moment. For example, when my son is at school and I am at work, I am engaged in other roles besides parenting. One day he will grow up and move away and my role as a mother will look completely different even while this role remains permanent in my life. However, I still exist when I am doing something besides parenting, and I will exist when my son grows up and moves away from home.

Here are some more examples from students, clients, colleagues, and friends. You may find that what some people rank as a low identity statement feels more integral to your identity and vice versa. See which ones you identify with and rank them for yourself as low, medium, or high identity statements. A low identity statement has little bearing on your self-identity—the situation can change and your sense of self will easily remain intact and unaffected. A moderate identity statement holds more attachment, yet you can imagine these aspects changing and you will move on without it. A high identity statement reflects attachments that feel integral to your sense of self and potentially crushing when you imagine yourself without that identity. Perhaps it is uncomfortable or even threatening to your sense of self to imagine yourself without this high-intensity piece of your conceptualized self. See Table 8.1 for examples of low, moderate and high identity.

Table 8.1: Low, moderate, high identity examples

Low identity	Moderate identity	High identity
I am standing	I am 6 feet tall	I am Latinx
I am drinking coffee	I am a skateboarder	I am in the world
I am wearing blue	I am a graphic artist	I am LGBTQ+
I am sleepy	I am good	I keep getting abused

I am hungry	I am a student	I am male
I am writing	I am...	I am a religious person
I am...		I am...

Write three "I am" statements about you that are low, moderate, and high identity statements.

1. Low identity: I am . . . .

2. Moderate identity: I am . . . .

3. High identity: I am . . . .

Try to imagine you have some distance from the high identity statement in the same way that you have some distance from the low identity statement. Grab a pen and answer the following questions:

- What does it feel like to de-identify with your high identity statement?

- Who are you if you are unable to be that?

- Who would be left?

- If any of the parts you identified as "I am" were gone, what would remain?

Tricky questions! Your answers to the I am statements relate to your conceptualized self/persona/ego identity. Your answers to the questions about what remains if you are unable to be your conceptualized self give you some clues as to your *essence* and the part of you that is the *context* of all your life experience. If the parts you identified above were gone, what would remain? Did you identify your soul? Your essence? Your spirit? Perhaps you identified your way of being when there is a lack of attachment to how you are "supposed" to be or how you like to be? What remains is the self as *context* for all your life experiences.

The self as context is the part of you that has seen and lived all of your experiences, the part of you that has existed long before now, exists now, and will continue to exist after this moment has passed. The self as context is nonjudging and always with you, even when you are unaware of it. If it feels uncomfortable to reflect on your self as context, I encourage you to keep looking—everyone has this core self. Remember to ensure that your client has sufficient ego strength to manage the sometimes frustrating aspects of peeling away layers of self-identity to reveal the self as context.

Self as context links to the concepts of defusion discussed earlier. If you are willing to make space between you and some of your core identity concepts, might you also consider creating even more distance between you and your thoughts? You may wish to review defusion concepts to deepen your experience in letting go of rigid or unhelpful belief systems and understand how self as context is linked to defusion.

Remember, the goal in ACT is to increase psychological flexibility in our thinking. Continued practice will allow you to discover other thoughts and aspects of your conceptualized self from which you are ready to distance yourself. Being psychologically flexible in any moment includes being aware of thoughts and feelings without trying to avoid or control them, without believing them as fact, or using them as a rationale for our behavior. When we get in touch with our self as context and begin to let go of our conceptualized self, the stance of psychological flexibility becomes easier. When we are unattached to ideas about ourselves, we have less need to defend our conceptualized self and we can just be in the moment.

Wait, some "I am" statements are really true!

Some "I am" statements are helpful in navigating the world safely. For example, someone saying, "I am allergic to peanuts," provides parameters around what to safely eat. This "I am" statement is a good example of a thought that is important, true, and *should* be believed. However, most "I am" statements lack this kind of clarity. Let's go a little deeper and explore why our attachment to these other identity statements might be limiting our psychological flexibility.

Let's go back to the statement, "I am a parent." This statement seems challenging to shift for a lot of parents and it remains the most challenging to me. I see myself *as* a mom. However, if I remain attached to that identity, I am limiting myself by reducing the number of possible psychological and behavioral options in any given moment. Creating psychological distance from this identity can give perspective and flexibility to act freely, choosing different behaviors in any given moment. The role of mom remains important and my commitment to parenting remains strong—these will continue, even when I have some psychological distance from thinking that "I am a mom." I would be better off changing the statement from "I am a mom" to, "one of my most important roles is being a parent."

Why create distance? Distance from our thoughts about a particular role we play brings freedom. This is the freedom to choose how much attention we give our thoughts that emerge. I imagine many parents might have thoughts of doubt in parenting, such as, "I am a bad mom/dad" or, "I am doing this all wrong." The distance from thoughts brings the freedom to choose from a wide variety of behavioral responses in any given moment. So, while my commitment to parenting remains strong, my choices increase when I have the psychological space to untangle my attachment to this role. I may have the thought, "I am doing this wrong" and with psychological distance, be able to retain all the behavioral options of how I want to respond in that moment.

There was a time before I was a mother so I know I exist and have existed before I took on the role of mother. There are times I am doing other things besides being a mother—being a therapist, a daughter, a wife, a neighbor, an artist. If I respond as if I were a mom while I am teaching, doing therapy, or talking with my partner, I may have some significant pushback and challenges in successful communication! My role stays important, yet I have psychological flexibility to take on other roles and who I am really has nothing to do with the roles I have. The point is to create some distance between you and your roles/self-concept so you can think and respond clearly with perspective in a way of your choosing. You can apply these same concepts to whatever role or conceptualized self you feel most attached to from the list you made.

Bringing your awareness to these as part of your identity naturally invites reflection on how others and how society views you.

You probably have a strong attachment to your race and culture, your family identity, your sexual orientation, your job, your body, and so on. Society reinforces value on certain races, bodies, cultures, genders, and jobs. When you begin to get in contact with yourself as context, you can even see society's expectations and judgments more clearly. You will likely even feel more engaged in movements important to you related to your identity—you will be able to engage in activism and advocacy from a deeper place within yourself. Being detached from our self as content means the roles we play and the identities we embrace are positioned as external and our self becomes elevated to the context of our lives. We become liberated from the trappings and limitations of roles and labels from both society and ourselves. Clients can begin to free themselves from the tyranny of unhelpful thoughts as well as societal and personal judgments.

The lived experience of an act practitioner

Corrie Mazzeo brings extensive experience working for the VA hospital using ACT. We co-facilitated ACT art therapy groups for several years at the VA (Backos & Mazzeo 2017). Mazzeo currently works as a CBT expert consultant with technology companies. She writes content for applications that promote wellbeing in the area of health psychology. She reflects here about the importance of integrating of ACT concepts, both in the therapy process and in the personal life of the therapist. Furthermore, she highlights the challenges inherent in the self as concept components of ACT as she and her clients humorously grapple with metaphors for this obtuse concept.

One of the most difficult ACT concepts for me and many therapists to work with is self as context. When I first began using ACT as my primary approach with clients, I was just out of school and I really tried to push each concept separately within a specified session, following a protocol by the book. What I found over time is that this did not work for me or the client. It felt awkward and forced, as if I was a robot therapist placing a narrative on the client and trying to force them into it. It wasn't natural and both myself and the clients felt it. I remember one session with a client when I tried the chess board metaphor for self as context with my little crafted paper chess board. Luckily, we had a solid therapeutic relationship, and he said to me while laughing, "This is weird."

We laughed together at the failure of the intervention. That experience grounded me in recognizing that it's not just the concept or theory we present in therapy but that we always must bring these things into session from a genuine, lived in space. Ultimately, ACT is most successful when you understand it not just as a standardized therapy approach, but as an experience, as a way of looking at life, a philosophy. I use ACT not just in professional settings, but also in my friendships, relationships with family, and in my relationship with myself. What I realize now is that one of the best things about ACT is that it is truly dynamic. My connection to it continues to grow and change over time as I see the use of it in so many different life situations and experiences. It's to be lived in, by both the therapist and the client. It's not just worksheets and specifically designed perfect interventions. It can be brought into our work in many different ways, weaving in and out of sessions seamlessly and organically.

For those of us who may not be tied to organized religion, or who may even be atheist, I believe it supports a spiritual connection to ourselves and others. We can use the concepts of this approach to identify what we value in ourselves, what's important about who we want to be in the world and in our various life roles, to approach ourselves and others with compassion and nonjudgment, to see ourselves and others as beings outside our thoughts, emotions, and actions. Ultimately, I find that for me, self as context is "taught" to most clients through this natural progression of the relationship we share with them, that we are helping them recognize that their past experiences, thoughts, emotions, and actions are not what we judge them by. We rather think of them as who they are deep down, in their heart and soul. Isn't that one of the greatest honors of this work, that we get to see people, really see people, for who they are and make space for them and hold them with unconditional acceptance and warmth? So really, our willingness to see them and accept them for exactly who they are at their core gives them the experience of self as context.

One example that sits with me as quite possibly the purest connection I've ever had with a human was when I was listening to a person recount the worst thing they had ever done, and while the act was truly one of the most heinous things I have ever heard in my entire life, I felt no judgment or disgust, just compassion for this human in front of me; it in no way changed anything about who I saw them to be. This client was willing to show me everything, hiding nothing, and trusted that I saw who they were regardless of what they'd done. And what that tells me is that self as context may be honestly the most important concept we ever show a client and also that it is much more powerful if we show them through our actions, approach, genuine connection, and lived experience than through a carefully crafted paper chess board.

Conclusion

Relating to ourselves might come in the form of content, process, or context. Awareness of the interactions between our inner content (thoughts, feelings, and bodily sensations) and our conceptualized self (ego-driven ideas about the self, societal and self-descriptions) allows us to explore the process of ourselves and how our mind works. We can take a step back to view the self as a context for all our lived experiences, which increases contact with the present moment and improves our psychological flexibility to choose behaviors consistent with our values. Self as context brings the soul/spirit into the therapy office and this awareness facilitates how we can allocate our attention and behavior in any moment. Moving away from our conceptualized self (ego-driven self-concepts) to a more spirit-driven self-concept (self as context) frees us to respond in ways of our choosing and engage with our values instead of reacting to what is happening around us.

Recommended resources

1. *The Big Book of ACT Metaphors* offers stories and ideas to bring to clients and these can be a great source of inspiration in

generating art interventions tailored to your clients: Stoddard, J.A. & Afari, N. (2014). *The Big Book of ACT Metaphors: A Practitioner's Guide to Experiential Exercises and Metaphors in Acceptance and Commitment Therapy.* Oakland, CA: New Harbinger Publications.

CHAPTER 9

What Matters Most: Getting in Contact with Values

Defining values promotes direction, clarity, and positive behavioral action. Value-based statements describe individual, personally chosen principles to guide one's life decisions and inspire daily behavior. In this chapter, value domains will be explored, highlighting interventions to identify personal, self-directed values and codes of behavior, as well as shared values, such as professional ethics, cultural humility, and service. Several value domains using verbal and art interventions are included that will help us and our clients move towards our individual and shared values.

Do you hope to express and act on the values for which you stand? Do you want to spend more of your time in meaningful ways? Do you wish to further explore and actualize what is most important to you and engage fully with your life? Most of us do, and we can do this through identifying, understanding, and expressing our unique set of values.

Values are a person's deep desires for what they want to stand for and do during their short time on earth (Harris, 2009). Values include the people and things that matter most to a person in conjunction with their personally chosen principles and standards (Gordan & Borushok, 2017). Values as guiding principles are embodied by purposeful action that is freely chosen in any given moment. Values are beliefs that guide behavior, and actively choosing one's personal values offers vital information for selecting how to behave.

The more you are able to align your behaviors with your values, the more your life will be satisfying, vital, and joyful (Harris, 2007; Hayes *et al.*, 2012). Each person has a unique set of values, which are important and distinct from their sense of what others want. Acting on values moves us closer to meaningful relationships, a happy family life, or a sense of ease and purpose in life. We are unable to check off a value on our to-do list. Instead, values serve as a sign-post, guide, or lighthouse that points the way to where we most want to go. You move towards your values each day by engaging in actions that are in line with what is most important to you. Acting on values is called *committed action* and I will go into more detail about putting values to work for you and your clients in Chapter 10.

Without a clear understanding of what we personally value, we become sidetracked into thinking we value what others want us to value. We may adopt values that our parents chose for us or we may pursue values we think we should have to be a good member of society. Fortunately, there is always a time in life to drop the socially prescribed values and identify personal values to start living a meaningful and satisfying life! Regardless of your age or any regrets you have about how you have lived your life, now is a great time to begin forging your worthwhile and authentic set of values, which may be similar or dissimilar to what our family or society values.

What and who do you most value and cherish in your life right now? What core principles drive your work and passions? For example, why are you reading this book right now? Perhaps you want to learn more to help yourself and your clients. Dig deeper and you likely find that you value the dignity and sacredness of yourself and your clients, you value access to mental health care, you want to support a particular community, and you support social justice and equality. Perhaps you, or someone you love, lives with a mental health issue and you want to "give back." Maybe you love being around people and art therapy is a natural extension of your love of art. Perhaps you want to share with others the wonderful feelings you experience using ACT or making art. Maybe you feel a calling to be a therapist or art therapist and you want to actualize your full potential while earning a living. All of these are important values in the domains of career, family, social justice, and education.

Remember, ACT teaches the importance of making nonjudgmental contact with ourselves and the world so that we can allocate our attention and behaviors in a way of our choosing (Gordon & Borushok, 2017). We all strive for survival and much of our goal-driven behavior is to make sure our needs, such as safety, belonging, and connection, are met. However, once our survival needs are met, we are free to choose our priorities in life. Values provide the direction we want to travel in, and they guide us in how we want to make contact with the present moment. By helping us regain or maintain control over our behavior, they assist with the often-challenging aspects of therapy—implementing our value-based behaviors (Hayes *et al.*, 2012). Values interact with all the other previously mentioned concepts in the hexaflex to provide us with a clear rationale for our choices and guide our responses to whatever is happening in any given moment. Values move us towards a more vital engagement with our lives.

Value domains: What do you stand for?

"The process of making close experiential contact with one's values is one of the most intense, intimate clinical experiences in ACT" (Hayes *et al.*, 2012, p.308). Value domains include the categories of life that are the most significant and meaningful for each of us. Hayes *et al.* (2012) noted that we "intuitively know" (p.308) what we care most about. They are the areas where you interact or act. The utility of the categories is to spark ideas and help you identify your own cherished areas of worth. Remember, values help us select our behaviors from many alternatives and ultimately, your values can inform your choices. Table 9.1 shows some examples of value domains and you can certainly add more to suit you and your clients.

Table 9.1: Potential value domains

Family	Social justice	Creativity	Health
Romantic relationship	Spirituality	Education	Parenting
Friends	Work/vocation	Community	Environment

Note: Examples of areas in which you have values that guide you.

Values vs avoidance

Values are distinct from feelings (Hayes *et al.*, 2012). We may feel we value our relationships with friends or family. However, *feeling* we value them might mean we engage with them in positive ways when we have the emotional sensation of valuing and appreciating them, whereas we may interact with them in negative ways when struggling or disagreeing with them. *Valuing* means taking action that is consistent with our values, regardless of how we *feel* in any given moment (Hayes *et al.*, 2012). For example, if we value our creativity, acting on it means we frequently engage in the creative process, regardless of how we may feel. Some people seem to place a high value on their social media presence, drinking alcohol, online shopping, earning or saving money, or exercise. By virtue of how much time they spend engaged in these activities, they appear to hold these activities in high esteem and as an end point to their valued life. However, engaging in these behaviors for the sake of a short-term mood boost or avoidance of unwanted feelings leaves us chronically empty and seeking more external ways to feel good and avoid feelings. Although none of these behaviors are inherently damaging to oneself or others when done in moderation, many of them can be done compulsively and lead us away from our true values. Too much time scrolling social media, drinking, or working might leave little time for our loved ones, passions, and hobbies. Overspending can lead to financial struggles or insufficient funds to support our true values. Over-exercising might cause injury or serve to mask negative self-image.

Conversely, any of these behaviors can be value-based behaviors when done consciously and intentionally. A person might care for their business and use social media to connect with customers. They may value their friends and meet up after work to spend quality time at the pub. Love of fashion and art might include carefully selecting beautiful clothes. Physical fitness and exercise are essential for health, our longevity, and survival. Without the careful consideration of what is important, we can easily fall into mindless, short-term hedonic behaviors, leading ultimately to dissatisfaction and unhappiness.

Experiencing connection to our values offers fulfillment and satisfaction. It eases our experiences of frustration and futility by realigning us with our purpose and intentions. For example, why do you go to work? If you are a therapist, teacher, or in a similar service profession, you likely care deeply for others and want to make the world a better and happier place by uplifting others. Furthermore, you work to pay rent/mortgage, buy food, and otherwise support yourself. Tapping into your values elevates awareness of purpose in our lives and creates more meaningful ways of engaging with others.

Call to mind three or four people you admire; they can be people you know or famous people, living or deceased. What do you admire about them? You might admire political or civil rights leaders who work to implement changes in legislation to further equality and change. You might admire a friend or family member for their dedication to their family, religion, volunteer service, or community. You might admire your parents or the parents of a friend for taking such good care of their children. You might admire athletes for their dedication to their sport. The shining qualities you have in mind when you think about why you admire the people you do likely exclude attributions, such as spending lots of time on social media, exercising too much, drinking, or working too many hours.

We admire people who engage with their values regularly and commit to whatever they value. They are committed to what is important to them—writing, sports, family, caring for children, or bringing justice to society. The people we admire may have values quite different from our own values, yet we are continually inspired by their hard work, dedication, and behaviors in service of their values. For example, an athlete's performance in the Olympics generates our collective admiration, even if we fail to share the that athlete's values. We are inspired and appreciate it when people engage in their values. The good news is that we can be just as dedicated to what we find most important in our lives, and act accordingly.

Values vs goals

Goals are specific and achievable and you know when you achieve them. A goal might be to run a mile in a certain time. Once you accomplish this goal, you can cross it off your list. Goals help us break down what we want to accomplish into smaller, manageable actions, which can be easily identified. Accomplishing a specific goal is re-enforcing and helps us move on to the next goal. It feels *good* to achieve a goal.

When goals are linked to values, we gain meaning, purpose, and motivation for our actions. While certainly satisfying in and of itself, running a faster mile can be linked to a value of feeling healthy and strong through the speed-related goal of exploring the limits of one's endurance and speed. Athletes know the thrill of accomplishing new physical goals and an existential crisis of identity may arise when their college or professional athletic career comes to an end if their reasons and behaviors are unconnected to their values. This is true of many people who reach a milestone goal in their career and then wonder why they feel disappointed or empty instead of happy and elated.

In contrast to goals, values point you in the right direction and help you to identify and to set your goals. "In order for valuing to occur, it is critical that values not be confused with decisions and judgments—values must instead be choices" (Hayes *et al.*, 2012, p.300). The time to act on your values is *now*, while you are working on your goals. You may have specific goals you are trying to reach and the process can be so much more meaningful and rewarding if they are linked to your values. Behaviors driven by values instead of goals offer meaning, purpose, and motivation. While you are working on your specific, long-term goals, such as getting married, parenting, buying a house, graduating, or being physically healthy, you can engage with your values every day. Each of these goals connects to values, which helps us to manage relationship challenges, display patience with children, persist in school, or stick with whatever we are trying to accomplish. For instance, maintaining mental and physical health is time consuming, and like any worthwhile goal, challenging. Weathering the ups and downs of being healthy can be met more easily when in daily, mindful contact with values, such as being physically strong or having longevity to see one's grandchildren. Making behavioral choices in line with one's values (e.g., healthy eating, daily exercise) creates the value of daily internal satisfaction, regardless of how quickly or slowly each specific goal is met.

The value of cultural humility

Akin to ACT's emphasis on values, cultural humility includes a lifelong pursuit of substance and significance in how we relate to ourselves and others. As such, cultural humility offers "not a discrete endpoint, but a commitment and active engagement in a lifelong process that individuals enter into on an ongoing basis with patients, communities, colleagues, and with themselves" (Tervalon & Murray Garcia, 1998, p.118).

A cherished value of therapists is to respect their patients and regard them with dignity. This standard (value) calls therapists to demonstrate these beliefs (committed action) through honesty with oneself, clients, community, and society by learning and practicing cultural humility. If you take an inventory about the origins of your current attitudes and beliefs, as well as your sources for new information, you may discover some aspects of your practice that are culturally encapsulated (Doby-Copeland *et al.*, 2013; Sue & Sue, 1999).

Through exploring your values, you will be able to defuse from your beliefs, observe them with curiosity and acceptance, and then mindfully make changes to your knowledge and skills. With zero personal judgment (mindfulness and acceptance) about each of our current states of cultural encapsulation or humility, it matters that we take steps now to engage in an ongoing critique of attitudes, beliefs, skills, and sources of information to increase our cultural humility (Jackson, 2020).

Integration of cultural humility, ACT, and art therapy

Claudia Mezzera provides art therapy and expert testimony for historically marginalized youth in Northern California. Her past research includes archetypical art with Latinas for fostering and applying strengths for growth, insight, and change. Mezzera works extensively in the area of cultural humility and cultural attunement, teaching and supervising master's and doctoral research students at Dominican University of California. In her essay, "Cultural humility and acceptance and commitment therapy in art therapy," she reflects on how cultural humility necessarily intersects and ultimately enhances ACT and art therapy.

Cultural humility, or the "ability to maintain an interpersonal stance that is other-oriented (or open to the other) in relation to aspects of cultural identity that are most important to the [person]" (Hook, 2013, p.2), is an essential component required for working efficaciously with multicultural populations while using ACT in art therapy. Clinicians who facilitate therapeutic practices that galvanize clients to embrace and express their thoughts and feelings, as well as their histories, cultural symbols, and stories, allow clients to actively utilize them for their own healing. Clients and communities that draw wisdom directly from their cultural values, beliefs, experiences, and principles can re-establish a sense of collective harmony and resiliency (Aponte & Bracco, 2000; de Young, 1998; Lefley, 2002; Ling & Vasquez, 2000; Sue & Sue, 1999). Art therapy combined with ACT provides a utilitarian approach for aiding clients in recognizing their own intrinsic wisdom in drawing new connections as well as integrating greater flexibility and adaptability via accepting, attending to, and exploring the symbolic and artistic messages that hold historical and personal significance. In this way, cultural symbols can become therapeutic tools for personal growth that serve to translate the language and cognition of clients' histories and their hearts into their own legacies of self-advocacy, regeneration, and healing.

"Cross-cultural work requires the understanding of symbols and myths when working with individuals and groups" (McNiff & Barlow, 2009, p.100). The content of historical images and ancestral stories can provide both clients and clinicians with a deeper understanding of themselves, of others, and of the conditions that enhance recovery and inspire life-enriching advocacy and valiancy. Clients who have a history of cultural trauma can benefit from learning to honor their beliefs and values and to reclaim them. Therapists can encourage their clients to actively harness and incorporate their customs and traditions as strength-based tools for treatment. Integrating and facilitating culturally relevant art directives can provide clients with a healing connection to their eugenic and symbolic languages. This can be done by providing culturally appropriate materials and enabling clients to create imagery relevant to their heritage. However, when doing so, it is critical that therapists remain careful not to repress other cultures by superimposing their own cultural ideology and instead honor clients' cultural values whether they fully understand or agree with them or not.

Researchers and clinicians must remain diligently aware of how their personal biases, projections, cultural experiences, and core values are influenced by their education and training via a Westernized theoretical lens. This requires an ongoing professional and personal commitment to remaining mindful and observant about how their education, systemic approaches, and preconceptions are demonstrated in their relational interactions with and within other cultures (McNiff, 1984). "Attaining cultural competence is an ongoing process requiring constant self-awareness and examination to increase an understanding of how our biases, values, and cultural customs affect interactions with culturally diverse populations" (Doby-Copeland, 2006b, p.177). Culturally sensitive ACT paired with art therapy can serve as an avenue of insight and healing. Art therapy and ACT can be instrumental in helping traumatized clients create an integrated appreciation of their cultural strengths and values in a way that empowers them to create meaning from their lived experiences.

Art therapy ethics and ACT values

A discussion of values would be incomplete without exploring our personal and professional ethical standards. In this section, you can begin to utilize the ethical principles of art therapy as a tool to understand your professional values. You can begin or continue to explore your professional values by using these examples to help flesh them out. Take special notice of the areas to which you already feel committed and the areas in which you feel less interested or that the standard is less important to your practice. These are the areas where you can grow and emerge a stronger, more culturally humble therapist, scholar, and researcher.

The aspirational, ethical principles of art therapy professional organizations and interest groups coincide with ACT's definition of values. In this case, the values shape our professional behavior and decision-making when interacting with clients. Included here are four examples of professional ethics for therapists, art therapists, and creative art therapists, with the hope of inspiring you to create your own tailored set of professional values that surpass those dictated by your professional organization. Identifying meaningful personal values in conjunction with the ethics of your profession provides direction for your behavioral choices in your value domain of work/profession.

The *Ethical Principles for Art Therapists* from the AATA (2013) include autonomy, nonmaleficence, beneficence, fidelity, justice, and creativity. The preamble asserts that, "art therapists are guided in their decision-making by core values that affirm basic human rights" (2013, para. 1).

The *Art Therapy Multicultural Diversity Competencies* from AATA (2011) offer more precise direction for counseling in our diverse world. Specific areas include awareness of personal values, biases, assumptions; knowledge of client worldview; and skill in developing and implementing appropriate interventions that are sensitive to language, religion, and biculturalism. These competencies offer clear standards for awareness, knowledge, and skill in each area.

The BAAT's (2014) *Code of Ethics and Principles of Professional Practice* calls for the highest ethical standards in competence, integrity, safety, fairness, and accountability. These encompass understanding one's scope of practice and cultural competence, including knowledge of community and cultural art practice, as well as providing choice and autonomy to clients. The BAAT code also provides standards for safe, effective, and good practice to support art therapists as well as to inform and protect their clients (BAAT, 2014).

Creative expression is a human right according to the Australian, New Zealand and Asian Creative Arts Therapy Association (ANZACATA; 2021). In particular, the ANZACATA (2018) noted, "Creative arts therapists are committed to the absolute welfare of their clients and to the preservation of their clients' human rights and privileges" (para. 2). Furthermore, the ANZACATA identifies additional values of the professional organization, including art being of central importance in therapy, valuing art-based research, embracing diversity, promoting human potential and wellbeing, and following ethical guidelines and safety standards. The *Standards of Professional*

Practice and Code of Ethics (ANZACATA, 2018) highlight three areas, including professional responsibility, confidentiality, and responsibility to creative arts therapy colleagues.

These aspirations and goals of our ethical practice comprise part of our personal values about our work as therapists. You likely have more personal and heartfelt values that inspire your work, such as compassion, creativity, and service, among other values. Incorporating ethical standards into our professional values statement offers integrity and a connection to the shared values of our profession. These principles are not only necessary to our profession in order to retain our credentials, but they also offer art therapists far more than simply rules to follow to protect our clients and ourselves. They provide guidance for how best to assist our clients through actions inspired by these values. When utilized, these professional principles assist art therapists in making optimal behavioral choices in their work.

Because the ethical principles provide an excellent example of ACT's professional values, we will explore six main concepts with an emphasis on how the principles inspire value-based behavioral choices and cultural humility. Remember, values are the aspirational direction we move towards when we select our behaviors in any given moment. They help guide each of our behavioral choices. Furthermore, these values are applicable in every aspect of our work, including self-reflection, care for clients, interactions with colleagues, and other professional capacities including education, research, and community engagement. When we link our behavior to our values as a professional, our choices become more meaningful and our work more effective. We can inform our clients of our chosen personal and professional values, and our living example provides opportunities for deepening our relational experience in the therapy space. The six art therapy values are explored in detail in the text that follows. It is my hope that this detailed exploration of our shared professional values will inspire and inform your work in each of your values, and in turn support your work with clients as they explore their values.

Independence and autonomy

This ethical principle pertains to how we support our clients in making their own choices regarding "life direction, treatment goals, and options" (AATA, 2013, para. 1). We are obligated to assist clients in obtaining information so they can make "informed choices, which further their life goals and affirm others' rights to autonomy" (AATA, 2013, para. 1). Art therapists "assist clients in understanding their options in making their own decisions, and will respect the choices they make" (BAAT, 2014, pp.2–3). These values dictate that we will help clients make their own choices, even if we would make a completely different decision for ourselves.

Behavior choices informed by autonomy include informed consent and information about services, as well as obtaining ongoing consent and helping clients gain the information or personal reflection they need to move forward in their life goals. How we demonstrate our committed action includes overt actions, such as initial paperwork and other obligations, as well as our word choices, tone of voice, and nonverbal cues to show we support our clients in their right to freely choose their actions.

Nonmaleficence

The ethical principle of nonmaleficence means the art therapist's behavior avoids harm to individuals, families, groups, and communities. Harm can be intentional and willful or based in negligence and ignorance. Cultural humility plays an important role in nonmaleficence because assumptions based on culture, as well as unexamined biases, cause significant harm to clients, students, and fellow therapists. Utilizing outdated and biased approaches or relying on one's unexamined biases negates choices.

Therapists' microaggressions inflict pain on People of Color, those from the LGBTQ+ community, women, and other historically underrepresented people in the therapy space (Nadel, 2018). Furthermore, aspects of psychological theories and education can be harmful to minority clients and students. For example, giving a diagnosis of depression to a woman who has experienced a lifetime of sexism and racism implies that the problem resides within the individual rather than the problem being the results of the system perpetuating male, White superiority. Furthermore, we are obligated to avoid misusing clinical or research findings (BAAT, 2014). The misuse of findings has been a significant and ongoing problem that perpetuates systems of racism and White supremacy in the field of psychology and art therapy. These are concerns that affect every therapist and client.

To uphold our commitment of nonmaleficence in art therapy, we can look to the principles of cultural humility (Jackson, 2020) and multicultural ethics (AATA, 2011) discussed earlier. Committed actions include engaging in lifelong critical self-reflection, addressing power imbalances in the therapy space, creating mutually beneficial partnerships with communities in which we work, and advocating for institutional accountability (Jackson, 2020). These strategies support our work to prevent us from engaging in harmful behavior towards clients.

Beneficence and wellbeing

The ethical principle of beneficence includes promoting the wellbeing of individuals, families, groups, and communities (AATA, 2011, 2013; ANZACATA, 2018). This is the value that brings many to the profession of psychology—we wish to help others improve their circumstances. Art therapists enhance welfare by identifying practices, approaches, attitudes, and institutions that actively benefit others. Cultural humility also supports the art therapist value of beneficence. When considering that we can avoid harm by adopting a culturally humble stance, this approach becomes an ethical obligation to promote wellbeing for our clients and communities (Jackson, 2020).

Fidelity

The ethical principle of fidelity addresses our responsibility to accept our role as art therapists by behaving responsibly and acting with integrity towards our clients, students, colleagues, and our community (AATA, 2013; ANZACATA, 2018; BAAT, 2014). Furthermore, fidelity means we work honestly and with integrity to be faithful to our promises about art therapy. Our value of fidelity includes working within our scope of practice and avoiding an overreach of our expertise. We are obligated to work with clients using techniques and information gathered from our professional training, rather than offering information or advice gleaned from the news, nontherapy-related professions, popular culture, or personal experience. Assuming we can offer assistance to clients based on only our experiences is an act of hubris. For example, we might have had a divorce, miscarriage, abortion, children, or benefited from a certain diet, exercise, or herbal/nonprescribed medicines, yet personal experience alone fails to qualify us to advise clients in these areas. We are obligated to seek training and supervision in areas within our scope of practice in which we will be offering interventions.

Justice

The ethical principle of justice teaches art therapists to commit themselves to treating each person with fairness (AATA, 2011, 2013; ANZACATA, 2018; BAAT, 2014). Art therapists ensure that clients have equal access to services. Cultural humility principles include advocating for institutional accountability, which means working within our agencies to create safe and supportive practices that are accessible to everyone by removing barriers and being open to learning how to identify and reject oppressive approaches and techniques (Jackson, 2020). Feminist ethics encourage art therapists to de-emphasize the "more personal focus of their work in order to give prominence to the political aspects, thereby engaging in a more politically edified practice as a way of transforming lives and affecting social change" (Wright & Wright, 2013, p.2).

This shift to a systemic understanding of how society affects people and their mental health brings justice to the therapy office through critical analysis of the causes of mental health problems, stigma, and barriers to care. Many are working to decolonize therapy and art therapy, exploring and dismantling areas in which the field of psychology rests on biased assumptions, White supremacy, capitalism, and individualism (AATA, 2021; Talwar, 2019). The critical analysis of the theories on which our practices rest creates greater safety in the therapy office; we create that safety by utilizing ideas that are truly welcoming and applicable to the strengths of clients and communities. Our committed actions in the area of justice include ongoing learning and self-reflection, as well as training and incorporating theories that emphasize social and community aspects in therapy.

Creativity

Creativity, a hallmark ethical principle for art therapists, supplies the tools to "cultivate imagination for furthering understanding of self, others and the world" (AATA, 2013, para. 1). Specifically, art therapists utilize creative thinking and artistic expression to assist clients in cultivating mental health healing, solving problems, and making meaning from their experiences (AATA, 2011; ANZACATA, 2018; BAAT, 2014). Considering the concept of values in ACT, creativity and creative expression are paramount to our work. I believe art therapists are obligated to maintain a creative and artistic process to support their professional practice. The aspirational ethical principle of creativity transitions easily into maintaining our own art practice. Avoiding an overly clinical stance in art therapy necessitates our ongoing value and committed actions of artmaking. Staying engaged in our personal art practice is vital to our sustainability and vitality in the field of art therapy. Personal artmaking benefits our work as a necessary instrument for understanding ourselves and our work. Furthermore, artmaking offers an important strategy in the critical self-reflective process of cultural humility (Jackson, 2020).

So...what are YOUR professional values?

In addition to our shared values and ethical principles (AATA, 2011, 2013; ANZACATA, 2018; BAAT, 2014), each of us has a unique set of values that guides us in our work. Reviewing the ethical standards above from AATA, BAAT, ANZACATA, as well as feminist and multicultural ethics, we can each begin to craft our own guiding principles in the value domain of work. Students and emerging therapists first learn the laws and ethics and how to apply them to clinical practice. After examining what has been laid out for us by professional organizations and leaders in the field, we are then able to explore our personal values more deeply. Here is my values statement in the domain of professional work.

> I value the dignity and sacredness of each person with whom I work. Kindness, cultural humility, and gratitude infuse my daily practice within my communities. I uphold the ethics of my profession and feminist standards in offering creative, supportive, and efficacious care to my clients, students, and art therapy community. I value helping people self-actualize, being accountable for my actions, and acknowledging and addressing power imbalances within the systems in which I work. Curiosity and learning guide me in the areas of art therapy, psychology, art, research, self-growth, and professional standards.

Using what you have read earlier about ethical principles, as well as those put forth by your specific state or regional and professional boards, begin to craft a statement about your values as a therapist. You might wish to include specific standards mentioned earlier that are of special importance to you or inspire you (e.g., human rights, creativity, cultural humility, feminist principles) and then build on these to include your own unique standards. I hope this exercise inspires you to re-engage with the ethical standards of your profession in a new and lively way and to come to a greater awareness of your personal values.

Exercise: Identifying values

Now that you have crafted your own values statement about your professional work, this next exercise provides an opportunity to explore the rest of your values. After you complete your own values statements and art, you can teach your clients about values and tailor the exercise to fit the needs of your clients. This should take time to complete and I recommend you spread out your writing over a few days to allow for reflection and a creative process. Your values are a living statement of what is important to you and they can and should be modified as you grow and change.

1. Make a list of all your value domains. These may include family, romantic relationships, friends, spirituality, creativity, education, community, mental and emotional health, physical health, parenting, or spirituality. Begin with the one that feels most relevant to you. In each of the categories, jot down a list of as many aspirational words as you can think of to describe what is important to you and what you want in each value domain. For example, in the area of family, you might list love, trust, protection, authentic, sharing, support, laughing, caring, fun, and lifelong. These are what you *aspire* to now and in the future, which may or may not relate to what you have experienced in the past. Skip the ideas and words you feel you are *supposed to* value based on what your family or society has taught you. The list is only for you, and it should reflect *your* beliefs, regardless of what others may think. Naturally, our values overlap with what we have been taught; however, the point of this exercise is to identify the ones that truly feel authentic to you right now. If you are unsure, you might ask yourself, "Who else shares this value?" and "How important is this value to me on a scale of 0 to 100?"

2. After you have created your list, it is time to refine it through writing—you can work at the computer, in your journal, on a big piece of paper, or even record it on your phone. Set a timer for five minutes of free writing. Write whatever comes to mind to answer these two questions: What do you value in each domain? How will you demonstrate that value in your behavior? For example, the value domain of family addresses four areas:

   a. Authenticity: I value a calm and happy family life, where we can all feel free and comfortable to be ourselves in our apartment. I am authentically myself in interactions with my family.

   b. Laughter and fun: Fun and laughter are important to me and I bring a good sense of humor to my family, especially when things are stressful.

c. Trust: I value a reliable and predictable family life where I am supportive and caring, and my family can expect trustworthy and reliable actions from me.

d. Caring, sharing, and protection: It matters to me that all our voices are heard, considered, and valued. I listen carefully to my family and I also have clear boundaries to make sure my voice is heard.

3. In each value domain, create a meaningful statement, crafting and modifying your value statements so that they feel bona fide, genuine, and uniquely authentic to you. There are no right or wrong ways to describe your values—they just need to be an accurate description of what you value right now and for the immediate future. For example, using the list of words above in the area of family (love, trust, protection, authentic, sharing, support, laughing, caring, fun, lifelong), you can craft a statement that embodies your feelings about how you want to be in your family. "I value a supportive and trusting relationship with my family that thrives on caring, laughter, and love."

4. Finally, hone the values using art materials. A collage is a wonderful place to start, and you can use words and images from magazines to create images reflecting each value. I have also helped clients create a visual of their value domains by making mobiles and playing cards. A mobile is an ideal metaphor for working on values, since working on one value typically influences other values in the same way that pulling on one portion of a mobile moves the rest. Additionally, values change over time and so this should be considered a living document of what you care about most of all.

This exercise might initially feel quite challenging for both you and your clients. Remember, values work is considered the most intensive and intimate aspect of ACT (Hayes *et al.*, 2012). You might worry that others might look down on what you value, which can feel shameful; such worries may have even stopped you from articulating and acting on your values in the past. Or perhaps you feel quite uncertain about true authentic values, having quickly adopted you family's or society's values with little support for exploring what matters most to you. Some people grow up with their needs and wishes being disregarded, so articulating their values and wishes feels foreign. Many others may have been in such stressful life circumstances that survival was paramount, and such contemplation seems a luxury they could hardly afford.

Some clients have reported being reluctant to articulate a value for fear of being wed to it forever. Remind clients that values are a living, breathing, flexible statement, which helps guide us right now and in the foreseeable future. However, the statements can be modified and changed as clients grow and gain more clarity about their values. You can support clients in identifying what they value by describing instances in which you have observed their values in action. For example, you might highlight their value and action towards good mental health by choosing to work with you, or perhaps you can assist them in recalling their values as a friend, parent, or partner based on what you have worked on in therapy. If clients remain stuck, you may want to explore areas of cognitive fusion that are getting in the way of their ability to articulate their values. This can be done through conversation or quick expressive line drawings, scribbles, or bilateral drawings using both hands at once to draw.

Integration of values for sustainability

When we pursue professional values of being a great, ethical, compassionate, and dedicated therapist without fully fleshing out what is required to be a healer, we may eventually feel exhausted, uninspired, and even burnt out. Rejuvenating and replenishing what we give away in our work requires rest, relaxation, fun, creative expression, and relationships, as well as personal healing and growth. Without these, being the best therapist we can be will be impossible and we will become depleted, unhappy, and ineffective in our work.

Sustainability of our value-based and engaging lives is indeed possible when we value our mental health and integrate our personal needs to thrive with our values. The ACT goal of psychological flexibility includes making adjustments when the environment changes and as we begin to observe how all of our values intersect. This next section provides examples and an exercise to integrate our professional and social justice values with our needs and standards around our own mental health.

I hope to inspire therapists to reframe the traditional model of a work ethic, which suggests that to be effective, valuable, and success-ful, we must work excessive hours, take on more clients than we can genuinely care for, offer free services when asked, and engage in other unsustainable activities. Typically, these strategies include sacrificing our creativity and vitality, as well as our physical and mental health. In a depleted state, we are unable to do our best work and we fail to be healthy examples for our clients. If you have found yourself in this state, or you wish to be proactive in preventing burnout, you can focus on your values to help you live and work sustainably.

Many business models and work expectations in nonprofits, hospitals, and private practice lack sustainability, relying heavily on therapists taking lower paying jobs with an unmanageable caseload. The expectation that therapists should be so giving of themselves that they burn out offers a poor business model and is destructive to therapists and clients and ultimately to the financial stability of the agency. Missed days of work, loss of productivity, staff turnover, and hiring and training new staff sap financial and human resources at any agency. The traditional model, in conjunction with a capitalist and puritanical work ethic, often leaves therapists feeling joyless and uninspired when faced with increasing paperwork, grant obligations, and client load, coupled with a loss of autonomy over their work prac-tices and free time.

It is time for we as therapists to stop the tradition of depleting ourselves to serve others! If depletion and scarcity sound like your work ethic and business model, you can approach change in two ways. The first strategy includes making personal, value-based decisions and taking action based on them, and the second includes tackling institutional problems that perpetuate burnout.

Beginning with the personal, identify your work and personal values. For example, I wish to work in a career where I am able to provide art therapy and psychology to clients in hope of resolving their traumas and improving their lives and the lives of their families and communities. To do this, I need the following: ongoing education, personal growth, strong mental and physical health, creativity, empathy, and passion. More specifically, for my education and personal growth, I need access to ongoing continuing education classes that are intellectually stimulating and relevant to my work. For strong mental health, I require my own therapist, nutritious food, eight to nine hours of sleep, healthy and nourishing relationships, and physical exercise. To maintain my creativity, empathy, and passion, I need an abundance of time and opportunities for creativity, rest, and daydreaming, insight into my own psychology, as well as activities and thoughts that stimulate joy and excitement. For our work to be its best, we must believe these elements are necessary to sustain our work. Furthermore, we must believe that we are deserving of this foundational, personal attention.

Many therapists have confessed they easily teach clients how to care for themselves, yet the therapists feel unworthy of their own basic self-care. However, as you see from the example above, my work is of a quality and sustainable only when I am at my best. Do you believe this type of personal balance is necessary for your clients? Do you believe it to be true for yourself as well? If you find that you are facing burnout or vicarious trauma from your work, seek more information about these conditions and engage in healing practices of rest, creativity, and personal therapy. Your clients and you will both benefit from these actions.

Personal sustainability exercise

Grab a pen and paper and some art supplies. Spend 30–90 minutes on this exercise to discover what you require for sustainable professional practice. There is a "before" art intervention and writing assignment, an "after" art intervention, and a written response. Find some time and get comfortable to let your creativity take over as you imagine how to keep your values and committed actions alive in the work/ career domain.

Art 1: Create a piece of art using lines, shapes, and colors, depicting your current state of emotional, physical, and psychological sustainability. Work quickly and intuitively without much contemplation. Title your picture and write three words or phrases to describe it.

Write 1: Reflect for a few minutes about the most important aspects of your career, including what drew you to your work. Answer each of the questions in writing with a pen or pencil. Avoid just thinking about the answers—these need to be written down.

1. What do you value in your career and what attracted you to it?

2. How do you want to feel when doing your work?

3. What behaviors do you currently engage in that demonstrate this value and feeling state?

4. What elements are required of you to sustain these values in the long run (e.g., sleep, exercise, nutrition, personal growth and healing, spiritual connection, education, relationships)? Describe these in detail and what the ideal version of these elements would be.

5. Look at your answers in Question 4. Rate yourself on a scale of 1–10 on each of the sustainability practices you listed.

   a. A rating of 0 means you are not engaged in this activity at all.

   b. A rating of 5 means you engage in the activity, yet the level is insufficient to truly sustain your work.

   c. A rating of 10 means you are actively working on this element at a level that sustains you and your work.

6. What happens if you disregard the sustainability practices you wrote about in Question 4? In other words, what are the personal and professional consequences of failing to take action on the sustainability steps?

7. What new committed actions are required of you to sustain

your work values? Describe them specifically (e.g., sleep eight to nine hours a night, keep a regular sleep schedule).

8. Which of these actions will you commit to work on first? Rank them in the order of where you will start. Write down *specifically* what you will do and when and where you will you do it. How will you know if you have been successful in the commitment? Who will you tell about your new sustainability commitment? What will you do when you skip a day?

Art 2: Create a second piece of art using lines, shapes, and colors, depicting your *ideal* state of emotional, physical, and psychological sustainability. Work quickly and intuitively without much contemplation. Title your picture and write three words or phrases to describe it.

Write 2: Reflect on your observations of your art and writing. How does it feel to now have an action plan and specific steps to make your career more emotionally, physically, and psychologically sustainable? It probably feels pretty great!

Implement your plan right away, starting today. Take the first step and the motivation will follow. When you think about rest and sustainability for yourself, it is normal to have feelings of doubt, guilt, or agitation, as well as thoughts related to futility or personal lack of time. Society has offered you few examples of how to feel proud of your work while employing boundaries to protect yourself, your loved ones, and clients. Notice and defuse from these thoughts and move straight to action with a 28-day commitment to your behavior.

Document your progress towards sustainable and balanced work practice each day on your planner. This step is vital for your success. For example, I have a small calendar book in my favorite color which I keep at my desk. The book serves to hold me accountable to my writing—the only thing I write in this book is the amount of time I write each day. Personal and professional writing is one of my current committed actions, and documenting my time spent writing holds me accountable and demonstrates my commitment. Each time I enter a number I get a dopamine reward, so I feel compelled to continue. Use your planner to record your committed action related to your sustainability goal: for example, the number of hours you sleep or the time you spend exercising or making art. After demonstrating your committed action and documenting it for 28 days, pick your next action and keep building on your sustainability plan. One you have seen success yourself, introduce the concept, art, and writing prompts to your clients, help them identify their most important priority in any value domain, and create a committed action plan and documentation strategy.

The value of institutional sustainability

A business model for an agency includes financial sustainability as an objective, and good business practice necessitates strategies to ensure the support and balance of the people within an agency. Once you have used the strategies described earlier to create your personal committed actions towards your own longevity at work, it is time to explore your workplace to support a culture of emotional sustainability, satisfaction, and endurance for you and your colleagues. One individual is quite capable of enacting cultural change at work. You may find yourself acting solo for a while; however, people who want to thrive like you will eventually join you. Pick an area in which you can make committed actions and jump in, inviting your co-workers. If it is common to eat lunch at your desk, take your lunch to the break room and invite a colleague to join you. If fatigue sets in in the afternoon because nobody is taking their breaks, go for a short walk and invite a friend. Remember to keep a calendar and mark down the days you complete your committed action. Remember, your committed action is worthwhile, and you get to document what you accomplish yourself, regardless of how your colleagues react. Even if nobody joins you for lunch, you will have increased your attention to your values and your vitality! Once you have attempted small changes, such as a community lunch or a walk, you can take more actions in areas of increasing importance.

When facing business practices that you find depleting and unmanageable at your place of employment, education and advocacy become necessary. Advocacy might include asking for an increased vacation allowance, negotiating caps on the number of clients they assign you, and realistic goal setting for paperwork and reports. These types of changes may seem insurmountable when working at agencies in which government funding depends on the number of client contact hours. However, change has to begin somewhere, and certainly it can begin with you and advocacy. Reflect on your satisfaction as an employee, exploring the nourishing, as well as the depleting aspects of your work. Strategize about what you require to feel satisfied, productive, and empowered in your job and imagine your ideal workplace. Talk with colleagues about your ideas for a more ideal workplace and work-life balance. See if others feel the same way and enlist your colleagues in advocacy. Make a list of specific requirements similar to what you wrote about in the personal sustainability section.

When to move on

If you find that you are exhausted by extended efforts at advocacy and find your personal work values are compromised by demanding business models, unsustainable practices, and experiences of racism, sexism, homophobia, ageism, ableism, discrimination, or harassment, you may wish to leave. You are under zero obligation to remain at your place of employment, working to provide healing and support for individuals and communities when you are burned out or when your physical and mental health is sacrificed for "the work." If you are facing harassment at work, the workplace model is likely to be unsustainable for you, as well as your colleagues and clients. You may wish to pursue other avenues of work and you can leave with zero guilt. It may be difficult to find other work because of finances, insurance, location, and emotional connections to colleagues and clients. It may be time to enlist support to help you consider options, including therapy, legal counsel, employee assistance programs, or other people and organizations with knowledge about what you are experiencing. You deserve to be working at a place that aligns with your values.

Conclusion

Our chosen values provide direction for our behavior so that we can engage in meaningful and purposeful behaviors regarding our self, family, community, spirit, and work. Values are aspirational and inspire us to engage in committed action.

Defining our values promotes direction, clarity, and positive behavioral changes to inspire our lives. Daily behavioral choices are crafted by our values, and behaviors that are out of line with our values become less important and less common. Using language and art to define our values provides a clear map towards the life we want to live. Professional ethics can inform our vocational values and inspire us to identify a sustainable work practice and place of employment.

Recommended resources

Reviewing the ethical principles of our professional organizations helps us stay connected to our professional values and avoid drifting away from core tenets of our work. The four standards reviewed in this chapter are included below.

1. To further engage in your professional values and help you identify how and where you want to work, read *Find your Blissful Calling* by Aymee Coget (2020). This workbook enables you to discover work you love for a new career or for building on your current career to transform it into your blissful calling. Complete the workbook and you will probably find it a welcome resource for clients as well. www.amazon.com/Blissful-Calling-Ph-D-Aymee-Coget/dp/B086Y4SH6Q. You can read more about Aymee Coget at www.happinessforhumankind.com.

2. To understand the difference between values and goals, check out this four-minute animated video by ACT leader, Russ Harris: www.youtube.com/watch?v=T-lRbuy4XtA.

3. The *Code of Ethics and Principles of Professional Practice for Art Therapists* from the BAAT can be found here: www.baat.org/Assets/Docs/General/BAAT%20CODE%20OF%20ETHICS%202014.pdf.

4. The *Ethical Principles for Art Therapists* from the AATA can be located here: https://arttherapy.org/wp-content/uploads/2017/06/Ethical-Principles-for-Art-Therapists.pdf.

5. The *Art Therapy Multicultural Diversity Competencies* from the AATA can be found here: https://arttherapy.org/wp-content/uploads/2017/06/Multicultural-Competencies.pdf.

6. The *Standards of Professional Practice and Code of Ethics of the Australian, New Zealand and Asian Creative Arts Therapy Association* are located here: www.anzacata.org/ethics-and-standards.

CHAPTER 10

Time to ACT:
Committed Action

Creating a value-based creative life involves acting on our personal
values and engaging in committed actions to do what is most import-
ant to us. Strategies for action support clients in their commitment to
engage in daily behaviors to create a more satisfying life, even when
external problems or mental health symptoms remain present. ACT
offers the opportunity to engage in a meaningful, value-based life
while continuing to work on mental health challenges.

Now comes the time to ACT! To commit and follow through with living your values means you are embodying psychological flexibility to do what you want and love, regardless of whatever else is happening inside you or around you. Action means making daily choices to remain flexible and maintain constant movement towards your values. This final step on the ACT hexaflex is where we finally see sustained behavioral change in ourselves and our clients. It means acting on what *you* find to be most important in your life. In this last area of the ACT hexaflex, you are living your value-based life with zest and vitality.

ACTion!

You are probably already choosing to act on many of your values—being a committed therapist, parent, friend, artist, worker, neighbor, sibling, athlete, appreciator of nature, or whatever is most important to you right now. Getting fully on board with your committed actions means you notice and continue to do what you are doing in service of your values and you commit to actualizing the rest of your values. More specifically, by using *committed action*, you will find that psychological flexibility manifests as behavioral change. These new behaviors reflect each person's unique movement towards their values. In ACT, "the ultimate goal is to develop patterns of behavior that work for the client and nothing less will be counted as success" (Hayes *et al.*, 2012, p.327).

To make space for values to manifest, we have to let go of the choices and behaviors that reflect other people's values. First, we examine the values of those around us (e.g., parents, society, culture, and religion). Most people find worth in at least some of some of the values they have been taught, such as we discussed in Chapter 9. Next, we work to recognize and commit to acknowledging the attitudes, thoughts, and behaviors we have unconsciously adopted from society, such as unrelenting work standards, conventional standards of beauty, racism, sexism, or homophobia. Finally, we make daily behavioral actions towards our values.

Sometimes following other people's values is important to the family unit and the value of family harmony. Other times it can bring about great dissatisfaction and distress. For example, when focused on fulfilling our parent's values of being "good," we may end up with only conditional acceptance of ourselves as a worthwhile person. Fulfilling the wishes of our family and friends to marry the "right" person means we might find a great partner or it might mean we miss out on a relationship with someone we love. Following a generational tradition to work in the family business may yield satisfaction and pride, or it might leave us pursuing a career ill-suited to our personality and interests. Only *you* can decide the most important values and actions for you in any given moment, and the way you manifest your values in behavioral actions will change as you grow and age.

What is committed action?

Recall that ACT is a "hard-core form of behavior therapy" (Hayes *et al.*, 2012, p.327), because it is based on behavioral principles and the outcome of success is measured in behavioral terms. In other words, all the aspects of the hexaflex (i.e., present moment awareness, acceptance, defusion, self as context, contact with values, and committed action) support the goal of psychological flexibility and the outcome of committed behavioral actions that support and reflect values.

Hayes *et al.* (2012) noted that "committed action is a choice to behave in a particular way on purpose" (p.330). Actions express a person's values in each moment and a committed action can be an internal mental operation or an external, observable behavior. They added, "Committed action is a values-based action that occurs at a particular moment in time and that is deliberately linked to creating a pattern of action that serves the value" (p.328). For example, you might commit to loving your partner and that commitment is made externally and internally. You can observe your commitment internally and others can observe it externally. A committed action is different from the value itself. Whereas values involve "freely chosen, verbally constructed qualities of ongoing action," value-based actions "embody a particular value and are intrinsically reinforced" (p.328). In other words, we feel our best when we consistently act on our values!

Sometimes we blame ourselves or others for our choices and pass judgment on past conduct we perceive as "bad." In ACT, we avoid blame and judgment about ways of behaving. Instead, the focus is on helping clients see choices available to them and then seeing the powerful position of linking behavioral choices to values. Committed action linked to values relates to present moment choices and is distinct from future goals.

Future oriented goals suggest that one may reap happiness or satisfaction through achievement and such states inevitably lie perpetually in the times ahead (Hayes *et al.*, 2012). Focusing on goals means happiness is dependent on successive accomplishments, which leaves zero room for contentment and joy in the moment. Focusing only on goals means living on a treadmill of pursuing external satisfaction, which could potentially be found with the right person, job situation, place, or object. Once we achieve a goal, the thrill quickly wears off, and we start all over again with a new goal, seeking pleasure in the future and the external (Coget, 2020). Conversely, committed action relies on present moment actions, which bring satisfaction and vitality; happiness and satisfaction are always within reach since they exist in the present.

Making art exists in the space of committed action because creating and expressing one's self links to multiple values. Creative expression is the embodiment and product of the value of creativity. In other words, by using committed action, the act of artmaking is transformed into the embodiment of the value. The value itself is being expressed in the moments of drawing, painting, sculpting, or photographing. The goal of completing a piece of art is distinct from being in the present moment and acting on one's values in a committed, moment-by-moment situational choice.

Commitment in verbal therapy

Following through on committed action and discussing one's dedication to values regularly in therapy utilizes positive psychological strategies to celebrate success. When clients skip their committed action homework, discussion includes identifying what got in the way, including ambivalence, substance use, fatigue, apathy, or "forgetting" about the homework. Attending both to accomplishments and lack of success assists clients in dissecting barriers and new strategies. It furthermore increases motivation and willingness to engage in value-based behaviors. Therapists can adjust their strategies to ensure that clients establish truly meaningful committed actions, without undue pressure from the therapist.

Asking for a committed action at the end of each session helps our clients concretely move towards their values. Clients come to rely on my question at the end of each session and begin to integrate the need for committed action in conducting their lives according to their values. Action planning perhaps looks similar to the CBT technique of behavior planning. The goal for the client encompasses targeting one value, choosing a behavior in service of that value, and identifying specific actions in support of the value. Here I facilitate conversation to elicit (1) the value, (2) target behaviors, (3) barriers to success, and

(4) strategies to ensure success. Below is an example of how this might look in a session:

> Therapist: As our session comes to a close, what value do you intend to focus on this week?
>
> Client: I have a few I want to focus on—family, work, health.
>
> Therapist: You can work on all of those—pick one for your homework this week so we have a specific example to talk about next time we meet.
>
> Client: I guess I will focus on family. I want to spend some time with my kids. (*Value*)
>
> Therapist: Great! What do you value about spending time with your kids and how do you want to show that to them?
>
> Client: I value giving them some of my time—they will only be at home a few more years, and I want to appreciate them. I want to give them guidance and let them know they can talk to me or my wife about any problems they might have. (*Value*)
>
> Therapist: How can you demonstrate that to the kids? What will that look like?
>
> Client: I guess being able to hang out without an event to go to— just make time to talk without pressure. I could take them to the park and kick the soccer ball around or go and get an ice cream. I guess nothing big like going to a game or the science center—you know, just hanging out. (*Committed action ideas*)
>
> Therapist: That sounds like fun for all of you. Which of those things do you want to commit to for next week? And when will you do it?
>
> Client: I think going to the park and kicking the soccer ball around. I could do it on Sunday morning. (*Committed action*)
>
> Therapist: And how will you demonstrate your values when you are with the kids?

Client: I probably need to leave my phone at home for our trip. Or not pull it out of my pocket when we are at the park. [pauses]. I think I need to leave it at home! (*Barriers to action*)

Therapist: Anything else you need to do to make sure you are successful at being present with your kids on Sunday morning?

Client: Make sure I am awake enough to be patient with them. I guess I need to not have any drinks the night before and go to bed early enough. (*Identify barriers*) Okay, wait, I know your next question. I will go to bed at 10 the night before. (*Committed action*)

Therapist: Great! You know the routine for picking your values and committed action! What is the plan then?

Client: I guess I do! So, I am going to bed at 10 on Saturday, no drinks that night. Sunday morning around 9 or 10 I am taking the kids to the park with the soccer ball and leaving my phone at home. See you next week, and I will tell you how the soccer went!

Here is another example of identifying committed actions in therapy.

CASE EXAMPLE

DD, a single White mother, reported that she highly values her family and tween-age daughter, yet she struggles to express this to her daughter in words or actions. She stated they had become very close after her divorce from her husband of 15 years but she now misses spending time with her "little girl" and feels sad and "shut out" from her daughter's life since she turned 12. DD reported a significant loss in her personal support since her daughter shifted her focus more towards her friends at school. When asked to clarify her values as a parent, she identified "making sure she has what she needs, showing up for her when she needs it, and spending time together doing fun things."

I asked DD what was getting in the way of her demonstrating

these values to her daughter. "It feels like my daughter does not want to spend as much time together as she used to, and it has gotten confusing and frustrating to talk with her when she seems so bored with me. I just kinda gave up asking, since she seems happier talking to her friends. I have been prioritizing time with my friends after I get out of work, and it is great to catch up with them. I don't know, maybe I am making too much of this. I valued my own independence growing up so maybe she just needs space to figure herself out and make mistakes."

I asked her to then make a list of three behaviors she could do in the next two weeks to demonstrate in action her values and commitment to her daughter. She identified having dinner together, attending her daughter's sport event, and attending her teacher conference. I asked about the last time she and her daughter had dinner together. She said it was "awkward, quiet, and my daughter jumped up from the table a few times when she heard her phone." We discussed setting limits with the phone during dinner.

The conversation helped to identify DD's values, committed actions, and barriers to these actions with respect to her tween daughter:

Personal values: "Being loving, showing up for her when she needs it, loving, spending time together, and doing something fun."

Cultural values: "Giving my daughter independence and freedom."

Committed action: "Providing for her financially, having dinner together, attending her sport event, and attending her teacher conference."

Psychological barriers to committed action: DD tried to talk herself out of making a change in her behavior by saying there were benefits for her and highlighting a value common for those who grow up within individualistic cultures—independence. "I don't know—I have been prioritizing time with my friends after I get out of work, and it is great to catch up with them. I really valued my own independence growing up so maybe she needs space to figure herself out and make mistakes."

In this case example, it is clear that there may be some conflict between DD's personal values and cultural values. It is important to identify cultural values and recognize possible barriers which might interfere with committed action. This conflict arises when cultural and personal values do not align with one another. For similar reasons, therapists must identify their own personal and cultural values to ensure they are able to clearly differentiate them from those of clients. This also points to the importance of having an ongoing commitment to cultural humility. When we are unwilling to explore the aspects of identity related to intersecting identities of race and culture, we run the risk of creating rigidity in our approach, or worse, disempowering our clients.

Commitment to cultural humility

As we have discussed throughout this book, cultural humility offers each of us the opportunity to learn about ourselves and grow in order to create a shared, loving, and accepting therapy approach. When we make an internal commitment and then engage in actions of cultural humility, we are embodying our personal value.

Kamaria Wells shares her values and committed actions in the context of cross-race friendships in a racially complex society. She is a member of the AATA research committee, and her research and clinical work focuses on healing from racial traumas, especially as they pertain to the traditional curriculum. Wells' path to art therapy encompassed growth and discovery in the fields of education, social services, mental health, community organizing, vocational rehabilitation, political, and legal fields. During these varied experiences, she was introduced to artmaking and discovered the therapeutic nature of art through personal process. Her essay, "Social justice and social circles: Cultural humility in practice," was inspired by her experiences and growth in friendships with an array of people throughout her journey in various regions of the United States and time spent abroad.

> Growing up navigating predominately White spaces allowed me to acquire the social aptitude necessary to accommodate the dominant culture, when needed. This was an imperative survival skill in order

to dodge stereotypes and confining boxes that may have otherwise penalized me for being a Black woman. This also provided the opportunity for me to develop various acquaintances on the friendship spectrum with vastly different people. I have always enjoyed variety in my friendships; rotating between various tables in middle and high school, I was one of the few students who never claimed a clique. I have had the fortune of participating in Ramadan, lighting a Torah, and celebrating a number of other religious and cultural festivals and holidays that I would not have experienced had I not chosen diversity and inclusion for my social life. It helped that my parents always had a diverse group of friends, in every respect. There is significant literature to support the movement of fostering cross-race friendships among youth to combat racism, but the correlating literature for their parents is lacking.

Friendships with people of the same ethnic or racial background can be a transforming and enlightening experience when there is also an element of light that facilitates personal growth. A genuine fellowship can transform one's world. This is why it is imperative, especially for therapists, to have profound diverse relationships. While I am not at all suggesting you go out and find a "fill-in-the blank" friend to check off a box, I am challenging you to look closely at your closest and oldest friendship circle. How diverse is it? How comfortable do you feel in groups different from your own? How many intimate conversations have you shared with cross-race friends about racism? Significant research shows that cross-racial friendships will allow you to improve perceptions of other groups, while also ultimately, impacting implicit bias and reducing anxiety (Korol, 2017; Page-Gould, 2004; Page-Gould et al., 2008).

The anxiety symptom is key because it is the reason so many people avoid interracial relationships: the fear of getting something wrong and inadvertently offending someone (Daniel Tatum, 1997). Daniel Tatum (1997) describes an account of a White woman who was intimidated by racial dialogue in classroom settings because the Students of Color spoke of it so eloquently and articulately, while she stumbled and fumbled over her words. The uncomfortable White student did not have a lens of critical consciousness; the ease with which the Students of Color were able to articulate their encounters with racism grew from practice. Having these dialogues with family, friends, and loved ones, beginning in childhood, prepared them for this discourse in academic settings. "The Talk" for Black children, as young as three and four, encompasses an explanation of the subpar treatment we will encounter in most settings throughout our lifetime, because we are not White. I have found it particularly interesting that in class, peers will trip over one another to provide condolences for a family member or friend with mental illness or addiction or encounters with death. Interestingly, accounts of encounters with racism are greeted with a pin drop. It is a deafening silence that rings the alarm of trouble. If future therapists cannot have a dialogue about racism in class, how can they support clients who are People of Color who deal with racism daily?

Unfortunately, problems never simply disappear; we have to work with them and through them, which requires discussion. Naturally, problems can be complicated and uncomfortable to discuss; nonetheless, they can only be resolved via awkward and uncomfortable conversations. Racism and its impact can be an emotionally charged and intense dialogue. The question remains, if the therapist has only homogeneous social circles, how can they have the cultural humility needed to navigate discussions around race and the interconnected roles it plays in our lives and those of our clients?

In 2014, the Public Religion Research Institute (PRRI) determined that 75 percent of White US Americans maintained homogeneous social groups. All other ethnic and racial groups on average have cross-racial friendships (Page-Gould, 2004). In 2019, the PRRI found that 62 percent of US Americans stated that diversity strengthens this country. These statistics are extremely interesting and telling. Many people state they are supportive of movements such as Black Lives Matter; however, data and the socio-political climate suggest much of this may be performative.

Envision social justice and social circles as a Venn diagram, because they are. The cultural humility that is imperative in quality therapy also translates into thriving social connections in one's personal life. Cultural humility has been identified as practicing equity with respect and being focused on the other, instead of one's self (Hook *et al.*, 2013); this is a tenet of a quality friendship that also has the potential to enlighten professional interactions. Friendships are a safe space to have difficult and confusing conversations about tough topics like race relations. Everyone makes mistakes; it is more about how the mistake is handled and one's subsequent actions. Overcoming fears of getting something wrong is essential for social justice to prevail.

I have had five friends, who happen to be White, with whom I had the fortune of sharing the space of an uncomfortable dialogue around racial systems. These conversations have facilitated healing and making peace with our shared intergenerational trauma from the past, and I am profoundly grateful for them. Most significantly, they dedicate their time, energy, and resources to supporting Communities of Color. There is nothing superficial or performative about these relationships. They are my accomplices and genuine people I love. My artwork, a three-dimensional mixed media piece that was created by sculpting paper and later painting it, is a deconstructive and reconstructive piece that artistically and metaphorically correlates with the process of growth within transformative relationships (Figure 10.1). The hues of gold in the sea of blue illustrate a transcendence of being and knowing.

The lessons we learn in our personal lives indubitably impact our professional lives, especially in art therapy. It is imperative that we practice cultural humility constantly and diligently, stepping outside our comfort zones for everlasting growth in humanity and compassion.

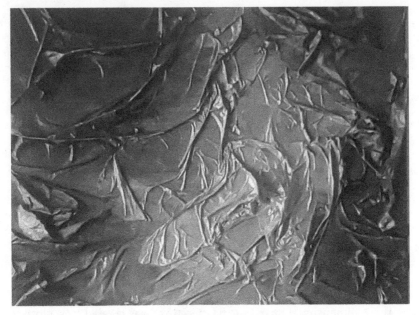

FIGURE 10.1: THE PROCESS OF GROWTH WITHIN
TRANSFORMATIVE RELATIONSHIPS

Barriers to committed action

Relapse prevention in ACT includes an exploration of barriers to each of the hexaflex components (Hayes *et al.*, 2012). Inviting clients to plan in advance how they will react to barriers, doubt, and uncertainty in their commitment is good practice and gives them the tools they need to manage future challenges. According to the transtheoretical model of change (Porchaska *et al.*, 1993), which explains the process of change, relapse is a part of any type of habit altering we might make in life. With preparation, we can assist clients in using any relapse from following through on their commitment to value-based behaviors as a learning opportunity. Relapse prevention potentially helps inoculate clients against unnecessary suffering.

What makes us stop short of pursuing a dream or making our daily life happier? What happens when we consider taking a risk in line with our values? ACT addresses these questions through the hexaflex. We may stop short because of fusion to our thoughts, avoidance, lack of contact with the present moment, nonacceptance, excessive focus on self as content, and loss of awareness of the self as context and personal values (Hayes *et al.*, 2012). Sometimes acting on one's values conflicts with what other people want from us. In pursuing our dream career or changing professions, we may struggle with balancing our professional values with what family and friends think we should do. Additionally, our inner discomfort and fears about change can create a significant barrier to moving forward towards our value-based life choices.

Helping clients address their barriers starts with revisiting each area of the hexaflex. Exploring defusion again will allow clients to recognize self-doubting thoughts as just thoughts, and support their movement forward regardless of their thoughts. Reviewing acceptance and being present to our internal events, including negative self-talk, assists in accepting discomfort and unease as a part of change. Returning to these areas of the hexaflex can relieve qualms, new uncertainty, and loss of conviction. Revisiting values and attending to the actions that support those values is a lifelong process, and assisting clients in resolving any apparent conflicts in values can reduce suffering and help them engage in their committed actions. Remember, ACT is effective in treating multiple problems at once, and clients can still engage in value-based behavioral choices even while experiencing internal/external problems or chronic mental health problems.

Conclusion

Committed actions are the final, integrative aspect of ACT therapy. ACT's bottom line is to help people orient their lives around their personally chosen values and engage in committed actions that embody those values. Acting on values by taking committed actions creates a unique and satisfying life doing what is most important to us. Committed actions can exist even when we are aware of unwanted feelings, thoughts, and memories, or are facing chronic mental or physical conditions. Using personally chosen values as a guide to our behaviors brings about satisfaction because we center our lives on what is most important to us, rather than acting in response to our unwanted feelings, thoughts, or memories or attempting to avoid, control, or escape them.

Engaging in a creative process in art therapy assists clients and therapists in exploring each step of the hexaflex. Additionally, art becomes an action-oriented behavioral choice when clients and therapists commit to engage in self-expression and creative process as part of their value expression.

Recommended resources

1. This ten-minute video by Nesh Nikolic teaches committed action: www.youtube.com/watch?v=q1ISW4JrErU.

2. This two-minute animated video from the Veterans Health Administration in the US uses a boat in a storm metaphor to describe committed action. The simple graphics and written description offer a great clip to share with clients: www.youtube.com/watch?v=yoVmoOnjscM.

CHAPTER 11

ACT Art Therapy:
Bringing it All Together

This chapter will summarize how the integration of ACT and art therapy works to promote psychological flexibility and value-based living. How to develop a creative ACT art therapy practice is addressed, using art examples and case examples to illustrate how ACT art therapy becomes a part of the therapist's way of being and the lens through which we view life and therapy.

Integrating the evidence-based practice of ACT with creative expression facilitated through art therapy fashions a powerful approach to healing and transformation. As you have learned throughout the previous chapters, the two approaches of ACT and art therapy complement one another beautifully. It is hoped that you now see the two styles as a seamless approach to helping both therapists and clients live a value-based and creative life. The benefits of committed action to create a meaningful life are accomplished through creative, cognitive, emotional, and behavioral processes designed to increase psychological flexibility. The specific ACT strategies in this approach include artmaking to facilitate (1) engaging mindfully in the present moment; (2) accepting what is truly happening without attempting to avoid, control, or escape private experiences; (3) defusing from thoughts; (4) viewing the self as the context of our lives; (5) defining values and what we care about; and (6) living values according to what is most important to create a meaningful life. Art therapy practice rests on the belief that accessing creativity helps us know ourselves, others, and our communities (Allen, 1995), and that creative expression has evolutionary advantages (Dissanayake, 1992).

Art and ACT approaches both rely on centuries-old wisdom, including present moment awareness and acceptance (Hanh, 2010; Tolle, 2004), as well as artmaking for storytelling and personal expression (Dissanayake, 1992). Building on generations of wisdom about how human beings can construct a meaningful life and advance themselves and their families, ACT and art therapy synergistically promote authentic behaviors to help people heal and move towards what they determine as valuable. The strategies assist us in detangling ourselves from unwanted or unhelpful thoughts and old stories that no longer serve. Furthermore, the positive and optimistic approach to living a value-based life can both inspire therapists and clients and offer them ways to take pragmatic action to sustain their inspiration and gratification.

Another beautiful quality of this combined approach is that anyone can benefit and move towards their values, even when experiencing symptoms of a mental health disorder or memories of a traumatic past. ACT and art therapy provide true action-oriented interventions designed to beget change straightaway—in the office and in one's life. Creative expression offers action-oriented opportunities for healing via exploring and generating new feelings, thoughts, and stories. There are zero prerequisites for clients to engage in art therapy and ACT to feel better, and multiple diagnoses can be addressed simultaneously using this approach.

ACT emphasizes actions that help clients to drop their struggle with mental health symptoms by accepting the symptoms while at the same time engaging in value-based behaviors. Skills learned in ACT and art therapy easily transfer to all areas of life. For example, proficiency in acceptance benefits the individual, as well as their family and romantic relationships, because dropping expectations and defusing from thoughts assists the person using the tools as well as the people around them. The aptitudes of cognitive defusion operate universally, regardless of thought content. By alleviating tensions built up from expectations, predictive thoughts, and early, problematic narratives, defusion techniques relieve internal struggles, such as impostor syndrome and public-speaking fears, as well as external stressors.

A therapist's choice of psychological theory emerges from personal philosophies, as well as our understanding of the mechanisms of change in our own lives and the lives of our clients. Integrating theory into our clinical practice and our worldview evolves over the course of our careers. When practitioners initially apply ACT theory, or any theory for that matter, it may appear awkward, linear, fragmented, and even frustrating for both therapist and client. However, becoming a master practitioner of one theory brings many benefits to both the therapist and their clients.

While it might be tempting to integrate other theoretical approaches when confused or frustrated in the face of clinical challenges that make us feel incompetent or triggered, maintaining our theoretical understanding offers security and support for both therapists and clients. Jumping around and dabbling with other theories can undo our previous work with a client. Alternatively, creating consistent interventions and narratives, reflection, self-exploration, consultation, and supervision are ways to maintain the integrity of our approach.

What next?

We have addressed the philosophical underpinnings of an integrated ACT and art therapy approach and we have explored the practical application in a clinical setting. The next section includes ideas for personal action, clinical application, and ongoing academic research.

Personal action

Now that you have studied the ACT hexaflex and have seen how art therapy illuminates its principles, you are prepared to integrate art therapy and ACT into your practice. While this book offers an introduction to the concepts, I highly recommend that you pursue the ongoing education suggestions in each chapter, which offer recommendations for relevant art therapy and ACT. What committed actions will you be taking to extend your understanding of the depth and breadth of these two approaches? Remember, ACT is a behavioral approach and success is evaluated by the extent to which behavioral change through committed action linked to values leads to psychological flexibility. Some ideas for committed action as an ACT therapist include intensifying your commitment to a mindfulness practice or asking yourself daily, "What truth can I accept today?" The hexaflex and creative process work only when we are *ACTing* on them, rather than thinking about them.

Clinical

Attention to the whole person, with their unique context and values, is a significant strength of ACT and art therapy. The two approaches provide intense focus on the uniqueness of each person, their self as context, and personal expression. ACT art therapy offers a unique contribution to the behavioral sciences. The functional integration of the ACT concepts creates psychological flexibility and, ultimately, behavioral change (Callaghan *et al.*, 2004). Moving fluidly around the hexaflex, using art material, elucidates the whole person in all our complexities and illuminates creative ways to increase psychological flexibility.

Robust literature exists separately for ACT and art therapy. Clinically focused research is needed to confirm how the integrated approach affects and facilitates change for clients. Initial case examples may offer insight into what the two approaches together in clinical practice might manifest. More rigorous studies might begin with art therapy as an adjunctive therapy to understand the ways in which the addition of art therapy might enhance existing ACT protocols and approaches. Finally, an integrated ACT art therapy approach needs to be compared to other approaches and to ACT alone. Though an abundance of literature exists in art therapy related to mindfulness (Rappaport, 2008, 2013) and flow in the creative process (Csíkszentmihályi, 2008), increased evidence in linking mindfulness and psychological flexibility in ACT to creative thinking would benefit clinicians and clients.

Academic

While the literature on ACT and art therapy is robust in terms of demonstrating their efficacy when they are applied separately, more research on the combined approach is needed to link the creative thinking necessary for psychological flexibility and the creative process in artmaking. In particular, greater understanding of the specific mechanisms of change most relevant to reducing mental health symptomatology and increasing psychological flexibility would be fruitful. The online resources from the Association for Contextual Behavioral Science (ACBS) offer a wealth of assessment and therapy tools, research articles, training, and community support for student and professional researchers. In a 2021 white paper report, the ACBS task force agreed that ACT research should be *multilevel, process-based, multidimensional, prosocial, and pragmatic* and it offered recommendations for ACT researchers to accomplish these goals (Hayes *et al.*, 2021). The call from ACBS for prosocial and pragmatic research suggests that more promising research will be emerging that will solve problems for the social good, including creating more access to schools and with historically underserved communities.

Committed action for integrating of ACT and art therapy

Let's further explore your role in using ACT and art therapy. Strategizing your clinical practice using ACT and art therapy requires practice, patience, and an ongoing commitment to personal growth and education. The training of an art therapist includes extensive studio art experience, as well as scholarly and clinical training. ACT training includes clinical and experiential knowledge of the strategies outlined in the hexaflex followed by practice and integration of the concepts. As you recall from previous discussion, acceptance is an ongoing process, and so too is the integration of theory into clinical practice. Without constant attention to developing our skill in using theory, we risk drifting away from evidence-based practice into using a hybrid of the evidence-based approaches in conjunction with other theories, self-help books, and personal interest. If we rest on our laurels and keep using the same approaches without building our learning, we naturally get bored and start switching around our approach and strategies. There is zero evidence that a mix of evidence-based practice, other theories, and self-help is effective in helping our clients. In fact, a cocktail of approaches is unlikely to effect the change your clients seek.

Our professional value of striving to be the best therapist we can be means committing to our ongoing education in a meaningful, personal, and engaged way. Committed action to our personal growth as ACT art therapists requires a mindfulness practice, our own therapy, engagement with the hexaflex strategies to increase our psychological flexibility, and living a value-based life. Furthermore, we must engross ourselves in personal artmaking, above and beyond what we might create in a class or with our clients. To be consistent with your values as a therapist, I encourage you to strategize three specific ways you can remain engaged in ACT art therapy. This includes taking committed actions to building your clinical and experiential knowledge through books, workshops, online training, and artmaking. Your daily commitments support your role as a congruent and consistent role model for your clients.

ACT psychoeducation for our clients

Sharing our clinical knowledge with clients deconstructs the outdated power structures that often exist in the therapy space. Psychoeducation about ACT, the goal of psychological flexibility, and the concepts in the hexaflex is an important part of building a caring, transparent, and egalitarian relationship. Furthermore, it allows our clients to continue learning from ACT resources in between sessions and, it is hoped, after therapy has ended. Providing education and a rationale for the interventions means taking the "mystery" out of the therapy process by empowering clients to take ownership of their own mental health.

Some ways we empower clients include genuinely ensuring that they have informed consent over the therapy process. Asking our clients to complete an intake assessment and an informed consent is only the beginning. It is critical that we review the information in the consent form with them and explain the process of therapy. This includes orienting them to therapy, what they can expect from the therapy in terms of outcomes, what to do if they want to cancel a session, the cost of a cancelled session, and what to do if they are having thoughts of hurting themselves.

The informed consent process can include providing them with a clear orientation to the theoretical direction and strategies the therapist will be using, as well as acknowledging the inherent power differential between someone coming to ask for help and the person offering help. Clients will have varying developmental levels and different understanding of the therapy lens, and so the language and descriptions need to be tailored to each client. We should be sure to make time to answer their questions. The therapist may have reviewed the form thousands of times; however, this will be your client's first time hearing it from you. Obtaining ongoing consent supports clients in their freedom to choose and change their mind.

Children may enjoy hearing the metaphor that you wear tinted glasses to think about challenges in therapy and you can invite them to "try on" your metaphorical glasses in therapy to look at their challenges in a new way. Adults have various ways of understanding therapy too, and the tinted glasses make for a good metaphor with them as well. With adults and children, I introduce them to the terms of ACT and teach them new concepts and terms each session. Many clients have observed that learning about therapy from a therapist is a novel approach and that learning about the interventions was helpful in regaining a sense of control over their own mind and mental health. As clients begin to see progress in their psychological flexibility, they may become interested in the ACT approach, which is so different from the ways they have experienced therapy before. I often ask if they would be interested in learning more about ACT, and I recommend books and online videos that might help them learn more about ACT and apply the learning outside the therapy office.

ACT and artistic parallel process for therapists

Jordan Anthony Gonzales, a painter and art therapist in the San Francisco Bay Area, works with resilient adolescents and their families in a residential facility. Gonzales received his bachelor's degree in studio art at San Jose State University and his master's in marriage and family therapy and art therapy from Notre Dame de Namur University, with clinical training in ACT. With a passion for art history and the creative process, Gonzales regularly includes these perspectives in his therapeutic work. Additionally, he incorporates a dialectical behavioral therapeutic lens infused with feminist and strength-based theories. Gonzales engages in a wide range of artmaking, including painting, drawing, ceramics, and photography, and he actively uses art as a way of learning and knowing. His process is reflected in the essay that follows, which is titled, "Navigational maps: How watercolor taught me acceptance and commitment therapy."

For most of my early artistic career, my chosen medium was acrylics. My early paintings were abstract—wild expressions of energy that only adolescence could fuel. As I worked my way through my college studio art courses, my work became devoid of the passionate impulses that characterized my earlier work—replaced by formal thinking and calculated movements. I reined in my natural painting tendencies and exercised control with every decision, doing my best to fit my creative process into the dominant narrative of fine art. It was cognitively exhausting and emotionally stifling. No surprise I stopped painting after graduating with my bachelor's in studio art. Oh, the irony!

A year and half later, after many unsuccessful attempts to reignite my interest in painting, I began my practicum year in graduate school and discovered ACT. I felt refreshed as I learned the versatility of ACT concepts and how they could be applied to a variety of situations, including those that a client may experience in the future. Living a value-driven life resonated with my own lived experiences, career choice, and future ambitions. Despite my initial attraction to ACT, fully understanding and using ACT with clients was challenging to say the least. I spent many months consuming ACT books, videos, podcasts, and webpages in my effort to understand the theory and apply it to my caseload.

At the same time I was investigating ACT, I was experimenting with watercolor. In painting terms, watercolor is the opposite of acrylic paints, and I found myself both intrigued and intimidated. I attempted to don my art therapy hat and make watercolor paintings for myself;

yet the fine art critic remained loud and insistent with each brush-stroke. I was in a battle between my practiced need to exert control and the innate insistence of watercolors to be free.

My breakthrough with watercolor came not in the studio but in a library. I was reading in depth on acceptance as I tried to piece together an ACT-oriented treatment plan. ACT teaches that acceptance is about demonstrating willingness and embracing experiences, rather than trying to exert psychological control over them. It dawned on me that to work with watercolor is to inherently work with acceptance. There is no controlling watercolor, it goes where it wishes, it mixes how it sees fit, and it dries in its own manner. The most beautiful watercolor works resulted because of the artists' ability to tolerate watercolor's autonomy while negotiating their own vision into the medium.

Soon after this realization, I found myself applying many ACT concepts to my own artmaking journey. Most obvious was the cognitive fusion I experienced as I painted—that inner critic who had a very specific definition of the fine artist and demonstrated a relentless determination to remind me as much. As ACT teaches, such cognitive fusion was pulling me out of the present moment as I painted. ACT teaches that resolving cognitive fusion starts with teaching individuals how to increase flexibility by practicing being in the present moment wholly.

One of my first acts of cognitive defusion for artmaking had already taken place through my physical medium choice. My re-engagement with painting through watercolor was inherently a decision to reject the ideas and constrictions that became tied to my acrylic work. Moreover, the mere fact I was engaging in the artmaking process, to say nothing of learning about clinical concepts through artmaking, demonstrated my own committed action to adhere to my chosen values.

It became clear to me that a parallel process had formed; my artistic growth and clinical growth had become linked through ACT and each informed and was enhanced by the other. As art therapists, we believe in the power of art as teacher and guide, but even so, it is easy to become absorbed in the cognitive thinking of academic and psychological theory. The creative process does not have to be the antithesis of such thinking but rather can be an equal partner. My watercolor work was a means to fully digest and practice the ACT principles and was by far the single most effective tool. In the second semester of my practicum year alone, I painted close to 150 watercolor works, most of which measured just 4 × 6 and 5 × 7 inches and were completed quickly in between the hectic moments of school and work. With each painting, I was rewarded as my understanding of ACT became a bit clearer and my connection to artmaking became stronger. It is of course no coincidence then that during such an extreme time of cognitive and artistic growth, all of my watercolor works resembled navigational maps. See Figures 11.1 and 11.2.

FIGURE 11.1: WATERCOLOR BY JORDAN GONZALEZ

FIGURE 11.2: WATERCOLOR COLLECTION BY JORDAN GONZALEZ

Conclusion

ACT art therapy has shown itself to be an exciting integration of both the linear and the abstract—the concrete and the metaphorical. The integration of art therapy and ACT creates a synergistic strategy to promote strong mental health and authentic creative expression. Combining the behavioral evidence base of ACT and the meaningful and insightful aspects of artmaking provides a practical and enjoyable structure to engage fully in life.

Artmaking provides the affective and experiential component of therapy and illuminates the somewhat cerebral concepts of ACT. Appreciating and striving for the goal of psychological flexibility includes an affirmative stance on living one's life with meaning and purpose. Engaging mindfully in one's chosen values and committing to action in the service of those values affirms that our lives can be filled with meaning and purpose. Indeed, meaning and purpose can exist alongside chronic medical and psychological conditions.

Remaining interested in our own values and lives provides vitality, despite the pain and sometimes suffering that exists within us and in the world. An engaged life can be created by following the strategies outlined in the ACT hexaflex: engage mindfully in the present moment; accept what is truly happening; defuse from our thoughts; view ourselves as the context of our lives; define our values and what we care about; and live according to what is most important (see Figure 11.3). As Lori Stevic-Rust (2013) reminds us, we all can be *greedy for life* and allow ourselves to fully experience what we most value in our lifetime. ACT art therapy delivers on the practical behaviors, as well as the affective response to living the life each of us wants for ourselves.

Fortified with the information and inspiring artwork in this book, it is my sincere hope that you will continue to learn about ACT and art therapy to meaningfully engage in your values and support your clients in doing the same.

FIGURE 11.3: THE HEXAFLEX
Note: By Jocelyn Fitzgerald, watercolor.

Recommended resources

Develop your ACT skills on your own and with a community of ACT practitioners. Remember ACT provides the opportunity for a lifetime of growth as a person and as a clinician. Commitment to ongoing training and learning is vital for your growth and for your clients' success in therapy.

1. For academic understanding, read the central ACT text: Hayes, S., Strosahl, K.D., & Wilson, K.W. (2012). *Acceptance and Commitment Therapy: The Process and Practice of Mindful Change* (2nd ed.). New York, NY: Guilford Press.

2. For experiential learning, complete the workbook: Hayes, S.C. & Smith, S. (2005). *Get Out of Your Mind and Into Your life: The New Acceptance and Commitment.* Oakland, CA: New Harbinger Publications. Once you complete this workbook, find an in-person workshop for an integrated experiential training.

3. To integrate all of your understanding and connect with others, consult the Association for Contextual Behavioral Science for recommendations on training, workshops, research articles, reports, and support. Consider joining the membership and engaging in the community. In-person training elevates your understanding and enhances your ability to integrate all the material: https://contextualscience.org/list_of_resources_for_learning_act.

References

ACT With Compassion. (n.d.). *Use of I/you perspective taking with highly self-critical and shame prone clients.* www.actwithcompassion.com/use_of_i_you_perspective_taking.

Alexander, A. (2020). The artopia program: An examination of art therapy's effect on veteran's moods. *Art Therapy: Journal of the American Art Therapy Association*, 37(2), 156–161.

Ali, S. & Lee, C.C. (2019). Using creativity to explore intersectionality in counseling. *Journal of Creativity in Mental Health*, 14(4), 510–518. doi:10.1080/15401383.2019.1632767.

Allen, P.B. (1995). *Art is a Way of Knowing: A Guide to Self-Knowledge and Spiritual Fulfillment through Creativity.* Boulder, CO: Shambhala.

American Art Therapy Association. (2011). *Art Therapy Multicultural Diversity Competencies.* https://arttherapy.org/wp-content/uploads/2017/06/Multicultural-Competencies.pdf.

American Art Therapy Association. (2013). *Ethical Principles for Art Therapists.* https://arttherapy.org/wp-content/uploads/2017/06/Ethical-Principles-for-Art-Therapists.pdf.

American Art Therapy Association. (2017). *About Art Therapy.* https://arttherapy.org/about-art-therapy.

American Art Therapy Association. (2021). *Statement from the AATA diversity, equity, and inclusion committee: Revisiting our values during the coronavirus pandemic.* Retrieved February 23, 2022, from https://arttherapy.org/about-art-therapy.

American Psychiatric Association. (2000). *Diagnostic and Statistical Manual of Mental Disorders* (4th ed., text rev.). Washington, DC: Author.

Aponte, J.F. & Braccco, H.F. (2000). Community Approaches with Ethnic Populations. In J.F. Aponte & Wohl (eds), *Psychological Intervention and Cultural Diversity* (pp.131–148). Boston, MA: Allyn & Bacon.

Assaz, D.A., Roche, B., Kanter, J.W., & Oshiro, C.K. (2018). Cognitive defusion in acceptance and commitment therapy: What are the basic processes of change? *The Psychological Record*, 68(4), 405–418. https://doi.org/10.1007/s40732-017-0254-z.

Association for Contextual Behavioral Science. (n.d.). *Homepage.* https://contextualscience.org/#.

Australian, New Zealand and Asian Creative Arts Therapies Association (ANZACATA). (2018). *Standards of Professional Practice and Code of Ethics of the Australian, New Zealand and Asian Creative Arts Therapy Association.* www.anzacata.org/ethics-and-standards.

Australian, New Zealand and Asian Creative Arts Therapy Association. (ANZACATA) (2021). *About ANZACATA.* www.anzacata.org/About-ANZACATA.

Babouchkina, A. & Robbins, S.J. (2015). Reducing negative mood through mandala creation: A randomized controlled trial. *Art Therapy: Journal of the American Art Therapy Association,* 32(1), 34–39.

Bach, P. & Hayes, S. (2002). The use of acceptance and commitment therapy to prevent the rehospitalization of psychotic patients: A randomized controlled trial. *Journal of Consulting and Clinical Psychology,* 70, 1129–1139. http://dx.doi.org/10.1037/0022-006X.70.5.1129.

Backos, A. (2018). Philosophical Foundations of Art Therapy. In R. Carolan & A. Backos (eds), *Emerging Perspective in Art Therapy: Trends, Movements & Developments* (pp.3–16). London: Routledge.

Backos, A. (2021). *Post-Traumatic Stress Disorder and Art Therapy.* London: Jessica Kingsley Publishers.

Backos, A. & Mazzeo, C. (2017). Group Therapy and PTSD: Acceptance and Commitment Therapy Groups with Vietnam Veterans with PTSD. In P. Howie (ed.), *Art Therapy with Military Populations: History, Innovations and Applications* (pp.165–176). London: Routledge.

Bahattab, M. & AlHadi, A.N. (2021). Acceptance and commitment group therapy among Saudi Muslim females with mental health disorders. *Journal of Contextual Behavioral Science,* 19, 86–91. https://doi.org/10.1016/j.jcbs.2021.01.005.

Belkofer, C.M. & Nolan, E. (2016). Practical Applications of Neuroscience in Art Therapy: A Holistic Approach to Treating Trauma in Children. In J. King (ed.), *Art Therapy, Trauma and Neuroscience: Theoretical and Practical Perspectives* (pp.157–172). London: Routledge.

Bell, C.E. & Robbins, S.J. (2007). Effect of art production on negative mood: A randomized, controlled trial. *Art Therapy: Journal of the American Art Therapy Association,* 24(2), 71–75. doi:10.1080/07421656.2007.10129589.

Bennington, R., Backos, A., Harrison, J., Etherington-Reader, A., & Carolan, R. (2016). Art therapy in art museums: Promoting social connectedness and psychological well-being of older adults. *Arts in Psychotherapy,* 49, 34–43. https://doi.org/10.1016/j.aip.2016.05.013.

Blenkiron, P. (2005). Stories and analogies in cognitive behaviour therapy: A clinical review. *Behavioural and Cognitive Psychotherapy,* 22, 45–59.

Boston, C. (2005). Life story of an art therapist of color. *Art Therapy: Journal of the American Art Therapy Association,* 22, 189–192. www.tandfonline.com/doi/abs/10.1080/07421656.2005.10129519.

British Association of Art Therapists (BAAT). (2014). *Code of Ethics and Principles of Professional Practice for Art Therapists.* www.baat.org/Assets/Docs/General/BAAT%20CODE%20OF%20ETHICS%202014.pdf.

Brown, W.K. & Ryan, R.M. (2003). The benefits of being present: Mindfulness and its role in psychological well-being. *Journal of Personality and Social Psychology,* 84(4), 822–848. doi:10.1037/0022-3514.84.4.822.

Callaghan, G.M., Gregg, J.A., Marx, B.P., Kohlenberg, B.S., & Gifford, E. (2004). FACT: The utility of an integration of functional analytic psychotherapy and acceptance and commitment therapy to alleviate human suffering. *Psychotherapy: Theory, Research, Practice, Training*, 41(3), 195–207.

Campbell, M., Decker, K.P., Kruk, K., & Deaver, S.P. (2016). Art therapy and cognitive processing therapy for combat-related PTSD: A randomized controlled trial. *Art Therapy: Journal of the American Art Therapy Association*, 33(4), 169–177. doi:10. 1080/07421656.2016.1226643.

Campenni, C. E. & Hartman, A. (2020). The effects of completing mandalas on mood, anxiety, and state mindfulness. *Art Therapy: Journal of the American Art Therapy Association*, 37(1), 25–33. doi:10.1080/07421656.2019.1669980.

Carolan, R. & Backos, A. (2018). *Emerging Perspectives in Art Therapy: Trends, Movements and Developments*. London: Routledge.

Carolan, R. & Hill, A. (2018). Art Therapy and Neuropsychology. In R. Carolan & A. Backos (eds), *Emerging Perspectives in Art Therapy: Trends, Movements and Developments* (pp.33–47). London: Routledge.

Carolan, R. & Stafford, K. (2018). Theory and Art Therapy. In R. Carolan & A. Backos (eds), *Emerging Perspective in Art Therapy: Trends, Movements and Developments* (pp.17–32). London: Routledge.

Chandra, S, Huebert, C.S., Crowley, E., & Das, A.M. (2019). Impostor syndrome: Could it be holding you or your mentees back? *Chest*, 156(1), 26–32.

Chapman, L. (2014). *Neurobiologically Informed Trauma Therapy with Children and Adolescents: Understanding Mechanisms of Change*. New York, NY: W.W. Norton & Company.

Chapman, R. & Evans, B. (2020). Using art-based acceptance and commitment therapy (ACT) for an adolescent with anxiety and autism. *Clinical Case Studies*, 19(6), 438–455. https://doi.org/10.1177/1534650120950527.

Craig, C. (2009). *Exploring the Self Through Photography: Activities for Use in Group Work*. London: Jessica Kingsley Publishers.

Crenshaw, K.W. (1989). Demarginalizing the intersection of race and sex: A black feminist critique of antidiscrimination doctrine, feminist theory and antiracist politics. *University of Chicago Legal Forum*, 1(8), 138–167. doi:10.4324/9780429500480-5.

Csíkszentmihályi, M. (2008). *Flow: The Psychology of Optimal Experience*. New York, NY: Harper Perennial.

Coget, A. (2020). *Find Your Blissful Calling*. San Francisco: Happiness for Humankind.

Coget, A. (2021). *Happiness for Humankind Playbook: Sustainable Happiness in Five Steps*. San Francisco: Happiness for Humankind.

Collard, J.J. (2019). ACT vs CBT: An exercise in idiosyncratic language. *Journal of Cognitive Therapy*, 12, 126–145. https://doi.org/10.1007/s41811-019-00043-9.

Cook, D. & Hayes, S.C. (2010). Acceptance-based coping and the psychological adjustment of Asian and Caucasian Americans. *International Journal of Behavioral Consultation and Therapy*, 6, 186–197.

Cookson, C., Luzon, O., Newland, J., & Kingston, J. (2020). Examining the role of cognitive fusion and experiential avoidance in predicting anxiety and depression. *Psychological Psychotherapy: Theory, Research & Practice*, 93(3), 456–473. https://doi.org/10.1111/papt.12233.

Crawford, M. (2020). Ecological systems theory: Exploring the development of the theoretical framework as conceived by Bronfenbrenner. *Journal of Public Health Issues and Practices*, 4(2), 170. https://doi.org/10.33790/jphip1100170.

Daks, J.S. & Rogge, R.D. (2020). Examining the correlates of psychological flexibility in romantic relationship and family dynamics: A meta-analysis. *Journal of Contextual Behavioral Science*, 18, 214–238. https://doi.org/10.1016/j.jcbs.2020.09.010.

Daniel Tatum, B. (1997). *Why are All the Black Kids Sitting Together in the Cafeteria?* New York, NY: Basic Books.

Darrell W. Krueger Library, Winona State University. (2021). *Research Hub: Evidence Based Practice Toolkit: Levels of Evidence*. https://libguides.winona.edu/c.php?g=11614&p=61584.

Davis, S. & Tungol, J. (2019). Efficacy of the transactional model of acceptance art therapy program on psychological distress among parentally bereaved female adolescents. *Indian Journal of Health & Wellbeing*, 10(10–12), 301–307.

de Botton, A. & Armstrong, J. (2013). *Art as Therapy*. New York, NY: Phaidon Press.

Decker, K.P., Deaver, S.P., Abbey, V., Campbell, M., & Turpin, C. (2018). Quantitatively improved treatment outcomes for combat-associated PTSD with adjunctive art therapy: Randomized controlled trial. *Art Therapy, Journal of the American Art Therapy Association*, 35(4), 184–194. doi:10.1080/07421656.2018.1540822.

de Young, M. (1998). *Collective Trauma: Insights From a Research Errand*. www.aaets.org/traumatic-stress-library/collective-trauma-insights-from-a-research-errand.

Dissanayake, E. (1992). *Homo Aestheticus: Where Art Comes From and Why*. New York, NY: Free Press.

Doby-Copeland, C. (2006a). Things come to me: Reflections from an art therapist of color. *Art Therapy: Journal of the American Art Therapy Association*, 23(2), 81–85. www.tandfonline.com/doi/abs/10.1080/07421656.2006.10129646.

Doby-Copeland, C. (2006b). Cultural diversity curriculum design: An art therapist's perspective. *Art Therapy*, 23(4), 172–180.

Doby-Copeland, C., Talwar, S., Vance, L., & Potash, J.S. (2013). *Art Therapy Ethical Practice and Multicultural/Diversity Competence*. The 44th Annual Conference of the American Art Therapy Association. Creative Commons: Attribution 3.0 Hong Kong License, Seattle, WA, 26–30. http://hdl.handle.net/10722/187371.

Edwards, C. & Hegerty, S. (2018). Where it's cool to be Kitty: An art therapy group for young people with mental health issues using origami and mindfulness. *Social Work with Groups*, 41(1–2), 151–164.

Etherington-Reader, A. (2018). Global Art Therapy. In R. Carolan & A. Backos (eds), *Emerging Perspective in Art Therapy: Trends, Movements and Developments* (pp.134–154). London: Routledge.

Eyal, C. & Lindgren, H.C. (1977). The house-tree-person test as a measure of intelligence and creativity. *Perceptual and Motor Skills*, 44(2), 359–362. doi:10.2466/pms.1977.44.2.359.

Farris, P. (2006). Mentors of diversity: A tribute. *Art Therapy: Journal of the American Art Therapy Association*, 23(2), 86–88. www.tandfonline.com/doi/abs/10.1080/07421656.2006.10129645.

Feenstra, S., Begeny, C.T., Ryan, M.K., Rink, F.A., Stoker, J.I., & Jordan, J. (2020). Contextualizing the impostor "syndrome." *Frontiers in Psychology*. https://doi.org/10.3389/fpsyg.2020.575024.

Filho, R.V.T. (2020). Hermann Rorschach from klecksography to psychiatry. *Dementia e Neuropsychologia*, 14(1), 80–82. doi:10.1590/1980-57642020dn14-010013.

Foa, E.B., Keane, T.M., & Friedman, M.J. (eds). (2000). *Effective Treatments for PTSD*. New York, NY: Guilford Press.

Follette, W.C. & Callaghan, G.M. (2011). Behavior Therapy: Functional-Contextual Approaches. In A.S. Gurman & S.B. Messer (eds), *Essential Psychotherapies: Theory and Practice* (3rd ed., pp.1–37). New York, NY: Guilford Press.

Gantt, L. & Tinnin, L. (2009). Support of a neurobiological view of trauma with implications for art therapy. *The Arts in Psychotherapy*, 36, 148–153.

Gantt, L. & Tripp, L. (2016). The Image Comes First: Treating Preverbal Trauma with Art Therapy. In J. King (ed.), *Art Therapy, Trauma, and Neuroscience: Theoretical and Practical Perspectives* (pp.67–99). London: Routledge.

Gibson, N. (2018). *Therapeutic Photography: Enhancing Self-Esteem, Self-Efficacy and Resilience.* London: Jessica Kingsley Publishers.

Gipson, L. (2015). Is cultural competence enough? Deepening social justice pedagogy in art therapy. *Journal of the American Art Therapy Association*, 32(3), 142–145. https://doi.org/10.1080/07421656.2015.1060835.

Gipson, L. (2017). Challenging neoliberalism and multicultural love in art therapy. *Art Therapy: Journal of the American Art Therapy Association*, 34(3), 112–117. https://doi.org/10.1080/07421656.2017.1353326.

Gloster, A.T., Walder, N., Levin, M.E., Twohig, M.P., & Karekla, M. (2020). The empirical status of acceptance and commitment therapy: A review of meta-analyses. *Journal of Contextual Behavioral Science*, 18, 181–192. https://doi.org/10.1016/j.jcbs.2020.09.009.

Godbee, M. & Kangas, M. (2020). The relationship between flexible perspective taking and emotional well-being: A systematic review of the "self-as-context" component of acceptance and commitment therapy. *Behavior Therapy*, 51(6), 917–932.

Gómez, N.N. (2020). Acceptance and commitment therapy for stigma: A systematic review. *Revista Argentina de Clinica Psicologica*, 29(3), 40–46.

Gordon, T. & Borushok, J. (2017). *The ACT Approach: A Comprehensive Guide for Acceptance and Commitment Therapy.* Eau Claire, WI: PESI Publishing.

Hanh, T.N. (2010). *You Are Here: Discovering the Magic of the Present Moment.* Boulder, CO: Shambhala.

Harris, R. (2006). Embracing your demons: An overview of acceptance and commitment therapy. *Psychotherapy in Australia*, 12, 2–8.

Harris, R. (2007). *The Happiness Trap: How to Stop Struggling and Start Living.* Boulder, CO: Trumpeter Books.

Harris, R. (2009). *ACT with Love: Stop Struggling, Reconcile Differences, and Strengthen your Relationship with Acceptance and Commitment Therapy.* Oakland, CA: New Harbinger Publications.

Harris, R. (2010). *ACT with Love: Stop Struggling, Reconcile Differences, and Strengthen Your Relationship with Acceptance and Commitment Therapy.* Oakland, CA: New Harbinger Publications.

Harrison, J. (2018). Art Therapy and Social Change. In R. Carolan & A. Backos (eds), *Emerging Perspectives in Art Therapy: Trends, Movements and Developments* (pp.123–133). London: Routledge.

Hass-Cohen, N. & Carr, R. (2008). *Art Therapy and Clinical Neuroscience.* London: Jessica Kingsley Publishers.

Hay, L. (2020). *You Can Heal Your Life.* Carlsbad, CA: Hay House Inc.

Hayes, S.C. (n.d.). *Does ACT Work for Minorities or the Poor?* https://contextualscience.org/does_act_work_for_minorities_or_the_poor#.

Hayes, S.C. (2004). Acceptance and commitment therapy, relational frame theory, and the third wave of behavioral and cognitive therapies. *Behavior Therapy*, 35, 639–665. http://dx.doi.org/10.1016/S0005-7894(04)80013-3.

Hayes, S.C. (2011). *Mindfulness and Acceptance in Evidence-Based Psychotherapy*. https://stevenchayes.com/mindfulness-and-acceptance-in-evidence-based-psychotherapy.

Hayes, S.C. (2016). *Psychological Flexibility: How Love Turns Pain into Purpose*. TEDx University of Nevada. www.youtube.com/watch?v=o79_gmO5ppg.

Hayes, S.C. (2017). *Using the Hexaflex in Publications—Copyright*. https://contextualscience.org/using_the_hexaflex_in_publications_copyright.

Hayes, S.C. (2021). *Acceptance and Commitment Therapy Exceeds 600 Randomized Controlled Trials!* https://contextualscience.org/news/acceptance_and_commitment_therapy_exceeds_600_randomized_controlled_trials.

Hayes, S.C., Barnes-Holmes, D., & Roche, B. (eds) (2001). *Relational Frame Theory: A Post-Skinnerian Account of Human Language and Cognition*. New York, NY: Plenum.

Hayes, S.C., Merwin, R.M., McHugh, L., Sandoz, E.K., *et al.* (2021). Report of the ACBS Task Force on the strategies and tactics of contextual behavioral science research. *Journal of Contextual Behavioral Science*, 20, 172–183. https://doi.org/10.1016/j.jcbs.2021.03.007.

Hayes, S.C. & Smith, S. (2005). *Get Out of Your Mind and Into Your Life: The New Acceptance and Commitment Therapy*. Oakland, CA: New Harbinger Publications.

Hayes, S.C., Strosahl, K.D., & Wilson, K.W. (2012). *Acceptance and Commitment Therapy: The Process and Practice of Mindful Change* (2nd ed.). New York, NY: Guilford Press.

Hayes, S.C., Wilson, K.G., Gifford, E.V., Follette, V.M., & Strosahl, K. (1996). Experimental avoidance and behavioral disorders: A functional dimensional approach to diagnosis and treatment. *Journal of Consulting Clinical Psychology*, 64(6), 1152–1168. www.ncbi.nlm.nih.gov/pubmed/8991302.

Hayes-Skelton, S.A. & Eustis, E.H. (2020). Experiential Avoidance. In J.S. Abramowitz & S.M. Blakey (eds), *Clinical Handbook of Fear and Anxiety: Maintenance Processes and Treatment Mechanisms* (pp.115–131). Washington, DC: American Psychological Association. https://doi.org/10.1037/0000150-007.

Henshilwood, C.S., d'Errico, F., van Niekerk, K.L., Dayet, L., Queffelec, A., & Pollarolo, L. (2018). An abstract drawing from the 73,000-year-old levels at Blombos Cave, South Africa. *Nature*, 562, 115–118. https://doi.org/10.1038/s41586-018-0514-3.

Hinz, L. (2020). *Expressive Therapies Continuum: A Framework for Using Art Therapy* (2nd ed.). London: Routledge.

Holt, N.J., Furbert, L., & Sweetingham, E. (2019). Cognitive and affective benefits of coloring: Two randomized controlled crossover studies. *Art Therapy: Journal of the American Art Therapy Association*, 36(4), 200–208. https://doi.org/10.1080/07421656.2019.1645498.

Hook, J. (2013). Cultural humility: Measuring openness to culturally diverse Latinas. *Journal of Counseling Psychology*, 60(3), 353–366.

Hook, J.N., Davis, D.E., Owen, J., Worthington Jr., E.L., & Utsey, S. (2013). Cultural humility: Measuring openness to culturally diverse clients. *Journal of Counseling Psychology*, 60(3), 353–366. doi:10.1037/a0032595.

Howie, P. (2017). *Art Therapy with Military Populations: History, Innovation & Application*. London: Routledge.

Hudson Banks, K., Goswami, S., Goodwin, D., Petty, J., Bell, V., & Musa, I. (2021). Interrupting internalized racial oppression: A community based ACT intervention. *Journal of Contextual Behavioral Science*, 20, 89–93. https://doi.org/10.1016/j.jcbs.2021.02.006.

International Expressive Arts Therapies Association (n.d.). *Who we are*. www.ieata.org/who-we-are.

Jackson, L. (2020). *Cultural Humility in Art Therapy: Applications for Practice, Research, Social Justice, Self-Care, and Pedagogy*. London: Jessica Kingsley Publishers.

Jackson, L. Mezzera, C., & Satterberg, M. (2018). Wisdom Through Diversity in Art Therapy. In R. Carolan & A. Backos (eds), *Emerging Perspectives in Art Therapy: Trends, Movements and Developments* (pp.105–122). London: Routledge.

Joseph, C. (2006). Creative alliance: The healing power of art therapy. *Art Therapy: Journal of the American Art Therapy Association*, 23(1), 30–33. www.tandfonline.com/doi/abs/10.1080/07421656.2006.10129531.

Kabat-Zinn J. (1990). *Full Catastrophe Living: Using the Wisdom of Your Body and Mind to Face Stress, Pain and Illness*. New York, NY: Delacorte.

Kagin, S.L. & Lusebrink, V.B. (1978). The expressive therapies continuum. *Art Psychotherapy*, 5(4), 171–180. https://doi.org/10.1016/0090-9092(78)90031-5.

Kandel, E.R. (2012). *The Age of Insight: The Quest to Understand the Unconscious in Art, Mind, and Brain, from Vienna 1900 to the Present*. New York, NY: Random House.

Kapitan, L. (2013). Art therapy's sweet spot between art, anxiety, and the flow experience. *Art Therapy: Journal of the American Art Therapy Association*, 30(2), 54–55. https://doi.org/10.1080/07421656.2013.789761.

Kashdan, T.B. & Rottenberg, J. (2010). Psychological flexibility as a fundamental aspect of health. *Clinical Psychology Review*, 30(7), pp.865–878. doi:10.1016/j.cpr.2010.03.001.

Killingsworth M.A. & Gilbert D.T. (2010). A wandering mind is an unhappy mind—supporting online material. *Science*, 330(6006), 932. https://doi.org/10.1126/science.1192439.

King, J.L. Kaimal, G., Konopka, L. Belkofer, C., & Strang, C.E. (2019). Practical applications of neuroscience-informed art therapy. *Art Therapy: Journal of the American Art Therapy Association*, 36(3), 149–156.

King, J.L. (2016). *Art Therapy, Trauma and Neuroscience: Theoretical and Practical Perspectives*. London: Routledge.

Klumpp, C.F.B., Villar, M., Pereria, M., & de Andrade, M.S. (2020). Reliability studies for the kinetics family drawing. *Avaliacao Psicologica*, 19(1), 48–55.

Korol, L.D. (2017). Is the association between multicultural personality and ethnic tolerance explained by cross-group friendship? *Journal of General Psychology*, 144(4), 264–282.

Krauss, D.A. (1983). The Visual Metaphor: Some Underlying Assumptions of Phototherapy. In D.A. Krauss & J.L. Fryrear, *Phototherapy in Mental Health* (pp.59–68). Springfield, IL: Charles C Thomas Publisher.

Kuri, E. (2017). Toward an ethical application of intersectionality in art therapy. *Art Therapy: Journal of the American Art Therapy Association*, 34(3), 118–122. https://doi.org/10.1080/07421656.2017.1358023.

Langer, K.S. (1942). *Philosophy in a New Key: A Study in the Symbolism of Reason, Rite, and Art*. Cambridge, MA: Harvard University Press.

Lanza, P.V., García, P.F., Lamelas, F.R., & González-Menéndez, A. (2014). Acceptance and commitment therapy versus cognitive behavioral therapy in the treatment of substance use disorder with incarcerated women. *Journal of Clinical Psychology*, 70(7), 644–657. https://doi.org/10.1002/jclp.22060.

Larmar, S., Wiatrowski, S., & Lewis-Driver, S. (2014). Acceptance & commitment therapy: An overview of techniques and applications. *Journal of Service Science and Management*, 7(3), 216–221. http://dx.doi.org/10.4236/jssm.2014.73019.

Lefley, H.P. (2002). Ethical Issues in Mental Health Services for Culturally Diverse Communities. In P. Backlar & D.L. Cutler (eds), *Ethics in Community Mental Health Care: Commonplace Concerns* (pp.3–22). New York, NY: Kluwer Academic/Plenum Publishers.

Levy, S. (2006). Your daddy is the boogeyman. *Art Therapy: Journal of the American Art Therapy Association*, 23(1), 136–138. www.tandfonline.com/doi/abs/10.108 0/07421656.2006.10129622.

Lillis, J. & Hayes, S.C. (2007). Applying acceptance, mindfulness, and values to the reduction of prejudice: A pilot study. *Behavior Modification*, 31, 389–411.

Ling Han, A. & Vasquez, M.J.T. (2000). Group Intervention and Treatment with Ethnic Minorities. In J.F. Aponte & J. Wohl (eds), *Psychological Intervention and Cultural Diversity* (pp.110–130). Boston, MA: Allyn & Bacon.

Lumpkin, C.L. (2006). Relating cultural identity and identity as art therapist. *Art Therapy: Journal of the American Art Therapy Association*, 23(1), 34–38. www. tandfonline.com/doi/abs/10.1080/07421656.2006.10129529.

Lundgren, A.T., Dahl, J., Melin, L., & Kees, B. (2006). Evaluation of acceptance and commitment therapy for drug refractory epilepsy: A randomized controlled trial in South Africa. *Epilepsia*, 47, 2173–2179.

Lusebrink, V.B. & Hinz, L.D. (2016). The Expressive Therapies Continuum as a Framework in the Treatment of Trauma In J. King (ed.), *Art Therapy, Trauma and Neuroscience: Theoretical and Practical Perspectives* (pp. 42–66). London: Routledge.

Martin, R. (1997). Looking and Reflecting: Returning the Gaze, Re-Enacting Memories and Imagining the Future Through Phototherapy. In S. Hogan (ed.), *Feminist Approaches to Art Therapy* (pp.150–176). London: Routledge.

Maujean, A., Pepping, C.A., & Kendall, E. (2014) A systematic review of randomized controlled studies of art therapy. *Art Therapy: Journal of the American Art Therapy Association*, 31(1), 37–44. https://doi.org/10.1080/07421656.2014.873696.

McLaughlin, J.E. (2019). Humanism's revival in third-wave behaviorism. *The Journal of Humanistic Counseling*, 58(1), 2–16. https://doi.org/10.1002/johc.12086.

McNiff, S. (1984). Cross-cultural psychotherapy and art. *Art Therapy: Journal of the American Art Therapy*, 1(3), 125–131. https://doi.org/10.1080/07421656.1984. 10758765.

McNiff, S. & Barlow, G. (2009). Cross-cultural psychotherapy and art. *Art Therapy Journal of the American Art Therapy Association*, 26(3), 100–106.

Merriam-Webster. (n.d.). *Hegemony*. www.merriam-webster.com/dictionary/hegemony.

Merriam-Webster. (n.d.). *Willing*. www.merriam-webster.com/dictionary/willing.

Messer, S.B. & Gurman, A.S. (eds) (2011). *Essential Psychotherapies: Theory and Practice* (3rd ed.). New York, NY: Guilford Press.

Molavi, P., Pourabdol, S., & Azarkolah, A. (2020). The effectiveness of acceptance and commitment therapy on posttraumatic cognitions and psychological inflexibility among students with trauma exposure. *Archives of Trauma Research*, 9(2), 69. https://doi.org/10.4103/atr.atr_100_19.

Monestes, J.L. & Villatte, M. (n.d.). Metaphors in ACT: Understanding how they work, using them and creating your own. *ACT Digest: Echos from Acceptance and Commitment Therapy*, 2. https://contextualscience.org/files/ACT_Digest_Special_Issue_nÂ°2.pdf.

Moradi, K. & Dehghani, A. (2018). Effectiveness of acceptance and commitment on happiness and social desirability of women in seminary. *Women and Family Cultural Education*, 12(42), 113–126. www.sid.ir/en/journal/ViewPaper.aspx?id=603731.

Moran, D.J. & Ming, S. (2020). The mindful action plan: Using the MAP to apply acceptance and commitment therapy to productivity and self-compassion for behavior analysts. *Behavior Analysis Practice*, 15, 330–338. https://doi.org/10.1007/s40617-020-00441-y.

Nadel, K. (2018). *Microaggressions and Traumatic Stress*. Washington, DC: American Psychological Association.

Naumburg, M. (1987). *Dynamically Oriented Art Therapy: Its Principles and Practice*. Chicago, IL: Magnolia Street.

Niles, A.N. Wolitzky-Taylor, K.B., Arch, J.J., & Craske, M.G. (2017). Applying a novel statistical method to advance the personalized treatment of anxiety disorders: A composite moderator of comparative drop-out from CBT and ACT. *Behaviour Research and Therapy*, 91, 13–23. https://doi.org/10.1016/j.brat.2017.01.001.

Ong, C.W., Hancock, A.S., Barrett, T.S., Lee, E.B., et al. (2020). A preliminary investigation of the effect of acceptance and commitment therapy on neural activation in clinical perfectionism. *Journal of Contextual Behavioral Science*, 18, 152–161. https://doi.org/10.1016/j.jcbs.2020.09.007.

Page-Gould, E. (2004, July 1). *Research on Cross-Race Relationships: An Annotated Bibliography*. https://greatergood.berkeley.edu/article/item/cross-race_relationships_an_annotated_bibliography.

Page-Gould, E., Mendoza-Denton, R., & Tropp, L.R. (2008). With a little help from my cross-group friend: Reducing anxiety in intergroup contexts through cross-group friendship. *Journal of Personality and Social Psychology*, 1080–1094.

Partridge, E. (2019). *Art Therapy with Older Adults*. London: Jessica Kingsley Publishers.

Peterson, B.D., Eifert, G.H., Feingold, T., & Davidson, S. (2009). Using acceptance and commitment therapy to treat distressed couples: A case study with two couples. *Cognitive and Behavioral Practice*, 16(4), 430–442. https://doi.org/10.1016/j.cbpra.2008.12.009.

Pinto-Gouveia, J., Dinis, A., Gregório, S., & Pinto, A.M. (2020). Concurrent effects of different psychological processes in the prediction of depressive symptoms: The role of cognitive fusion. *Current Psychology*, 39, 528–539. https://doi.org/10.1007/s12144-017-9767-5.

Porchaska, J.O., Diclemente, C.C., & Norcross, J.C. (1993). In search of how people change: Applications to addictive behaviors. *Journal of Addictions Nursing*, 5(1), 2–16.

Pratt, K. (2016). *Living in the Present Moment = More Happiness?* https://healthypsych.com/living-in-the-present-moment-more-happiness.

Puskar, K.R., Mazza, G., Slivka, C., Westcott, M., Campbell, F., & Giannone McFadden, T. (2012). Understanding content and process: Guidelines for group leaders. *Perspectives in Psychiatric Care*, 48, 225–229. https://doi.org/10.1111/j.1744-6163.2012.00343.x.

Rappaport, L. (2008). *Focusing-Oriented Art Therapy: Accessing the Body's Wisdom and Creative Intelligence*. London: Jessica Kingsley Publishers.

Rappaport, L. (2013). *Mindfulness and the Arts Therapies: Theory and Practice*. London: Jessica Kingsley Publishers.

Ravichandran, S. (2019). Radical Caring and Art Therapy. In S. Talwar (ed.), *Art Therapy for Social Justice* (pp.144–160). London: Routledge.

Rober, P. & De Haene, L. (2014). Intercultural therapy and the limitations of a cultural competency framework: About cultural differences, universalities and the unresolvable tensions between them. Culture and therapy. *Journal of Family Therapy*, 36, 3–20. https://doi.org/10.1111/1467-6427.12009.

Rosal, M.L. (2018). *Cognitive Behavioral Art Therapy: From Behaviorism to the Third Wave.* London: Routledge.

Ruiz, F.J. (2012). Acceptance and commitment therapy versus traditional cognitive behavioral therapy: A systematic review and meta-analysis of current empirical evidence. *International Journal of Psychology and Psychological Therapy*, 12(3), 333–357.

Ruiz, F.J., Peña-Vargas, A., Ramírez, E., Suárez-Falcón, J.C., *et al.* (2020). Efficacy of a two-session repetitive negative thinking-focused acceptance and commitment therapy (ACT) protocol for depression and generalized anxiety disorder: A randomized waitlist control trial. *Psychotherapy*, 57(3), 444–456. https://doi.org/10.1037/pst0000273.

Saad, L.F. (2020). *Me and White Supremacy: Combat Racism, Change the World, and Become a Good Ancestor.* Naperville, IL: Sourcebooks.

Sandmire, D.A., Gorham, S.R., Rankin, N.E., & Grimm, D.R. (2012). The influence of art making on anxiety: A pilot study. *Art Therapy: Journal of the American Art Therapy Association*, 29(2), 68–73. doi:10.1080/07421656.2012.683748.

Santos, A. (n.d.). *Mindfulness meditation courses with Dan Harris and Joseph Goldstein.* Ten Percent Happier. www.tenpercent.com.

Slayton, S.C., D'Archer, J., & Kaplan, F. (2010). Outcome studies on the efficacy of art therapy: A review of findings. *Art Therapy: Journal of the American Art Therapy Association*, 27(3), 108–118. https://doi.org/10.1080/07421656.2010.10129660.

Soyer, G.F. (2019). Urie Bronfenbrenner: The ecology of human development book review. *Journal of Culture and Values in Education*, 2(2), 77–80. doi:10.46303/jcve.02.02.6.

Spring, D. (2004). Thirty-year study links neuroscience, specific trauma, PTSD, image conversion, and language translation. *Art Therapy: Journal of the American Art Therapy Association*, 21(4), 200–209.

Stenhoff, D.A., Steadman, D.L., Nevitt, D.S., Benson, M.L., & White, D.R. (2020). Acceptance and commitment therapy and subjective wellbeing: A systematic review and meta-analyses of randomized controlled trials in adults. *Journal of Contextual Behavioral Science*, 18, 256–272. https://doi.org/10.1016/j.jcbs.2020.08.008.

Stevic-Rust, L. (2013). *Greedy for Life: A Memoir on Aging with Gratitude.* Cleveland, Ohio: Integrated Health Publishing.

Stoddard, J.A. & Afari, N. (2014). *The Big Book of ACT Metaphors: A Practitioner's Guide to Experiential Exercises and Metaphors in Acceptance and Commitment Therapy.* Oakland, CA: New Harbinger Publications.

Substance Abuse and Mental Health Services Administration. (2019). *Key Substance Use and Mental Health Indicators in the United States: Results from the 2018 National Survey on Drug Use and Health* (HHS Publication No. PEP19-5068, NSDUH Series H-54). Rockville, MD: Center for Behavioral Health Statistics and Quality, Substance Abuse and Mental Health Services Administration. www.samhsa.gov/data.

Sue, D.W. & Sue, D. (1999). *Counseling the Culturally Different: Theory and Practice.* New York, NY: John Wiley & Sons.

Suzuki, S. (2020). *Zen Mind, Beginner Mind: Informal Talks on Meditation and Practice*. Boulder, CO: Shambhala.

Swain, J., Hancock, K., Hainsworth, C., & Bowman, J. (2013). Acceptance and commitment therapy in the treatment of anxiety: A systematic review. *Clinical Psychology Review*, 33(8), 965–978. https://doi.org/10.1016/j.cpr.2013.07.002.

Talwar, S. (2010). An intersectional framework for race, class, gender, and sexuality in art therapy. *Art Therapy: Journal of the American Art Therapy Association*, 27(1), 11–17. https://doi.org/10.1080/07421656.2010.10129567.

Talwar, S. (2019). *Art Therapy and Social Justice: Radical Intersections*. London: Routledge.

Tervalon, M. & Murray Garcia, J. (1998). Cultural humility verses cultural competence: A critical distinction in defining physician training outcomes in multicultural education. *Journal of Health Care for the Poor and Underserved*, 9(2), 117–125.

Thompson, B.L., Luoma, J.B., & LeJeune, J. (2013). Using acceptance and commitment therapy to guide exposure-based interventions for posttraumatic stress disorder. *Journal of Contemporary Psychotherapy*, 43(3), 133–140. https://doi.org/10.1007/s10879-013-9233-0.

Tolle, E. (2004). *The Power of Now: A Guide to Spiritual Enlightenment*. Novato, CA: New World Library.

Twohig, M.P. & Levin, M.E. (2017). Acceptance and commitment therapy as a treatment for anxiety and depression: A Review. *Psychiatric Clinics of North America*, 40, 751–770.

United Nations. (1948). *Universal Declaration of Human Rights*. https://www.ohchr.org/EN/UDHR/Documents/UDHR_Translations/eng.pdf.

United Nations. (2021). *Artistic Freedom*. https://www.ohchr.org/en/issues/culturalrights/pages/artisticfreedom.aspx.

van der Vennet, R. & Serice, S. (2012). Can coloring mandalas reduce anxiety? A replication study. *Art Therapy: Journal of the American Art Therapy Association*, 29(2), 87–92. doi:10.1080/07421656.2012.680047.

Van Lith, T. (2020). Fostering client voice and choice through art therapy. *Art Therapy: Journal of the American Art Therapy Association*, 37(4), 167–168.

US Department of Veterans Affairs (2021). *Evidence-Based Therapy*. Retrieved February 21, 2022, from www.mentalhealth.va.gov/get-help/treatment/ebt.asp.

Walker, L.E. (2009). Battered women syndrome. *Psychiatric Times*, 26(7). www.psychiatrictimes.com/trauma-and-violence/battered-woman-syndrome/page/0/1.

Weiser, J. (1993). *Phototherapy Techniques: Exploring the Secrets of Personal Snapshots and Family Albums*. San Francisco, CA: Jossey-Bass.

Weiser, S. (2021). Zoom Art Program with Adults Living with Acquired Brain Injury: The Effect of Using Videoconferencing to Deliver Act Art Therapy Intervention. Unpublished master's thesis, Dominican University of California.

Wheeler, M. (2013). Fotos, Fones, & Fantasies. In D. Loewenthal (ed.), *Phototherapy and Therapeutic Photography in a Digital Age* (pp.40–52). London: Routledge.

Wilson, K.G., Bordieri, M., Flynn, M.K., Lucas, N., & Slater, R. (2011). Understanding Acceptance and Commitment Therapy in Context: A History of Similarities and Differences with Other Cognitive Behavior Therapies. In J. Herbert & E. Forman (eds), *Acceptance and Mindfulness in Cognitive Behavior Therapy* (pp.277–306). New York, NY: Wiley.

Wix, L. (2000). Looking for what's lost: The artistic roots of art therapy: Mary Huntoon. *Art Therapy: Journal of the American Art Therapy Association*, 17(3), 168–176. https://doi.org/10.1080/07421656.2000.10129699.

Woidneck, M.R., Pratt, K.M., Gundy, J.M., Nelson, C.R., & Twohig, M.P. (2012). Exploring cultural competence in acceptance and commitment therapy outcomes. *Professional Psychology: Research and Practice*, 43(3), 227–233. https://doi.org/10.1037/a0026235.

Wright, T. & Wright, K. (2013). Art for women's sake: Understanding feminist art therapy as didactic practice re-orientation. *International Practice Development Journal*, 3(5). www.fons.org/Resources/Documents/Journal/Vol3Suppl/IPDJ_03suppl_05.pdf.

Xplore. (n.d.). *Ansel Adams Quotes*. www.brainyquote.com/quotes/ansel_adams_100072.

Yalom, I.D. (1995). *The Theory and Practice of Group Psychotherapy*. New York, NY: Basic Books.

Ziller, R.C. (1990). *Photographing the Self: Methods for Observing Personal Orientations*. Newbury Park, CA: Sage.

Subject Index

Author Index

ACT With Compassion 173, 174, 175
Afari, N. 182, 192–3
Alexander, A. 67
AlHadi, A.N. 23
Ali, S. 29
Allen, P.B. 64
American Art Therapy Association
(AATA) 65, 79, 204, 206,
207, 208, 209, 221
American Psychiatric Association 27
Aponte, J.F. 202
Armstrong, J. 111, 112
Assaz, D.A. 155
Association for Contextual Behavioral
Science (ACBS) 241
Australian, New Zealand and
Asian Creative Arts Therapy
Association (ANZACATA)
204–5, 207, 208, 209, 221

Babouchkina, A. 25
Bach, P. 124
Backos, A. 26, 27, 31, 41, 47,
53, 54, 64, 67, 68, 69, 71,
95, 97, 102, 183, 190
Bahattab, M. 23
Barlow, G. 202
Belkofer, C.M. 73
Bell, C.E. 24
Bennington, R. 112
Blenkiron, P. 181
Borushuk, J. 19, 38, 39, 40, 150,
154, 155, 174, 195, 197

Boston, C. 63, 79
Bracco, H.F. 202
British Association of Art Therapists
(BAAT) 65, 66, 67, 79, 206,
207, 208, 209, 220
Brown, W.K. 103

Callaghan, G.M. 19, 20, 39, 55, 240
Campbell, M. 24, 25
Campenni, C.E. 103
Carolan, R. 31, 63, 64, 72,
73, 74, 105, 183
Carr, R. 68
Chandra, S. 48
Chapman, L. 63, 67, 68, 73, 84, 91
Coget, A. 97, 220, 225
Collard, J.J. 57
Cook, D. 23
Cookson, C. 151, 152
Craig, C. 137
Crawford, M. 46, 47
Crenshaw, K.W. 29
Csíkszentmihályi, M. 69, 102, 240

Daks, J.S. 42
Daniel Tatum, B. 231
Darrell W. Krueger Library 21
Davis, S. 84
de Botton, A. 111, 112
De Haene, L. 144
de Young, M. 202
Decker, K.P. 24, 25
Dehghani, A. 41